The Syntax Of Silence

Oxford Studies in Theoretical Linguistics

This series provides a new forum for cutting-edge work in theoretical linguistics. Its focus will be on the interfaces between the subcomponents of grammar and between grammar and other components of the mind. The books will be accessible at postgraduate level, and will be published simultaneously in hardback and paperback editions.

The Syntax of Silence

*Sluicing, Islands,
and the Theory of Ellipsis*

JASON MERCHANT

OXFORD
UNIVERSITY PRESS

OXFORD
UNIVERSITY PRESS

Great Clarendon Street, Oxford OX2 6DP

Oxford University Press is a department of the University of Oxford.
It furthers the University's objective of excellence in research, scholarship,
and education by publishing worldwide in

Oxford New York

Athens Auckland Bangkok Bogotá Buenos Aires Cape Town
Chennai Dar es Salaam Delhi Florence Hong Kong Istanbul Karachi
Kolkata Kuala Lumpur Madrid Melbourne Mexico City Mumbai Nairobi
Paris São Paulo Shanghai Singapore Taipei Tokyo Toronto Warsaw

with associated companies in Berlin Ibadan

Published in the United States
by Oxford University Press Inc., New York

British Library Cataloguing in Publication Data

Data available

Library of Congress Cataloging in Publication Data

Merchant, Jason.
The syntax of silence : sluicing, islands, and the theory of ellipsis / Jason Merchant.
p. cm.—(Oxford studies in theoretical linguistics)
Includes bibliographical references.
1. Grammar, Comparative and general—Ellipsis. 2. Extraction (Linguistics)
3. Grammar, Comparative and general—Syntax. 4. Semantics. I. Title. II. Series.
P291.3.M47 2001
415—dc21 2001021771
ISBN 0-19-924373-5 (hbk.)
ISBN 0-19-924372-7 (pbk.)

1 3 5 7 9 10 8 6 4 2

Typeset by Best-set Typesetter Ltd., Hong Kong
Printed in Great Britain
on acid-free paper by
T.J. International Ltd., Padstow, Cornwall

Contents

Oxford Studies in Theoretical Linguistics

General Preface

The theoretical focus of this series is on the interfaces between subcomponents of the human grammatical system and the closely related area of the interfaces between the different subdisciplines of linguistics. The notion of 'interface' has become central in grammatical theory (for instance, in Chomsky's recent Minimalist Program) and in linguistic practice: work on the interfaces between syntax and semantics, syntax and morphology, phonology and phonetics, etc. has led to a deeper understanding of particular linguistic phenomena and of the architecture of the linguistic component of the mind/brain.

The series will cover interfaces between core components of grammar, including syntax/morphology, syntax/semantics, syntax/phonology, syntax/pragmatics, morphology/phonology, phonology/phonetics, phonetics/speech processing, semantics/pragmatics, intonation/discourse structure, as well as issues in the way that the systems of grammar involving these interface areas are acquired and deployed in use (including language acquisition, language dysfunction, and language processing). It will demonstrate, we hope, that a proper understanding of particular linguistic phenomena, languages, language groups, or inter-language variation all require reference to interfaces.

The series is open to work by linguists of all theoretical persuasions and schools of thought. A main requirement is that authors should write so as to be understood by colleagues in related subfields of linguistics and by scholars in cognate disciplines.

We are pleased to present the first volume in the series. Jason Merchant examines ellipsis constructions, focusing on sluicing, and arguing for a perspective which involves both the syntax/phonetic form (PF) and syntax/semantics interfaces. He shows that a theory involving PF deletion under semantic identity allows for an explanation of a broad range of cross-linguistic data.

David Adger
Hagit Borer

Preface

This work is a revised version of my dissertation, written primarily in the years 1997–9, and filed in June 1999 at the University of California, Santa Cruz. My primary thanks therefore go to my supervisors Jim McCloskey and Bill Ladusaw. Jim's insightful comments on the many drafts and discussions that led to this work always demonstrated his unparalleled ability to see to the heart of an argument and to clarify it, and his astounding grasp of the literature. My meetings with Bill were also crucial to the development of the ideas presented here, and the work would be much poorer without the benefit of his ability to combine formal acuity with linguistic insight. I have also benefited from Sandy Chung's penetrating intelligence and healthy skepticism. I must also thank these three in particular for their willingness to generously entertain, and then to cheerfully encourage, the analysis of sluicing presented below, which runs counter to their own; few committees are faced with such a challenge, and none, I am sure, would have handled it with more grace and enthusiasm.

In general, I doubt that this work could have been completed without the stimulating environment for linguistics at Santa Cruz. I benefited enormously from my interactions with everyone in the community there, and am especially thankful to Judith Aissen, Chris Albert, Daniel Büring, Donka Farkas, Ted Fernald, Jorge Hankamer, Junko Ito, Chris Kennedy, Armin Mester, Line Mikkelsen, Eric Potsdam, Geoff Pullum, Jaye Padgett, Peter Svenonius, and Rachel Walker.

Over the course of writing and revising this book, I have amassed a large number of debts to colleagues around the world for their helpful comments, suggestions, reactions, and support. In the Netherlands, I am grateful to Norbert Corver, Marcel den Dikken, Jeroen Groenendijk, Jack Hoeksema, Helen de Hoop, Josep Quer, Henk van Riemsdijk, Eddy Ruys, Yoad Winter, Jan-Wouter Zwart, and Frans Zwarts. In Germany, thanks to Kerstin Schwabe, Satoshi Tomioka, Chris Wilder, Susanne Winkler, and Niina Zhang. In America and other places, I thank Mike Dickey, Edit Doron, Hana Filip,

Danny Fox, Dan Hardt, Hajime Hoji, Norbert Hornstein, Kyle Johnson, Mika Kizu, Anne Lobeck, Taisuke Nishigauchi, Maribel Romero, and Uli Sauerland. Numerous improvements are especially due to discussions with and comments from Daniel Büring and Chris Kennedy.

A special debt of gratitude is owed to Anastasia Giannakidou, whose comments, ideas, and collaboration over the years have been essential to this book's development.

A work of this scope, dealing as it does with a construction that is unknown in traditional grammars, could never have been completed without the active participation of numerous informants and discussants as well. For their indispensible aid, I am grateful to the following people for discussion of their various native languages and languages of expertise. Such a list unfortunately cannot do justice to the often painstaking and always patient work done in judging the numerous examples I was interested in.

1. Arabic (Moroccan): M'hamed Bennani-Meziane, Mohamed Damir
2. Basque: Arantzazu Elordieta
3. Bulgarian: Sevdalina Dianova, Lily Schürcks-Grozeva
4. Catalan: Josep Quer
5. Chinese (Mandarin): Niina Zhang
6. Czech: Hana Filip, Anna Pilátová
7. Danish: Line Mikkelsen
8. Dutch: Norbert Corver, Jelle Gerbrandy, Herman Hendriks, Petra Hendriks, Jack Hoeksema, Bart Hollebrandse, Iris Mulders, Henk van Riemsdijk, Rob van Rooy, Eddy Ruys, Frans Zwarts
9. Finnish: Dan Karvonen
10. French: Caroline Féry, Paul Hirschbühler, Marie Labelle
11. Frisian: Jelle Gerbrandy, Ger de Haan, Jarich Hoekstra, Oebele Vries
12. German: Daniel Büring, André Meinunger, Armin Mester, Hans Rott, Patrick Schindler, Susanne Winkler; and Philip Spaelti for Swiss German
13. Greek: Yoryia Agouraki, Artemis Alexiadou, Elena Anagnostopoulou, Kostis Danopoulos, Anastasia Giannakidou, Anna Roussou, Athina Sioupi, Melita Stavrou
14. Hindi: Rajesh Bhatt
15. Hebrew: Edit Doron, Danny Fox, Adam Sherman, Yoad Winter, Shalom Zuckerman
16. Hungarian: Donka Farkas, Genoveva Puskás
17. Icelandic: Höskuldur Thráinsson
18. Irish: Jim McCloskey
19. Italian: Maria Aloni, Gloria Cocchi, Paola Monachesi

20. Japanese: Motoko Katayama, Mika Kizu, Kazutaka Kurisu, Junko Shimoyama, Satoshi Tomioka
21. Norwegian: Peter Svenonius
22. Persian: Behrad Aghaei
23. Polish: Dorotha Mokrosinska, Adam Przepiórkowski
24. Romanian: Carmen Dobrovie-Sorin, Donka Farkas, Alexander Grosu
25. Russian: Sergey Avrutin, Dasha Krizhanskaya
26. Serbo-Croatian: Svetlana Godjevac
27. Slovene: Tatjana Marvin
28. Spanish: Rodrigo Gutierrez, Juan Mora, Josep Quer
29. Swedish: Kerstin Sandell, Peter Svenonius
30. Turkish: Dilara Grate
31. Tzotzil: Judith Aissen
32. Yiddish: Jerry Sadock, Elisa Steinberg

Parts of this work have been presented at various forums in Groningen, Paris, Berlin, Thessaloniki, Tübingen, Utrecht, Leiden, Austin, Los Angeles, Santa Cruz, Chicago, Vancouver, Evanston, and San Diego, and the present work has benefited from those audiences' reactions and comments.

The majority of this research was funded by a Fulbright scholarship at the Universities of Utrecht and Amsterdam and by a President's dissertation fellowship at the University of California, Santa Cruz. The final stages of the preparation of the manuscript were supported by a Mellon postdoctoral fellowship at Northwestern University and by an NWO (Dutch Organization for Scientific Research) postdoctoral fellowship at the University of Groningen. The support of these institutions is hereby gratefully acknowledged.

Finally, my deepest gratitude goes to my parents for their support over the years, and to Anastasia, για (τα) πάντα.

J.M.

Abbreviations

The following is a list of abbreviations used in the glosses thoughout.

I	1st person	lit.	literally
2	2nd person	LOC	locative
3	3rd person	NEG	negative (marker)
ACC	accusative	NOM	nominative
AGR	agreement	PFV	perfective
AUX	auxiliary	pl	plural
CL	clitic	PRES	present
DAT	dative	PROG	progressive
ENC	enclitic	PRT	(modal) particle
ERG	ergative	Q	question particle
FIN	finite	REFL	reflexive
FUT	future	sg	singular
GEN	genitive	SUBJ	subjunctive
INSTR	instrumental	TOP	topic

Στη γυναίκα μου Αναστασία

Introduction

Silence is the perfectest herald of joy

(*Much Ado About Nothing*, 2. 1. 286)

The primary goal of contemporary theoretical linguistics is to develop a theory of the correspondence between sound (or gesture) and meaning. Nowhere does this sound–meaning correspondence break down more spectacularly than in the case of ellipsis. And yet various forms of ellipsis are pervasive in natural language—words and phrases that by rights should be in the linguistic signal go missing. How is this possible?

It is possible because ellipsis is parasitic on redundancy: to paraphrase Wittgenstein, 'wovon man nicht sprechen muß, darüber kann man schweigen'. Elliptical processes capitalize on the redundancy of certain kinds of information in certain contexts, and permit an economy of expression by omitting the linguistic structures that would otherwise be required to express this information.

Such redundancy is a general property of biological systems, and is exploited by numerous other systems as well (compression algorithms being one contemporary example). But there will always be a competition between economy of expression (speaker-based least-effort principles) and the requirement that the output expression be usable (that is, interpretable) in the intended way (hearer-based least-effort principles). The use of ellipsis by a speaker is obviously more economical from the speaker's standpoint, by whatever metric of economy we may wish to employ (be it 'effort', however defined, number of words, phrases, and so on). By the same token, interpreting elliptical utterances is concomitantly more work for the hearer, since a meaning must be derived from no overt linguistic signal.

These competing demands on the language system ensure that it will resemble various other systems selected for optimizing resource allocation. The widespread use of ellipsis in natural languages is, from this standpoint, natural and expected: an obvious method to exploit redundancies in a system while maintaining usability.

Grammatical information is encoded redundantly in various ways in many languages. A simple example is subject–verb agreement—for example, English marks the verb as 3rd person even if the subject is unambiguously 3rd person: she_{3sg} is_{3sg} *smart.* Many languages mark the same grammatical information in various parts of the sentence: number is marked both on the negative auxiliary and verbal participle in Finnish, aspect is marked redundantly on each verbal head in serial verb constructions in Dagaare, tense and negation appear on each verb in serial verb constructions in Akan, and so on (these examples all taken from Niño 1997).

Such facts make the point that, although expressing redundant information may be a necessary condition to license the omission of linguistic structure, it is surely not a sufficient one. In fact, languages differ extensively in how they allow redundancies to be reduced by the grammar, in typically systemic ways. Because of this, the possibility for ellipsis, being language- and structure-specific, cannot solely be attributed to general principles of information redundancy, and must be encoded in some way in the grammar. Two issues arise here, which commonly go by the names 'licensing' and 'identification'. Licensing refers to local conditions on the omissibility of structures, while identification refers to the recovery of the information that would have otherwise been expressed if the structures had been overt.

A theory of licensing will be concerned with potentially quite parochial facts about local configurations and features of the categories involved. I will address this issue in Chapter 2. The problem of identification seems at first sight to be the more intractable one, since we come directly to the puzzle of generating meanings from silence.

This fact alone has inspired the considerable body of work done on ellipsis in the last thirty years, and is the primary reason that ellipsis continues to puzzle and challenge researchers, remaining an active topic of investigation. Most of this work has concentrated on the omission of verb phrases in English, spurred on by the remarkable results achieved in Keenan (1971) and Sag (1976a), and later works, who convincingly showed that this kind of ellipsis was sensitive to semantic conditions, not simply phrase structural ones as had been commonly assumed.

As productive and successful as the work based on VP-ellipsis in English has been, however, it has also been of necessity quite limited in scope. For reasons

that remain unclear, though presumably closely linked to the particular
properties of the auxiliary system, VP-ellipsis as attested in English seems to be
quite rare among the world's languages. Given the subtlety of the necessary
data (much of the literature is concerned especially with the possibilities of
anaphoric relations under ellipsis), most work on VP-ellipsis, and hence on
ellipsis in general, has been carried out by native speakers of English. While this
is a practical boon for researchers who *are* native speakers of English, resulting
in a near monopoly on theorizing in this domain, it goes without saying that
this limitation makes it impossible to know whether the conclusions reached
for English VP-ellipsis hold with any interesting generality cross-linguistically.

Fortunately, there are elliptical phenomena that are much more widespread
than VP-ellipsis, and it is the goal of this book to investigate certain properties
of one of these other types of ellipsis in a number of languages. The phenomenon that will engage our attention here is *sluicing*.

Sluicing is the name given by Ross (1969)[1] to the phenomenon exemplified
in (1) and (2)—sentences in which an interrogative clause is reduced to containing only a wh-phrase. This wh-phrase may correspond to an overt correlate
(italicized in (1)), or not (as in (2)).

(1)   a   Jack bought *something*, but I don't know what.
      b   *Someone* called, but I can't tell you who.
      c   *Beth* was there, but you'll never guess who else.

(2)   a   Jack called, but I don't know {when/how/why/where from}.
      b   Sally's out hunting—guess what!
      c   A car is parked on the lawn—find out whose.

These seem to have a structure like that in (3), where the struck-through IP
indicates that the sentential part of the interrogative CP is elided.

(3)

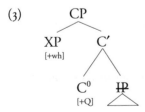

---

[1] Ross has always been known for his onomastic fecundity, though this particular example is
less transparent than many of his other christenings. It presumably picks up on the sense of the
verb *sluice* (Webster's 2nd edition gives the following etymology: from the Dutch *sluys, sluis* <

Although it is not widely recognized, sluicing may arguably be the most important of the commonly studied elliptical constructions, for one reason: the class of possible sluiced sentences seems to be a proper superset of the class of equivalent non-elliptical 'deaccented' sentences, as we will see immediately below.

This is the opposite of what has been observed for VP-ellipsis: many of the properties ascribed to VP-ellipsis are found in deaccented VPs as well; in other words, in VP-ellipsis the elliptical cases form a proper subset of the whole phenomenon. This has led many researchers, notably Tancredi (1992), Rooth (1992*a*), Chomsky and Lasnik (1993), Tomioka (1995, 1997), Asher *et al.* (1997), Romero (1998), and Fox (2000), to argue that the identity conditions on ellipsis would fall out (fully or in part) from a more complete investigation of the effects of focus and parallelism in certain grammatical environments (though it should be noted that earlier researchers had realized that theories concentrating solely on the identity of the missing VP and an antecedent VP—identity of predication theories—were not enough: Prüst and Scha (1990*a*,*b*), Prüst (1993), and Prüst *et al.* (1994) noted that *clausal parallelism* was the crucial component, constraining quantifier interactions even outside the ellipsis site). Thus the problem of *significatio ex nihilo* with which analyses of ellipsis have traditionally been concerned, employing syntactic identity mechanisms, seems to be a side issue: once we identify the conditions that license deaccenting in non-elliptical structures—so the conjecture goes—we can apply these to the cases of ellipsis, which is itself nothing more than the most radical form of deaccenting—namely, phonological deletion.

It is in this context, then, that the commonly accepted wisdom on sluicing looms large, despite its neglect in the general literature on ellipsis. This general wisdom regarding sluicing stems from Ross (1969) and has gone unchallenged to my knowledge. In his original investigation of this area, Ross noticed that wh-phrases stranded under sluicing could seemingly violate his island constraints, as the contrast between (4a) and (4b) shows (where the small italicized phrase in (4b) represents the low-flat F_0 intonation characteristic of deaccented material).

(4)   a   They want to hire someone who speaks a Balkan language, but I don't remember which.

OFr *escluse* < LLat *exclūsa*, the past participle of Lat *exclūdere* 'exclude, shut out'; the OED's etymology is comparable) meaning 'to wash off with a rush of water', metaphorically extended to the 'washing-away' of the sentence below the wh-phrase. A more fanciful interpretation would trace the origin of the term to the approximate sound-similarity of sluicing to 'S-losing', in the sense of 'losing' the S node under the wh-phrase (cf. S-lifting 'slifting' and wh-is 'whiz' deletion).

b *They want to hire someone who speaks a Balkan language, but I don't remember which *they want to hire someone who speaks.*

This insensitivity to islands, which received prominence in the analysis of Chung *et al.* (1995), is the major stumbling block to reducing elliptical structures to merely deaccented ones syntactically. If we assume that the degradation in acceptability of sentences containing extraction from islands is the result of a syntactic principle that operates to prevent such unbounded dependencies, the contrast between (4a) and (4b) is mysterious. Under the deletion approach, (4a) is derived from (4b) by a purely phonological process of deletion, operating at Phonological Form (PF). This PF operation should, under a purely *syntactic* approach to islands, have no bearing on the impossibility of extraction in this context.

One way to respond is to claim that islands are essentially PF phenomena after all, perhaps most plausibly a kind of processing constraint (on memory and associative domains), as often proposed in the literature (see Kluender 1998 for references and a recent approach). If an island falls within an ellipsis site but is deleted at PF, no violation will be triggered. This is essentially what Ross (1969) suggested—that island violations were calculated 'across the derivation' (globally), with extracted-out-of islands that remained at PF even worse than those that were deleted. But reducing island violations to processing difficulties in the case of overt extraction but not in ellipsis would, of course, also require some principled way to distinguish the processing of overt linguistic signals from the processing that must take place to assign elliptical structures their meaning. If human on-line language processing reflects anything about the actual comprehension of sentences, as it surely must if it is to have any interest at all, then this discrepancy is entirely unexpected and extremely worrying.

Even if this discrepancy could be resolved, however, the general strategy will fail, because there are cases where islands occur inside ellipsis sites and retain their force. For example, a VP-ellipsis version of (4a) is impossible:

(5) *They want to hire someone who speaks a Balkan language, but I don't remember which they do [$_{VP}$ ~~want to hire someone who speaks~~].

Another major reason to reject the idea that all islands are PF phenomena comes from the evidence that certain kinds of islands—including the relative clause of (4b)—are respected by covert movement as well (see Huang 1982, Nishigauchi 1986, and, for further references, May 1991). We can, therefore, set aside at least the possibility of reducing *all* islands to PF constraints (in particular, islands of the sort represented by (4b)).

We are then left with the problem posed by the contrast in (4): why does sluicing seem to be able to void islands? Although the most successful account to date of these facts—namely, Chung *et al.* (1995)—relies on an LF-copying mechanism supplemented by various matching and repair operations, I will show that the facts are in fact also compatible with a strictly deletion-based approach to ellipsis, sensitive to a partly novel condition on the focus structure of the deleted material (as proposed more generally for VP-ellipsis in Rooth 1992*b* and pursued for sluicing by Romero 1997*a*, 1998). My goal in what follows, in other words, is to rehabilitate the deletion account of sluicing.

Deletion accounts are often assumed to require that a morphosyntactic identity condition hold between the deleted structure and some antecedent. This is by no means, however, a necessary assumption, and it is not one that I will adopt. We will see, in fact, that any such syntactic isomorphism requirement runs into severe problems in both sluicing and VP-ellipsis, and must be avoided in any case. This historical link between deletion approaches and syntactic isomorphism is easily severed: there is nothing inherently contradictory in building a theory of ellipsis that imposes a semantic identity requirement on a PF operation; in fact, as we will see, such a theory provides a straightforward way of linking the syntactic (licensing) and semantic (identification) requirements.

But, if the syntax in the ellipsis site is the usual syntax of clauses, a major claim to be defended here, then we arrive back at the problem of the apparent island insensitivity. This fact, that some kinds of sluicing are not sensitive to islands, will be shown to require a revision in our understanding of the nature of some syntactic islands. In particular, I will argue that certain islands are indeed PF phenomenon, while others, like the relative clause in (4) above, are not. This means that not all islands are created equal: we need a pluralistic view of islandhood. The fact that sluicing is possible in cases like (4a) is misleading: I show that there is in the end no reason to assume that there is a corresponding island in the deleted IP, and that the observed interpretations can be generated without the island.

The general answer, then, to the question we began with—how the apparent lack of the usual correlation between sound and meaning is overcome in the case of ellipsis—is the more mundane answer given to this question when the items involved have phonetic (or gestural) exponence: this correlation is mediated by syntax. The fact that the syntax in these cases has no phonetic exponence certainly does make it more difficult to investigate, but it seems unlikely at this point that any other option will prove to be correct. It is the goal of the present study to argue for the conclusion that there is indeed syntax in the silence.

OVERVIEW OF THE BOOK

I will defend here the idea that there are two components to the derivations underlying the sentences in (1) and (2)—the movement rule that extracts a wh-phrase from an IP in interrogative structures in general, and an operation of deletion of the remaining IP fed by the movement. This gives a maximally simple syntax, since it is just the ordinary syntax of wh-clauses.

I begin in Chapter 1 by reviewing our current understanding of ellipsis, based primarily on VP-ellipsis in English. I show that the commonly assumed structural isomorphism condition imposed on deleted structures (supplemental to more general focus conditions on deaccenting) encounters a number of severe problems when applied to even simple cases of sluicing. It furthermore encounters a better-known problem regarding anaphora under ellipsis, dubbed 'vehicle change' by Fiengo and May (1994). I then define a novel focus condition on ellipsis sites, building in a two-way implicational relation, which allows us to abandon the additional structural isomorphism condition, solving the problems for sluicing and eliminating the need for a separate theory of 'vehicle change'. These general conditions apply to both VP-ellipsis and sluicing, and set the stage for the analysis of the data to come.

Chapter 2 examines the structural conditions on sluicing and investigates its external and internal syntax. I establish that sluicing involves a CP, with an IP missing, and discuss the licensing conditions on the null IP, building on work by Lobeck (1995). I show that these conditions can be captured under a deletion account, based on a single feature that triggers deletion; this feature, furthermore, provides the locus for imposing the semantic condition developed in Chapter 1. Finally, I document a novel generalization regarding the elements that can appear in the C-domain in sluicing, and propose that it follows under a natural interpretation of deletion and economy, and from general principles concerning the kinds of null elements that can follow complementizers.

In Chapter 3, I turn to the core novel data presented in this work, based on informant work on twenty-four languages. I begin by documenting the relevant island facts, mostly known from the literature. I continue by establishing the novel generalization that will be crucial in Chapters 4 and 5, relating to the form-identity required between the sluiced wh-phrase and its antecedent, in particular to the cross-linguistic availability of preposition-stranding under wh-movement.

In Chapter 4, I examine five different approaches to sluicing, representative of extant accounts, and show that these accounts fail to offer a way to deal either with the island insensitivity or with the form-identity generalizations of Chapter 3.

Finally, in Chapter 5, I turn to my account of the form-identity generalizations, and show that a deletion account of sluicing captures these facts, and that the island insensitivity in the crucial cases can be analyzed away, leaving only cases where no syntactic island is violated. It is shown that this analysis supports a division between syntactic islands such as relative clauses and adjuncts, and PF effects such as COMP-trace phenomena, certain coordinate structures, and left-branch effects. The ability of deletion to account for sluicing entails that one of the best arguments for an LF-copying approach to ellipsis resolution (or indeed, for more abstract semantic approaches) collapses. This result has the additional welcome consequence of making sluicing less mysterious from current theoretical perspectives, and will, I hope, make sluicing a respectable companion to VP-ellipsis in the typology of ellipsis.

NOTE TO THE READER

It is worth emphasizing at the outset that, while readers interested in an expanded domain of data for theorizing about ellipsis will find much of interest below, readers interested primarily in VP-ellipsis in English and the perennial questions concerning strict and sloppy identity will find very little. This is, on the one hand, due to time and space requirements: sluicing is sufficiently complex to need to be treated on its own, leaving a possible eventual complete unification for a better understanding of all the processes—although the unification that is achieved in Chapter 1 is quite general, many further, primarily VP-ellipsis-specific questions remain to be investigated from this perspective. On the other hand, it is difficult to investigate the question of strict and sloppy identity under sluicing, because speakers are quite uniform in finding sloppy readings under sluicing to be highly inaccessible.[2]

---

[2] Although Ross (1969) gives one example of fairly acceptable sloppy identity under sluicing, even the most cursory examination of a fuller range of cases reveals that something substantially different from VP-ellipsis is involved. In the following cases, which have been checked with three speakers, it is very difficult to get the sloppy reading (there was some variation, but in the range of 'impossible' versus 'very marginal').

    (i)   a   Abby said she'd stop smoking tomorrow, but Beth wouldn't say when.
            b   Alex said someone would visit him after Ben wondered who.
            c   Abby knew how fast she'd run, but Beth had to ask how fast.
            d   Abby knew how fast she'd run, but Beth even had to ask how far.
            e   Abby already knew which students were enrolled in her seminar, but Beth didn't even know how many.
            f   Abby knew who she saw, and Beth said she knew who, too.

For these reasons, I will turn the tables on most recent theorizing about ellipsis, relegating VP-ellipsis to the footnotes, and keeping sluicing on center stage throughout.

These should be compared to the following parallel cases of VP-ellipsis, where the sloppy reading is perfectly available. Similar contrasts can be constructed for all the above examples. The constrast is remarkable.

(ii)   a   Abby told us when she'd stop smoking, but Beth didn't.
        b   Abby already knew which students were enrolled in her seminar, but Beth didn't.

See Tomioka (1996, 1999) for discussion and references to the immense literature on sloppy identity under VP-ellipsis, and especially Hoji and Fukaya (1999) and Hoji (forthcoming) for relevant discussion in an expanded domain.

I

Identity in Ellipsis: Focus and Isomorphism

Despite the stated primary goal of this book to investigate sluicing, any discussion of the general conditions on ellipsis must begin with the best investigated case, VP-ellipsis in English. I therefore start with this case, describing the general results in this area, and then move on to see how these results apply to sluicing, returning only briefly to VP-ellipsis.

Since Tancredi (1992) and Rooth (1992*a*), it has been known that the problem of defining the conditions under which VPs can be elided in English is related to (these authors claim that it forms a subpart of) the problem of defining the conditions under which English VPs can be deaccented, or phonologically reduced. Both problems seem intimately related to general conditions governing the distribution of focus, and several authors have sought to define the appropriate focus conditions for regulating both deaccenting and ellipsis phenomena. While this unification is not entirely uncontroversial (see Winkler 1997 and López 2000 for dissenting views), the intuitions upon which it is founded are quite robust, and it seems like a promising strategy to explore the connections between the two. Nonetheless, as we will see, identifying the conditions under which a VP can be deaccented (treated as given, in the technical sense defined below) does not answer all the questions about the conditions under which a VP can be omitted—ellipsis of a VP has always been taken to be subject to an additional, usually structural constraint as well.

In this chapter, I review the general conditions on deaccenting as well as the evidence for an additional structural constraint. I show that this additional constraint raises numerous problems in a variety of domains, both under VP-ellipsis and, especially, under sluicing. (Perhaps the most widely known of these problems has been dubbed 'vehicle change' in Fiengo and May 1994, and in one of the most important of its manifestations concerns the conditions under which pronouns can be deleted under identity with R-expressions.) I then propose a revised focus condition that can handle the cases that were problematic for the more general focus conditions, while allowing us to abandon the structural isomorphism constraint that was so problematic (and eliminating the necessity for a separate theory of 'vehicle change' for these cases). Finally, I illustrate how this revised focus condition applies to a core set of data from sluicing, setting the stage for the investigation that follows, and in particular laying the groundwork for the analysis to be developed in Chapter 5.

In what follows, I anticipate several of the results of the following chapters, and refer to the constituent dominating the remnant wh-phrase as CP, to the missing material as IP, and to the process that derives the ellipsis as deletion. These terminological choices will be justified extensively later, but serve here only to facilitate discussion.

1.1 SEMANTIC BACKGROUND

In this section, I very briefly lay out some of the relevant background notions that will be assumed in what follows. The assumptions here are entirely standard, and readers familiar with semantics can proceed directly to the following section.

I will be assuming a type-driven translation of phrase-markers at Logical Form (LF), which are expected to encode all the relevant properties (up to context) for determining meanings of syntactic structures. LF expressions are assigned translations into a logical language L (we will use the standard predicate calculus for L), and these expressions of L are evaluated by an interpretation function $[\![\cdot]\!]$ relative to a model M and an assignment function g (ignoring intensionality for the moment), written $[\![\cdot]\!]^{M,g}$.

The relevant definition is given in (1).

(1)   Let $M = \langle E, I \rangle$, where E is the domain of individuals, and I is an interpretation function that assigns to each constant (individual or predicate) in L an extension in E.

If c is an individual constant, then $I(c) \in E$. If P is a n-ary predicate, then I maps P onto an ordered n-tuple of elements of E: $I(P) \subseteq E^n$. For example, for a one-place predicate P of type $\langle e,t \rangle$ and a constant c of type $\langle e \rangle$, P(c) is true in M if and only if $I(c) \in I(P)$. This is illustrated in the example in (2).

(2)   Let $M_1 = \langle E, I \rangle$, where
$$E = \{\, abby, ben \,\}$$
$$I = \begin{bmatrix} a \rightarrow abby \\ b \rightarrow ben \\ sing \rightarrow \{abby\} \end{bmatrix}$$

Now, $[\![\mathbf{sing(a)}]\!]^{M_1,g} = 1$ iff $[\![\mathbf{a}]\!]^{M_1,g} \in [\![\mathbf{sing}]\!]^{M_1,g}$, that is, iff abby $\in$ {abby}, which is the case in the model in (2).

While this works fine for formulas that contain only constants and predicates (and various logical connectives, whose definitions I will not go over here), something more is needed to interpret variables, which are used as translations of traces of movement and pronouns. Formulas with free variables are evaluated with respect to assignment functions. For present purposes, where variables will only be of type $\langle e \rangle$, an assignment function g is a function from variables to individuals in the domain E. As an example, consider the function g_1 in (3).

(3) $g_1 = \begin{bmatrix} x \rightarrow abby \\ y \rightarrow ben \\ z \rightarrow charlene \end{bmatrix}$

Using this assignment function, we can evaluate a formula such as **sing**(y). This formula will be true with respect to M and g if and only if the value that g returns for y is an element of the set given by I(**sing**). Using M_1 and g_1 as examples, we have $[\![\mathbf{sing(y)}]\!]^{M_1,g_1} = 1$ iff $[\![\mathbf{y}]\!]^{M_1,g_1} \in [\![\mathbf{sing}]\!]^{M_1,g_1}$; since $g_1(y) =$ ben, and since ben $\notin$ {abby}, the formula **sing**(y) is false under M_1 and g_1.

Note that there is no difference between $[\![\mathbf{sing(y)}]\!]^{M_1,g_1}$ and $[\![\mathbf{sing(b)}]\!]^{M_1,g_1}$. This simple fact will be the key to eliminating one of the core cases of 'vehicle change', as we will see below.

In general, the recursive definition for the semantics of $[\![\cdot]\!]$ relative to a model M and an assignment function g is given in (4).

(4)   If α is an individual constant or predicate, then $[\![\alpha]\!]^{M,g} = I(\alpha)$.
       If α is a variable, then $[\![\alpha]\!]^{M,g} = g(\alpha)$.

This brief overview should suffice for our purposes.

1.2 THE FOCUS AND ISOMORPHISM CONDITIONS

Rooth (1992*a*), following an early version of Fiengo and May (1994), distinguishes two different relations between an elided VP (call it VP$_E$) and its antecedent (VP$_A$), indicated schematically in (5), order irrelevant.

(5)   redundancy relation 2

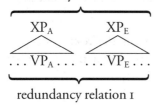

         redundancy relation 1

These authors claim that redundancy relation 1 is syntactic: in particular, to be identified with the notion of 'reconstruction' that Fiengo and May outline, which we return to directly. While Rooth accepts this premise, he is more concerned with redundancy relation 2, which Fiengo and May (1994) claim falls under their Dependency Theory (essentially imposing syntactic isomorphism on the parallel structures, modulo indices). Rooth argues that redundancy relation 2 is in fact a semantic relation, which he identifies with his ~ operator (see Rooth 1985, 1992*b*, 1996). The ~ operator attaches to an LF constituent α and requires that there be a set of alternatives of the same type as α; I will not go into the details here—the reader is referred to Büring (1997) for an especially lucid exposition of Rooth's theory of focus.

Rooth's hypothesis is as follows:

ellipsis should be possible exactly in configurations where
    1. a verb phrase can be syntactically reconstructed, and
    2. some phrase identical with or dominating the reconstructed phrase can be related by the ~ relation to some phrase identical with or dominating the reconstruction antecedent . . . (Rooth 1992*a*: 18)

The condition in 2, applied to the schema in (5), requires that XP$_A$ ~ XP$_E$, in Rooth's terms. Spelling this out, we can restate this condition as in (6) (as is usually done: see Johnson 1997 and Romero 1997*a*).

(6)   **R-Focus condition on VP-ellipsis** (Roothian version)
         A VP α in XP$_E$ can be deleted only if there is an XP$_A$, where $[\![XP_A]\!]^o$ either is or implies an element of $[\![XP_E]\!]^f$.[1]

---

[1] Simplifying somewhat, $[\![α]\!]^o$ is the ordinary value returned by $[\![\ ]\!]$ for α; $[\![α]\!]^f$ is the focus value of α, the set of alternatives to α, derived from α by replacing all F-marked constituents in α by variables of the appropriate type.

Rooth's insight can also be applied using Schwarzschild's (1999) theory of focus, based on his definition of GIVEN.

(7)   **GIVENness** (Schwarzschild 1999)
      1. If a constituent α is not F-marked, α must be GIVEN.
      2. An expression[2] E counts as GIVEN iff E has a salient antecedent A and, modulo ∃-type shifting,[3] A entails the F-closure of E.

(8)   **F-closure**
      The F-closure of α, written F-clo(α), is the result of replacing F-marked parts of α with ∃-bound variables of the appropriate type (modulo ∃-type shifting).

I will refrain from taking the reader through Schwarzschild's theory here; how it works will become evident as we examine various examples.

(9)   **S-Focus condition on VP-ellipsis** (Schwarzschildian version)
      A VP α can be deleted only if α is or is contained in a constituent that is GIVEN.

Let us illustrate this with an example.

(10) a Abby sang because [Ben]$_F$ did.
      b

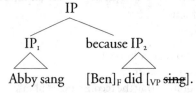

Example (10a) has the LF in (10b), where struck-through text is the diacritic for material that is not pronounced at PF (I will assume that the feature that triggers this deletion at PF is present at LF; see §2.2.1 for implementation).

The R-Focus condition requires that $[\![IP_1]\!]^\circ \in [\![IP_2]\!]^f$—that is, that $\lambda w.\mathbf{sing}_w(a) \in \{\lambda w.\mathbf{sing}_w(x): x \in D_e\}$. This latter set is equivalent to $\{\lambda w.\mathbf{sing}_w(a),$ $\lambda w.\mathbf{sing}_w(b)\}$ in M_1. (I ignore tense and aspect here and throughout.)

---

   [2] I use the term 'expression' in place of Schwarzschild's 'utterance' to abstract away from certain complications that he discusses, irrelevant here; see Schwarzschild (1999).
   [3] ∃-type shifting is a type-shifting operation that raises expressions to type ⟨t⟩ and existentially binds unfilled arguments.

The S-Focus condition is also satisfied: the deleted VP is given, since the antecedent *Abby sang* entails the ∃-type shifted deleted VP: ∃x.**sing**(x). Equivalently, we could compare the containing IPs—again, *Abby sang* entails the result of replacing the F-marked [Ben]$_F$ in IP$_2$ by an ∃-bound variable: ∃x.**sing**(x).

Consider now the example in (11a), which contains a pronoun *him$_2$*, which we translate with the variable *x$_2$*.

(11) a Abby saw him after [Ben]$_F$ did.

b

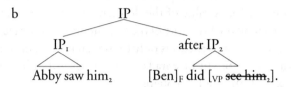

The LF in (11b) will meet the R-Focus condition iff ⟦Abby saw x$_2$⟧° ∈ ⟦[Ben]$_F$ saw x$_2$⟧^{f}—that is, if λw.**see**$_w$(**a**, g(x$_2$)) ∈ {λw.**see**$_w$(y, g(x$_2$)) | y ∈ D$_e$}. It meets the S-Focus condition iff IP$_1$ entails ∃x.**see**(x, g(x$_2$)); this will hold only if **see**(**abby**, g(x$_2$)) is true.

It is well known that certain kinds of VPs can be deaccented by satisfying a focus condition but not elided under the same conditions. The final VPs in (12) and (13), for example, can be deaccented because the preceding clause provides an appropriate antecedent. Here, capital letters represent focal stress, and italics indicate deaccenting (a low F$_0$ contour: see Hirschberg and Ward (1991) and Winkler (1997) for more detailed examination of this phenomenon and some important caveats). The cases in (13) are somewhat more extreme examples of the same phenomenon, dubbed 'implicational bridging' cases by Rooth.

(12) a Abby was reading the book while BEN *was reading*.
      b Abby ate a sandwich after BEN *ate*.
      c Abby left the party because BEN *left*.
      d Abby sang her hymn louder than BEN *sang*.

(13) a Abby called Chuck an idiot after BEN *insulted him*.
      b Abby ate a sandwich after BEN *had lunch*.
      c Abby left the party because BEN *took off*.

In each case, the antecedent implies a proposition that is in the focus value of the deaccented VP, satisfying the R-Focus condition.[4] This is shown in (14) for (12a):

---

[4] Similar remarks hold for the passive–active alternation under ellipsis, which raise numerous difficult questions that I will sidestep here. These have been extensively discussed in the litera-

(14)   [[Abby was reading the book]]° → [[Abby was reading]]° and
        [[Abby was reading]]° ∈ [[BEN$_F$ was reading]]^f

Similarly, since entailment[5] is built into the definition of Schwarzschild's
GIVEN, the computation is direct:

(15)   *Abby was reading the book* entails ∃x.x **was reading**

These should be compared with examples in which the antecedent does not
imply a proposition in the focus value of the deaccented VP, or, in Schwarzschild's terms, does not entail the F-closure of the IP containing the deaccented
VP (these following examples are felicitous only to the extent that, in the context of evaluation, the matrix predicate entails or implies the subordinate, e.g.
in a model where, if *x* reads the book, *x* coughs):

(16)   a   *Abby was reading the book while BEN *was coughing.*
        b   *Abby ate a sandwich after BEN *coughed.*
        c   *Abby left the party because BEN *coughed.*
        d   *Abby sang her hymn louder than BEN *coughed.*

(17)   a   *Abby called Chuck an idiot after BEN *coughed.*
        b   *Abby ate a sandwich after BEN *coughed.*
        c   *Abby left the party because BEN *coughed.*

However, the reasoning applied to the cases of phonological deaccenting
in (12) and (13) cannot be applied to VP-ellipsis. With VP-ellipsis, implications alone are not enough; rather, it seems we need identity of meaning, as a

ture (see Hardt 1993, Kehler 1993, 2000, and Fiengo and May 1994 for discussion and references).
Compare:

(i)   a   First, Abby picked Ben, and then CHARLIE *was picked.*
       b   *First, Abby picked Ben, and then CHARLIE *was fired.*
       c   *First, Abby picked Ben, and then CHARLIE was.

[5] What is intended by 'entailment' here is 'some kind of contextual entailment, where certain
background information is assumed' (Schwarzschild 1999: 151), with an obvious connection to
standard notions of presupposition. I assume that this somewhat laxer notion of entailment will
allow the necessary equivalences, as Schwarzschild assumes, for the reductions seen in the examples in the text. For example, (13b) is felicitous only if the context supports an 'entailment' (or
(perhaps accommodated) presupposition) that Abby ate the sandwich for lunch. The other cases
in (13) require less contextual support, since *leave* will always entail *take off* in the relevant sense,
and, if you call someone an idiot, you can virtually always be sure that you have insulted him
(perhaps unless he *really* is an idiot).

number of authors have proposed in varying forms (see Hardt 1992, 1993 for a recent approach and references). Take, for example, the VP-ellipsis in the sentences in (18) and (19); the elided VPs do not permit readings under which they would be equivalent to those in (12) and (13) above.

(18)   a   Abby was reading the book while BEN was.
        b   Abby ate a sandwich after BEN did.
        c   Abby left the party because BEN did.
        d   Abby sang her hymn louder than BEN did.

(19)   a   Abby called Chuck an idiot after BEN did.
        b   Abby ate a sandwich after BEN did.
        c   Abby left the party because BEN did.

Instead, in each of these cases, the elided VP must be identical in meaning to the antecedent. So (18a) is true only if Ben was reading the book, not simply if Ben was reading something.[6] Thus while the Focus conditions as stated apply to both VP-deaccenting and VP-ellipsis (and are responsible for the general parallelism of scope, etc.; see especially Tomioka 1995, 1997, Asher *et al.* 1997, and Fox 2000), the elliptical structure seems to be subject to an additional, stronger requirement.

This stronger requirement is often assumed to be some kind of structural isomorphism. The idea is to impose a further condition that requires a syntactically identical twin, an antecedent—an antecedent that does not just 'mean' the same as the deletion target, but has exactly the same structure as well (meaning actually plays no direct role in this approach, though a convenient byproduct of identity of structure will be identity of meaning in most circumstances, presumably). If no structurally identical antecedent is available, deletion will not be possible. This claim is made precise in Fiengo and May's (1994) notion of 'reconstruction', which they define as a 'set of token structures . . . [which are] occurrences in a discourse of a given (sub-) phrase marker over a terminal vocabulary' (p. 191); a deleted phrase must be a member of a reconstruction. The structural component of the theory of ellipsis consists, then, of the claim that an elided phrase must have a structurally isomorphic twin available. I will call this general claim the isomorphism condition on ellipsis.

Let us see how the isomorphism requirement applies to the cases at hand. For example, (18a) has the structure in (20).

---

[6] These facts are why the conditions are stated above as necessary but not sufficient conditions on deletion; they could be strengthened to biconditionals if we took them to apply only to deaccenting, not deletion.

(20)   Abby was

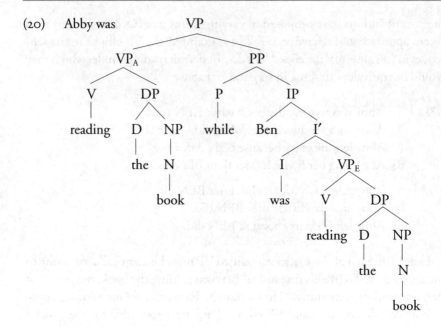

In this structure, VP$_A$ has the same structure as VP$_E$. By the isomorphism condition, then, VP$_E$ can be deleted.

The isomorphism requirement will prevent deletion of the embedded VP in a structure like (12a), as desired. That example has the structure in (21) (assuming that the implicit indefinite object of the intransitive *read* is not syntactically present):

(21)   Abby was

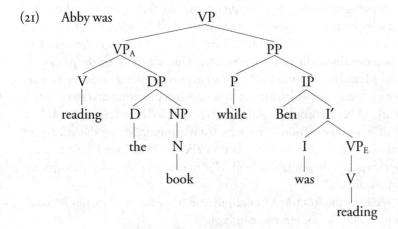

Since VP$_A$ ≠ VP$_E$, deletion is not allowed.

An isomorphism condition on deletion is thus successful in accounting for the basic facts presented above. Note that general considerations of inferability seem not to play a role here; even though *Abby was reading* is inferable from *Abby was reading the book*, this inference is not enough to make the structure available that is required to license deletion.

This condition also applies correctly to more complex examples, such as (22).

(22)   Abby [$_{VP_1}$ [$_{VP_2}$ left] after Ben did [$_{VP_3}$ ~~leave~~]], and Carla did [$_{VP_4}$ ~~leave after Ben did~~] too.

In this example, VP$_3$ is isomorphic to VP$_2$, while VP$_4$ is isomorphic to VP$_1$. This example shows that any segment of a VP can be used to satisfy isomorphism (see Merchant 2000*b* for an independent argument supporting this conclusion; see also Sag 1976*b*).

Of course, the example in (22) cannot be taken to show that adjuncts in general can be ignored for purposes of satisfying the isomorphism condition. Adjuncts internal to the minimal VP cannot be ignored, as (23) shows. Example (23) has only the reading given in (a), with the nominal adjunct in the ellipsis site, not that in (b), which ignores the adjunct.

(23)   Abby [$_{VP}$ met [$_{DP}$ [$_{DP}$ someone] from Kentucky]], and then Ben did.
        a   = ⟨meet someone from Kentucky⟩
        b   ≠ ⟨meet someone⟩

It seems that this fact must be a result of the isomorphism condition, because either focus condition would be satisfied by (23b), since ⟦Abby met someone from Kentucky⟧ → ⟦Abby met someone⟧. And indeed the isomorphism condition will rule out deletion of a VP like (23b), since it is not isomorphic to the antecedent VP [*meet someone from Kentucky*].

1.3 PROBLEMS FOR ISOMORPHISM

As successful as this is, it immediately runs into some problems. This section lays out a few of these problems, some potentially more serious than others, setting the stage for the semantic approach below.

One of the most evident problems comes from even simple cases of sluicing with implicit correlates, as in (24).

(24)   a Abby was reading, but I don't know what.
        b Ben called—guess when!

The relevant parts of the antecedent IP and CP of (24a) are given in (25).

(25)

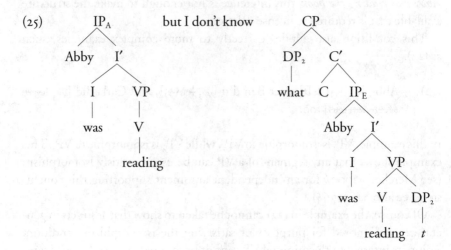

We have just seen that the intransitive use of *read* does not satisfy the iso-morphism condition for VP-ellipsis with the transitive use, which necessarily includes a direct object. The same holds for IP-ellipsis, obviously; here, $IP_A \neq IP_E$. The same kind of problem emerges for (24b), assuming that adjunct wh-phrases are generated internal to the IP (see Johnston 1994 for convincing argu-ments that this is the case).

Faced with this data, we might claim that traces of moved wh-phrases are not structurally present at LF, where the condition applies. This suggestion is reminiscent of various trace-pruning algorithms proposed to eliminate inter-mediate traces at LF (as in Lasnik and Saito 1984). But eliminating the traces structurally at LF goes directly against the grain of having an LF in the first place: if the trace is no longer structurally present, how do we know where the variable required by the wh-phrase should go? And how will the composition requirements of transitive *read* in (24a), for example, be satisfied? We would also have to develop an alternative account of the substantial data that suggests that traces maintain structure at LF, especially from work on reconstruction effects (Romero 1997*b*, Fox 1999; also Sauerland 1998, Merchant 2000*a*). In general, such a suggestion makes a hash of transparent LF, and reduces the iso-morphism condition to vacuity.

Even in sluicing, however, there is good evidence that the traces of moved elements should count for the purposes of ellipsis. A case in point is Dutch. Dutch is a V2 language, fronting the highest verb into C and some XP into SpecCP. Since in V2 structures these elements have vacated IP, if their traces could be eliminated or ignored, we would expect the deleted IPs in sluicing not to be required to have corresponding elements. This expectation is not borne out. In these examples, not only does the only sensible interpretation come from having the equivalents to the moved elements in the antecedent IP internal to the deleted IP; these are indeed the only grammatical possibilities:

(26) a [$_{CP}$ Nu gaat [$_{IP}$ zij t_{nu} t_{gaat}]], maar ik weet niet waarom.
          now goes she   but I know not why
       'She's going now, but I don't know why.'
   b *. . . waarom [$_{IP}$ ~~zij~~]
   c = . . . waarom [$_{IP}$ ~~zij nu gaat~~]

(27) a [$_{CP}$ Gisteren heeft [$_{IP}$ hij $t_{gisteren}$ met iemand gesproken t_{heeft}],
          yesterday has   he   with someone spoken

          maar ik weet niet met wie.
          but I know not with who
       'He spoke to someone yesterday, but I don't know who.'
   b *. . . met wie [$_{IP}$ ~~hij met iemand gesproken~~]
   c = . . . met wie [$_{IP}$ ~~hij gisteren heeft gesproken~~]

(Of course, this objection is mostly mitigated if one adopts a copy theory of movement; in that case, the question becomes, under what circumstances can moved material be ignored, and when must it—as above—be part of the resolution of the ellipsis?)

A second problem for isomorphism in sluicing comes from Romanian. As Dobrovie-Sorin (1993) and Grosu (1994: 224) discuss, clitic-doubling (here, with the clitic *l-* 'him') is obligatory in questions with certain (D-linked) wh-phrases, like *care* 'which':

(28) Pe care băiat *(l-) ai   văzut?
      ACC which boy   him have.2sg seen
      'Which boy did you see?'

Nonetheless, as C. Dobrovie-Sorin (p.c.) notes, a deleted IP under sluicing can correspond to a non-clitic-doubled correlate in the antecedent IP:

(29) Am   văzut pe un băiat dar nu ştiu   pe care.
      I.have seen ACC a boy   but not I.know ACC which
      'I saw a boy, but I don't know which.'

Here, the deleted but presumably present clitic double for the moved wh-phrase *pe care* would have no correspondent in the antecedent IP to satisfy isomorphism.

A further potential problem arises from the sluices in (30)–(32), most of which show a correspondence between a deleted infinitive and some other kind of structure: a gerund, a future auxiliary, a negated possibility auxiliary, present and past participles, an exceptive, an agentive noun, and imperatives.

(30)   Decorating for the holidays is easy if you know how!
        a   ≠ *. . . how [decorating for the holidays]
        b   = . . . how [to decorate for the holidays]

(31)   I'll fix the car if you tell me how.
        a   ≠ . . . how [I'll fix the car]
        b   = . . . how [to fix the car]

(32)   a   'I can't play quarterback: I don't even know how.'   (Bart, *The Simpsons*, 'Homer Coaches Football' episode)
        b   Invest now! We'll tell you how!   (BankOne advertisement)
        c   Eat (something), if you can figure out what!
        d   Two or three men were crying. Others couldn't remember how. (O'Brien 1994: 103)
        e   George . . . suffer[ed] . . . the very same sort of guilt trip he'd inflicted on countless others since he first learned how.   (Brin 1991: 316)
        f   He put his feet in the drawer, resting them on somebody's paper. He didn't look to see whose.   (Dexter 1988: 58)
        g   'Cut it loose,' she said.
             'I don't know how.'   (Dexter 1988: 203)
        h   'Do you know who the forger is?'
             'I talked to Seth Frank. Apparently Whitney learned how in prison.'   (Scott Glenn in *Absolute Power*, 1997 US film)
        i   'Nobody'll talk to you, except for old Wakasha. I have no idea why.' (from the context it's clear that this means 'I have no idea why old Wakasha will talk to you')   (Graham Greene in *Thunderheart*, 1992 US film)

The examples in (33) and (34) illustrate related problems. In (33), the gerund *meeting him* must license the deletion of a finite clause *I met him*. Likewise in the attested example in (34) (similar to one in W. Klein 1993), where the subjunctive form *würden* 'would' seems to be equivalent to the modal *sollten* 'should', since German does not have wh-infinitival questions (cf. (34*a*)), and the modal particle *gern* must not be present in the missing IP (the sluice does not have the readings given in (34*b,c*), only that in (34*d*)).

(33)   I remember meeting him, but I don't remember when. [= I met him]

(34)   Politiker   würden   gern helfen aber sie   wissen nicht, wie.
        politicians would.SUBJ PRT help   but they know   not   how
        (*Die Zeit*, 31 Aug. 2000)
        'Politicians would like to help but they don't know how.'
        a   ≠ . . . * wie [zu helfen].
                    how to help
        b   ≠ . . .   wie [sie   gern helfen würden].
                    how they PRT help   would
        c   ≠ . . .   wie [sie   gern   helfen sollten].
                    how they PRT help   should
        d   = . . .   wie [sie   helfen sollten].
                    how they help   should

Given these difficulties for the isomorphism condition, one might be tempted to claim that it simply does not apply in sluicing, holding perhaps only for VP-ellipsis, for the reasons discussed.[7] But the kinds of facts that motivated imposing the isomorphism condition on VP-ellipsis hold for sluicing as well. In particular, IP-deaccenting exhibits the same kinds of possibilities and restrictions we saw above for deaccented VPs. Thus, while (35a) and (35b) are possible, since they are entailed in the relevant sense by the first IP, (36) is impossible, as in the VP cases in (16) and (17).

(35)   a   Abby called Ben an idiot, but I don't know who else *she called an idiot.*
        b   Abby called Ben an idiot, but I don't know who else *she insulted.*

(36)   *Abby called Ben an idiot, but I don't know who else *she dated.*

By the same token, the sluice in (37) cannot have the structure in (37a)—rather, it must be related to (37b).

(37)   Abby called Ben an idiot, but I don't know who else.
        a   *Abby called Ben an idiot, but I don't know who else ~~she insulted~~.
        b   Abby called Ben an idiot, but I don't know who else ~~she called an idiot~~.

Thus it seems that the same difficulties that beset the VP-ellipsis cases that were solved by the isomorphism condition emerge for sluicing as well.

---

[7] But see especially Hardt (1993), who documents a wide range of apparent structural differences between antecedent and elided VPs, in the spirit of the problems noted for IP-ellipsis here.

The final, and perhaps the most important, problem for isomorphism comes from the equivalence between (potentially complex) R-expressions and pronouns under ellipsis, both in sluicing (see §5.2) and in VP-ellipsis, as in (38). Since this problem has been discussed only with respect to the latter, I will concentrate on these cases for the moment.

(38) a   They arrested Alex$_3$, though he$_3$ thought they wouldn't.
      b   They arrested [the guy who lives over the garage]$_3$, though he$_3$ thought they wouldn't.

As Fiengo and May (1994) point out, a perfect equivalence between the deleted VP and the antecedent VP would incorrectly predict (38) to have the same status as (39).

(39) a   *He$_3$ thought they wouldn't arrest Alex$_3$.
      b   *He$_3$ thought they wouldn't arrest [the guy who lives over the garage]$_3$.

In the examples in (39), the DPs *Alex$_3$* and *[the guy who lives over the garage]$_3$* are c-commanded in their respective clauses by the co-indexed pronoun *he$_3$*, in violation of Principle C of the Binding Theory, which we can take to be that in (40) (see Chomsky 1986 *b*).

(40) **Principle C**
      An R-expression α with index *i* must not be c-commanded by any expression β with index *i*, β in an A-position.

But the sentences in (38) are grammatical, apparently not violating Principle C. Fiengo and May (1994) propose an operation of 'vehicle change' that allows the value of the pronominal feature associated with nominals to vary within a 'reconstruction'. Although not all the details of their proposal are clear (see their pp. 218 ff. especially), they will not be crucial here (see Kennedy 1997, Giannakidou and Merchant 1998, Potts 1999, and Safir 1999, and also below, §5.2, for some discussion). In my terms, what they have discovered is that R-expressions in antecedents can license the deletion of pronouns in ellipsis sites. With reference to the example at hand, this means that the deleted VPs are not those in (41a,b), but rather that in (41c).

(41) a   *[$_{VP}$ ~~arrest Alex$_3$~~]
      b   *[$_{VP}$ ~~arrest [the guy who lives over the garage]$_3$~~]
      c   [$_{VP}$ ~~arrest [him]$_3$~~]

But such a deletion also would violate the isomorphism condition, since the terminal vocabularies of the deleted and the antecedent VPs differ. (For the case of the definite description, one could perhaps take this as indirect evidence that pronouns do have complex internal structures of exactly the kind required, varying their structure appropriately with context, but I regard this as a *reductio* in the absence of independent evidence for such internal structure, and it would not extend to the case of names in any case.[8] See McCawley (1998: ch. 11) for relevant discussion and references.)

So how is the non-equivalence between pronouns and such R-expressions to be reconciled with the apparent need for a structural isomorphism requirement we saw above? Fiengo and May, who are the only authors to have dealt seriously with this question, retain structural isomorphism and propose that values of features like [pronominal] can be treated as 'equivalence classes' for the purposes of structural comparison—that is, that, while the ellipsis site does indeed contain a structurally and lexically identical R-expression, this R-expression does not trigger a BT(C) violation because it is, exceptionally (that is, only in an ellipsis site) allowed to be [+pronominal], unlike its overt counterparts which must always be [−pronominal]. This featural mismatch, the heart of 'vehicle change', can be overlooked for purposes of deletion, by hypothesis. Although this is a workable analysis, and it is to Fiengo and May's credit to have highlighted this problem and addressed it seriously at all, it does not advance our understanding of the phenomenon very much, nor illuminate why this should hold only under deletion (and not deaccenting, which otherwise would seem to pattern with deletion). To pursue a theory of ellipsis based on structural isomorphism while considering the cases of 'vehicle change' to have been sufficiently dealt with simply by naming them is to confuse the diagnosis with the cure.

1.4 THE REVISED FOCUS CONDITION AND E-GIVENNESS

The other possible approach, and the one I will pursue here, is to revise or reject structural isomorphism as a condition on ellipsis. The strongest, and hence

---

[8] The same issue arises with respect to simple interrogatives in sluicing with complex antecedents:

(i) He talked to somebody from the Finance Department, but I don't know who.

Here [who] would have to be structurally isomorphic to [somebody from the Finance Department].

most interesting and most difficult, position to take is that there is no structural isomorphism condition on ellipsis at all. Because of the numerous problems that isomorphism encounters, I think it will be fruitful to abandon it entirely, and attempt to account for the data that it was introduced to handle in another way, one that does not at the same time force us to revise our notions of featural constancy or do violence to the syntax of wh-movement. The proposal to be developed below, in relying solely on a semantic, not structural, condition on ellipsis, shares the goal of a number of researchers who have also pursued purely semantic approaches, such as Dalrymple *et al.* (1991), Hardt (1993, 1999), Prüst (1993), Prüst *et al.* (1994), Shieber *et al.* (1996), Asher *et al.* (1997), Hendriks and de Hoop (forthcoming), and others; the proposal here, however, is original and differs from the majority of these in explicitly assuming syntactic structure in the ellipsis site.

1.4.1 e-GIVENness in VP-Ellipsis

Although it is not my intention to develop an entire theory of VP-ellipsis here, I will present a revised Focus condition that will capture the data given so far. My primary aim, however, will be to use a version of this new Focus condition as a condition on IP-ellipsis below. This condition is based on the definition of e-GIVEN in (42), and is stated in (43).

(42) **e-GIVENness**
 An expression E counts as e-GIVEN iff E has a salient antecedent A and, modulo ∃-type shifting,
   (i)   A entails F-clo(E),[9] and
   (ii) E entails F-clo(A)

(43) **Focus condition on VP-ellipsis**
 A VP α can be deleted only if α is e-GIVEN.

Several simplifications could be made here, which I omit for exposition. It should be clear that the only novel part of the definition is in (42ii); one could thus easily divorce this condition applying strictly to deleted structures from the more general conditions discussed above. Such a theory would be

---

[9] In general, of course, and perhaps on principled grounds (see §5.2.1 for some discussion), a deleted constituent will not contain any F-marked material; material extracted from the ellipsis site, on the other hand, will often—though not always—be F-marked. I will assume, as above, that traces of constituents moved out of the ellipsis site will be ∃-bound for purposes of satisfaction of the various Focus conditions.

equivalent to the one that forms the basis of my discussion here, and more par-
simonious in certain respects, since the more general Focus conditions of §1.2
will certainly apply to structures that contain ellipsis as well. For purposes of
exposition, however, I will collapse the two requirements on elliptical structures (the more general focus conditions plus clause (ii) of (42)) into one definition—this will allow us to refer to a structure as simply satisfying the
e-GIVENness requirement, though the careful reader may want to keep this
conflation in mind.

First let us see how (43) handles the examples in (18) and (19), repeated here,
which motivated the isomorphism condition.

(44) a Abby was reading the book while BEN was.
      b Abby ate a sandwich after BEN did.
      c Abby left the party because BEN did.
      d Abby sang her hymn louder than BEN did.

(45) a Abby called Chuck an idiot after BEN did.
      b Abby ate a sandwich after BEN did.
      c Abby left the party because BEN did.

To take one example, what is at issue here is making sure that the elided VP in
(45a) has the source in (46a), not that in (46b), in accordance with our intuitions about the possible meanings of (45a).

(46) a = . . . after BEN did ~~call Chuck an idiot~~.
      b ≠ . . . after BEN did ~~insult Chuck~~.

The first task is to see how the deleted VP in (46a) is e-GIVEN. The
antecedent here is the VP in the first clause [$_{VP}$ call Chuck an idiot]. This VP has
an open variable corresponding to the subject, so ∃-type shifting must apply,
yielding (47) (where α' stands for the result of applying ∃-type shifting to α).

(47) $VP_A' = \exists x.x$ called Chuck an idiot

The first question now is whether VP_A' entails the result of replacing F-
marked parts of the deleted VP by ∃-bound variables. Let us assume that the
VP-internal trace of the subject BEN is also F-marked, though at this point I
see nothing crucial riding upon this. Replacing this trace by an ∃-bound variable yields (48):

(48) F-clo(VP_E) = $\exists x.x$ called Chuck an idiot

Clearly, then, VP_A' entails $F\text{-clo}(VP_E)$. The second question is whether VP_E' entails the F-closure of VP_A, given in (49). Since the two are identical, the answer is yes.

(49) $F\text{-clo}(VP_A) = \exists x.x$ called Chuck an idiot

Consider now (46b). $F\text{-clo}(VP_A)$ remains the same, but the deleted VP itself is different—$\exists$-binding the subject trace yields (50):

(50) $VP_E' = \exists x.x$ insulted Chuck

Now the answer to the second question changes: VP_E' does not entail $F\text{-clo}(VP_A)$, since you can insult someone without necessarily calling him or her an idiot. Therefore the VP in (46b) is not e-GIVEN, by (42ii). As a result, this VP does not satisfy the revised Focus condition in (43), and cannot be deleted, as desired. The same reasoning applies to the examples in (44).

Eliminating the isomorphism condition also lets us claim that the deleted VP in the problematic cases of (38) (repeated here), which motivated having 'vehicle change' in the first place, simply contains a regular pronoun, as desired:

(51)   a   They arrested Alex$_3$, though he$_3$ thought they wouldn't ~~arrest him$_3$~~.
        b   They arrested [the guy who lives over the garage]$_3$, though he$_3$ thought they wouldn't ~~arrest him$_3$~~.

Consider the case in (51a). Does this deleted VP satisfy the Focus condition? It does, just in case *him* = *Alex*. This is because the result of $\exists$-type shifting the antecedent VP, given in (52a), entails the $F\text{-clo}(VP)$ of the deleted VP in (52b) just in case the value returned by the assignment function for the translation of *him* (x_3) picks out the same individual that is returned by the assignment function for the name *Alex*. (Schwarzschild 1999: 154 notes this result as well—namely, that a pronoun will count as GIVEN if it has an antecedent with the same index, since $[\![\text{John}_i]\!]^g = [\![\text{he}_i]\!]^g$ for any g, thus correctly allowing deaccenting equivalencies between names and pronouns.) This, of course, is the desired result.

(52)   a $VP_A' = \exists x.x$ arrested Alex
        b $F\text{-clo}(VP_E) = \exists x.x$ arrested him

The second condition, that the VP' of the deleted VP entail the $F\text{-clo}(VP)$ of the antecedent VP, is satisfied as well. (Some complications, resolvable under natural assumptions about epistemic compatibility and presuppositions, arise in the case of descriptions as in (51b), but I will not go into these here; I also pass over the issues involved with voice changes mentioned in note 4.)

The Focus condition in (43), then, handles the data that motivated vehicle change,[10] while ruling out illicit cases of 'implicational bridging' in the missing VP.[11] Our next question is whether this Focus condition can be applied with equal success to sluicing.

1.4.2 e-GIVENness in Sluicing

Answering this question requires a bit more background. In particular, it requires that we make some specific assumptions about what the alternatives to questions are, in order to determine what should count as GIVEN. Here I will use the results of Romero (1998),[12] who shows that versions of the more general focus conditions in (6) and (9) can fruitfully be applied to IP-deaccenting and sluicing, accounting for a wide range of data, especially concerning the nature of the antecedents and scopal parallelisms (issues that will not concern us to a great extent here, though see §5.4 for a brief return to some of them). For our purposes, the basics of her analysis will suffice. The basic idea is that the questions in (53) should all count as alternatives to one another.

---

[10] At least for the best investigated case of what goes under the rubric 'vehicle change' in Fiengo and May (1994) (equivalences between R-expressions and pronouns). The term 'vehicle change' is, however, widely applied in that work, being pressed into service in twelve different ways on pp. 201–30 to account for varieties of non-distinctness under ellipsis. Whether all these varieties can or should be accounted for in the same way will have to be taken up in later work. Note that the present approach also captures the equivalence of negative polarity items and indefinites under VP-ellipsis noted in Baker and Brame (1972: 62) and Sag (1976a), which Fiengo and May (1994) also label an instance of vehicle change.

[11] It will also ensure that the correspondent to the remnant XP in cases like (i) and (ii) (the latter a case of pseudogapping, which I assume involves VP-deletion, following many researchers— see Kennedy and Merchant 2000a for references) must bear focus:

(i)   I saw [Abby]$_F$, but [Bart]$_F$, I didn't.

(ii)   I want to see [the Simpsons]$_F$ more than I do [the X-Files]$_F$.

In (i), for example, VP$_E$' = $\exists x \exists y[x$ saw $y]$, and F-clo(VP$_A$) = $\exists x \exists y[x$ saw $y]$. Note that here, VP$_E$' does not entail VP$_A$', which is $\exists x[x$ saw Abby$]$. If no F-marking were present on *Abby* in VP$_A$, F-clo(VP$_A$) would not be entailed by VP$_E$' and VP$_E$ could not be deleted. It seems to be necessary as well that some overt material in the clause containing the deleted VP be present to indicate the possibility of F-closure in the antecedent; see Fox (2000) for related discussion.

[12] Page and example numbers are cited from a 1998 draft of chapter 2; I have not had access to the complete manuscript.

(53)   a   (know[13]) which P are Q
        b   (know) how many P are Q
        c   (know) whether any P are Q

She further adopts Schwarzschild's GIVENness condition, applying it to constituents that contain IP-ellipsis (she shows that the same results hold for Rooth's version as well, which I omit here). Modifying (9) above by replacing 'VP' by 'IP', we get the condition in (55) (the definition of GIVENness is repeated for convenience).

(54)   GIVENness (Schwarzschild 1999)
        An expression E counts as GIVEN iff E has a salient antecedent A and, modulo $\exists$-type shifting, A entails F-clo(E).

(55)   **S-Focus condition on IP-ellipsis** (Schwarzschildian version)
        An IP α can be deleted only if α is or is contained in a constituent that is GIVEN.

Concretely, supposing this will allow the null IP in (56):

(56)   I know how MANY politicians she called an idiot, but I don't know WHICH (politicians[14]).

In this case, the alternative questions are those in (57).

(57)   a   (know) which politicians she called an idiot
        b   (know) how many politicians she called an idiot
        c   (know) whether she called any politicians an idiot

The result of replacing F-marked parts of the CP that contains the missing IP by $\exists$-bound variables of the same type yields (58); here I use Q to represent the variable over wh-determiners (see Romero 1998: 18–22).[15]

---

[13] Here and below I use *know* as the embedding predicate, assuming that the conclusions reached for this case generalize (i.e. that semantically, *wonder*-type predicates will have some component equivalent to *know*—'want to know' or the like); see Romero's discussion. Using something like *I know* . . . as a leader to both the antecedent and CP containing the sluice allows us to avoid the multiple applications $\exists$-type shift that would be necessary to evaluate GIVENness; while these applications are routine, they clutter up the formulas considerably.

[14] I ignore for the most part the independent question of how the NP-ellipsis after *which*, etc., is resolved.

[15] The same result holds if we apply Rooth's condition, assuming that $E^f = [\![WHICH_F$ (politicians) she called an idiot$]\!]^f = \{$which politicians she called an idiot, how many politicians she

(58)   ∃Q[I know [Q-politicians she called an idiot]]

A similar computation gives us the desired result in the following case:

(59)   I know she called some politician an idiot, but I don't know WHICH.

Since knowing that she called some politician an idiot entails knowing whether she called any policitian an idiot (that is, *knowing whether she called any policitian an idiot* will be GIVEN), the S-Focus condition will be satisfied.

But again this is not enough for our purposes: using the one-way entailments in the definition of GIVENness in (54) will allow for the illicit IP-ellipsis in (60).

(60)   *I know how many politicians she called an idiot, but I don't know WHICH (politicians) [~~IP she insulted t~~]

Again, this is because *calling someone an idiot* entails *insulting someone*, in the relevant sense. Thus Romero, like others before her, adopts an LF-identity condition supplemental to the focus conditions in order to rule out these kinds of ellipsis. But we have already seen the difficulties associated with such an isomorphism requirement on IP-ellipsis. In line with the analysis of VP-ellipsis above, we can solve this problem by abandoning the isomorphism condition and instead adopting the revised Focus condition above, applied now to IP-ellipsis. Recall the definition of e-GIVEN in (42), repeated here.

(61)   **e-GIVENness**
        An expression E counts as e-GIVEN iff E has a salient antecedent A and, modulo ∃-type shifting,
        (i)   A entails F-clo(E), and
        (ii) E entails F-clo(A)

Using this, we now state the Focus condition on IP-ellipsis:

(62)   **Focus condition on IP-ellipsis**
        An IP α can be deleted only if α is e-GIVEN.

Consider how this requirement applies to the following example.

called an idiot, whether she called any politician an idiot} and A = *how many politicians she called an idiot*; therefore A ∈ E^f, as required. See Romero (1998) for detailed exemplification.

(63)   I know how MANY politicians she called an idiot, but I don't know WHICH (politicians).

First, we need to decide what to do with the traces of wh-movement, in this case, in both the elided and antecedent IP (again, for the time being, I will concentrate on cases where there is no F-marking inside the IP; I return to the other cases below). The same issue arose above with respect to the VP-internal subject trace; as I did there, I will translate them as simple variables, existentially bound. This is a convenient oversimplification that will make the exposition clearer, but it should be borne in mind that there is good evidence that traces have more structure than this notation indicates (this fact is actually crucial in accounting for several cases that I will not consider in detail here; see Romero 1997*b*, Sauerland 1998, Fox 1999, and Merchant 2000*a*).

Adopting this, then, gives us the following, in satisfaction of the first part of the definition of e-GIVENness, since IP_A' entails F-clo(IP_E).

(64)   a   F-clo(IP_E) = $\exists$x.she called x an idiot
      b IP_A' = $\exists$x.she called x an idiot

Secondly, IP_E' entails F-clo(IP_A), satisfying the second clause of the definition. Therefore, by the Focus condition in (62), IP_E can be deleted.

Likewise for the following example:

(65)   I know she called some politician an idiot, but I don't know WHICH.

Here again, we have the following for IP_A and IP_E, in satisfaction of (42i).

(66)   a IP_A' = F-clo(IP_A) = $\exists$x.she called x an idiot
      b IP_E' = F-clo(IP_E) = $\exists$x.she called x an idiot

Again, since these are identical, (42ii) will also be satisfied.

But note that (42ii) will rule out the cases discussed above that the original focus conditions allowed for:

(67)   *I know how many politicians she called an idiot, but I don't know WHICH (politicians) [~~IP she insulted t~~]

Now we have:

(68)   a   F-clo(IP_A) = $\exists$x.she called x an idiot
      b IP_E' = $\exists$x.she insulted x

Since (68a) gives rise to entailments that (68b) does not (since *she insulted x* does not entail *she called x an idiot*), IP_E is not e-GIVEN under (42ii). Therefore, by (62), IP_E cannot be deleted.

These definitions have the additional desirable result of accounting for the paradigm discovered by Chung *et al.* (1995) (their (21)), given in (68):

(69) a *She served the soup, but I don't know who(m).
          (cf. She served the soup, but I don't know to whom.)
      b She served the students, but I don't know what.

Chung *et al.* (1995), who adopt a structural isomorphism account implemented by LF-copying, propose to account for these contrasts by constraints on their LF-operation of 'sprouting'; essentially, they propose that sprouting is 'licensed by an extension of the particular argument structure used in the antecedent IP' (p. 262), given in Levin and Rappaport's (1988) representations for argument structure:

(70) a *serve₁*: server $\langle$ <u>meal</u> (diner)$\rangle$
                              DP PP_{to}
      b *serve₂*: server $\langle$ <u>diner</u> (meal)$\rangle$
                              DP   DP

I return to a discussion of their account in §4.4. But their essential insight—that argument structure alternations cannot occur under sluicing—can also be captured in the system proposed here. Under this system, assuming the lexical entries in (70), the question is the following: why should these two verbs differ in their ability to license sluicing over their unexpressed argument? In the proposed account, this contrast must follow from a contrast in inferability of existence of these unexpressed arguments (how the syntax–lexicon interface is to be handled appears to be irrelevant). And, in fact, just the desired contrast does exist. Note the differences in coherence in the following two discourses:

(71) a I served₁ the food, but there were no guests.
      b #I served₂ the guests, but there was no food.

The sentence in (71b) is a contradiction, since the use of *serve₂*, even without its optional argument, entails the existence of a theme argument. As seen by the felicity of (71a), on the other hand, *serve₁* does not similarly entail the existence of a goal argument (I may simply have put the food on plates on a table). These facts also account for the impossibility of deaccenting in (72):

(72)   *She served₁ the meal, but I don't know WHO *she served₁ it to.*
         (cf. She served₁ the meal, but I don't know who *she served₁ it* TO.)

The preposition in (72) cannot be deaccented, because it is not GIVEN. The relevant pieces of the computation are given in (73):

(73)   a IP_A = she served the meal
         b $F\text{-clo}(IP_E) = \exists x[\text{she served the meal to x}]$

By the Focus condition, IP_A must entail the F-closure of IP_E. Since this is not the case, the IP in (72) cannot be deaccented. *A fortiori*, it cannot be deleted, as would be required to derive (69a). Thus the observed contrast follows from the present system as well.

One last possibility must be considered, and dispensed with, before we can move on. From what does Chung *et al.*'s correct observation that *serve₁* is not equivalent to *serve₂* under sluicing follow in the present system? In other words, what rules out a derivation like (74)?

(74)   *She served₁ the meal, but I don't know WHOᵢ ~~she served₂ tᵢ the meal~~.
         (cf. She served₂ someone the meal, but I don't know whoᵢ ~~she served₂ tᵢ the meal~~.)[16]

The answer to this question lies, again, in the respective entailments generated, given in (75).

(75)   a IP_A = she served the meal
         b $F\text{-clo}(IP_E) = \exists x[\text{she served x the meal}]$

As we observed above, *serve₁* does not entail the existence of a recipient of the meal. But exactly this entailment is needed to license deletion of an IP containing a moved wh-phrase corresponding to the recipient of *serve₂*, since the ∃-closure of such an IP will entail a recipient.

A related question concerns examples like (76), brought to my attention by S. Chung:

---

[16] Note that the grammaticality of this second example indicates that the often-noted restriction on the extraction of the first object in a double object construction (as in (i); see Fillmore 1965 and Kuroda 1968) must similarly be located at the PF interface, and not built into the mechanisms of extraction in the syntax, as pointed out to me by M. den Dikken (p.c.) (essentially the same point is made by Baker and Brame (1972: 62) with respect to their example (31)).

(i)   ??Whoᵢ did she serve tᵢ the meal?

(76)   *Someone shot Ben, but I don't know by who(m) [$_{IP}$ ~~Ben was shot t~~]

This will be ruled out if the subject of the active transitive *shoot* induces entailments in the relevant sense that the object of the *by*-phrase does not. Although it is difficult to give specifics at this point, it does seem plausible that the active/passive difference in form corresponds to a difference in meaning, whether this be solely perspective-based (see Dowty 1991 for discussion and references) or actually found in lexical entailments. However these differences are characterized, it seems that the GIVENness conditions are sensitive to them. (Further complications, partly noted above, arise in the case of VP-ellipsis; note, however, that pseudogapping examples parallel to (76) have a comparable status: *Abby shot Ben {before/and} Chuck was by Dara.*)

Up to this point, we have concentrated on examples that contained no F-marking in the antecedent IP. But it is instructive to examine two of these cases as well.

The first of these is illustrated by examples like (77):

(77)   She called Ben an idiot, but I don't know who else [$_{IP}$ ~~she called t an idiot~~].

If there were no F-marking in the antecedent IP, clause (ii) of (42) would be violated, since simply existentially closing the apparent free variables in the deleted IP would give us IP$_E'$ = $\exists x.she\ called\ x\ an\ idiot$. But F-clo(IP$_A$) = *she called Ben an idiot*, which is not entailed by IP$_E'$. This should violate (42ii) and rule out the IP-deletion, contrary to fact.

But this problem is resolved once we take the necessary F-marking into consideration. Consider the interpretations of the pair in (78):

(78)   a   ABBY$_F$ called Ben an idiot, but I don't know who else.
        b   Abby called BEN$_F$ an idiot, but I don't know who else.

The interpretations of the sluices in (78a) and (78b) correspond to (79a) and (79b), respectively:

(79)   a   . . . but I don't know who else called Ben an idiot.
        b   . . . but I don't know who else Abby called an idiot.

This distribution is exactly that predicted by the Focus condition. Consider (78a) with respect to (42ii). The relevant elements for comparison are given in (80).

(80)   a $IP_E' = \exists x.x$ called Ben an idiot
        b $F\text{-}clo(IP_A) = \exists x.x$ called Ben an idiot

Since these are the same, the relevant entailments hold (namely, $IP_E' \rightarrow$ F-clo(IP_A)). This would not be the case if the antecedent IP were the first IP in (78b), though, since in that case $F\text{-}clo(IP_A) = \exists x.$*Abby called x an idiot*. The reverse holds, *mutatis mutandis*, for (78b): the F-marking on *Ben* ensures that the sluice can only derive from (79b), not (79a). (The fact that the implicit argument of *else* must be resolved to the F-marked constituent in these cases follows from a natural semantics for *else*, such as that in Romero 1998: 31 (81), and the more general Focus conditions; the reasoning is the same as that given for pronouns above.)

The second case where F-marking plays a role in sluicing is in cases like those in (81), which we can call 'contrast'-sluices.

(81)   a   She has five CATS, but I don't know how many DOGS.
        b   The channel was 15 feet wide, but I don't know how deep.
        c   Abby knew which of the MEN Peter had invited, but she didn't know which of the WOMEN.
        d   We know which streets are being repaved, but not which avenues.
        e   Max has five Monets in his collection, and who knows how many van Goghs.
        f   There are nine women in the play, but I don't know how many men.
        g   I know how many women are in the play, but I don't know how many men.
        h   She's an absolute idiot: unaware of who she is, or where. (Wallace 1986)

Consider (81a). We can assume it has the structure in (82).

(82)   She has [five CATS]$_F$, but I don't know how many DOGS [$_{IP}$ ~~she has *t*~~].

Here, the relevant computations are given in (82), which satisfy (42ii).

(83)   a $IP_E' = \exists x.$she has x
        b $F\text{-}clo(IP_A) = \exists x.$she has x

If we were to look only at IP_A without being able to abstract away from the material that contrasts with the descriptive content DOGS in the wh-phrase, we would incorrectly predict deletion to be impossible, since IP_E' does not entail *she has five cats*. In cases where there is no contrasting material in the wh-phrase, as in the usual cases with NP-ellipsis or the like, the more general Focus conditions employing GIVENness will ensure that the correct descriptive content is understood (as Romero 1998 shows)—it is only in these cases, where there is some contrast in the wh-phrase, that the necessity of the formulation in (42) becomes fully apparent.[17]

1.5 SUMMARY

This chapter has examined some of the general conditions on ellipsis, in particular the question whether the conditions regulating VP- and IP-deaccenting are the same as those that regulate VP- and IP-ellipsis. While the more general Focus conditions still apply to structures in which ellipsis has applied, we have seen that the interpretations of ellipsis sites are constrained in ways that go beyond their merely deaccented cousins.

While the majority of researchers either assume or have argued that these additional constraints on ellipsis reflect a structural isomorphism requirement, I have shown that such a requirement is extremely problematic in a number of domains. Even simple cases of sluicing fail it, and it leaves us without a satisfying account of the equivalence of elided pronouns to R-expressions in the antecedents to ellipsis. Instead, I have argued that the appropriate division in the data can be made by adopting an expanded definition of Schwarzschild's (1999) GIVENness which I called e-GIVENness.

Using this revised definition, I proposed the following simple constraint on the interpretation of ellipsis sites, generalized here over both VP- and IP-ellipses:

---

[17] Further important qualifications must be kept in mind: the F-marking must contrast with an element in the wh-phrase extracted from the deleted IP. Hence examples like (i) must be avoided:

(i)   A: Who did Abby see?
        B: *Abby [$_{VP:A}$ saw BEN$_F$], and Carla did $\frac{}{[VP:E\ \text{see someone}]}$ too.

Given the F-marking on BEN in the first conjunct licensed by the wh-question, F-clo(VP$_A$) = $\exists x\exists y[x$ saw $y]$ and VP$_E'$ = $\exists x\exists y[x$ saw $y]$, hence deletion would be licensed if nothing more were said. What has been ignored so far for ease of presentation is the fact that F-marking must be anaphoric, and that the GIVENness conditions must be sensitive to these relations; see Schwarzschild (1999) and Schwabe (2000) for discussion and proposals how to encode this. I will assume for the remainder that such a theory can be successfully implemented, and retain the simplified computations used thus far, keeping this complication in mind.

(84)   **Focus condition on ellipsis**
        A constituent α can be deleted only if α is e-GIVEN.

Because e-GIVENness incorporates 'two-way' entailment requirements (that is, checking the entailments of the antecedent XP against those of the deleted XP and vice versa, modulo the observed complications arising from focused constituents), the antecedent will not be able to vary from the deleted constituent in the ways it can when triggering mere deaccenting.

This system successfully accounts for those cases that were taken to motivate the structural isomorphism condition. Because it is fundamentally semantic in nature, it will allow for syntactic variation in the ellipsis site, just in case these can lead to satisfaction of the focus condition. This leads to a significant overall simplification of the theory, eliminating any need for an additional theory of 'vehicle change' or of the other kinds of deviancies from structural identity needed especially under sluicing.

2

The Syntax of Sluicing

In this chapter I examine the structural conditions on sluicing and investigate its external and internal syntax. The first issue, the external syntax, is by far the easier to tackle, and the answer reached there is straightforward: the 'sluice' is a CP. The second, which requires investigating the structure of ellipsis— that is, the syntax of silence—can be approached only by more indirect means and is, therefore, much more difficult; the answer defended here is that the ellipsis site contains syntactic structures of the kind familiar from overt syntax.

This chapter proceeds roughly in order of analytic difficulty. I begin with the simpler task, identifying the category of the sluice by looking at what the external distribution of sluiced wh-phrases is. The conclusion is unambiguous: sluices behave as CPs. This leads to the hypothesis that the sluice consists of a CP in which the sentential part, the IP, has gone missing. With this in mind, I turn to the more difficult question of what mechanisms in the grammar license this silent IP. We will see that the conditions are fairly parochial, being limited to certain feature combinations on the C sister to the null IP. To capture these, I propose a mechanism for triggering deletion at PF based on feature movement to C. I conclude by tackling a vexing analytic question raised by a novel generalization established in §2.2.2: nothing but the wh-phrase itself can appear overtly in the COMP domain under sluicing. I suggest that this fact is related to other, probably prosodic, limitations on the kinds of null elements that can immediately follow complementizers.

2.1 EXTERNAL SYNTAX: THE SLUICE AS AN INTERROGATIVE CP

I begin by investigating the external syntax of the sluiced material—that is, by addressing the following question: how does the wh-phrase that appears in sluicing behave with respect to the surrounding syntactic material? The arguments presented here, marshalled from selectional facts, number, case, syntactic positioning, and prosody, will support the *opinio communis* on this question—namely, that what appears to be a simple wh-phrase in isolation is in fact a CP. This is perhaps not a surprising conclusion, but it is one that has been challenged and must be established before we can move on to the elliptical puzzles it raises.

Many of the arguments originate with the initial investigation of sluicing, Ross (1969). Since much of the literature takes his conclusions for granted, I will attempt not to belabor the point here. But it has sometimes been specifically argued that sluicing need not involve a CP, most notably by van Riemsdijk (1978), and to some extent by Ginzburg (1992). What is at issue is whether a sluice like (1) has the structure of a CP as in (2), which I will defend here, or a more impoverished structure like the one in (3), defended in van Riemsdijk (1978) in particular, where wh-fragments are generated on their own, here as a complement to the verb *know*.

(1)   Anne invited someone, but I don't know who.

(2)   Sluices as interrogative CPs:

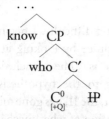

(3)   Sluices as 'wh-fragments':

        · · ·
           know   DP
                   |
                  who

   As we will see immediately, the sluiced wh-phrase behaves by all measures not as a direct argument of an embedding predicate, but as a full interrogative CP.

2.1.1 Selection

As Ross (1969) pointed out, the generalization about which predicates allow sluicing in their complements and which do not is quite simple to state:

(4)   All and only predicates that s-select questions and c-select CPs allow sluiced wh-phrases.

Although *know* in (1) above allows both interrogative and non-interrogative complement CPs, when we examine a verb like *wonder* that takes only interrogative complements, as the contrast between (5a) and (5b) shows, we see that sluicing is possible, as in (6).

(5)   a   *I wonder {the time/the answer/the question}.
      b   I wonder {what time it is/what the answer is/what Ben asked/who's coming}.

(6)   a   Ben wanted to ask something. I wonder what.
      b   Abby said someone's coming to dinner. We're all wondering who.

Indeed, when we examine predicates that are lexically ambiguous, like *know* or *remember*, we find that the sluiced reading is often the only one that is available in a given context. Although these can take DP objects as in (7) as well as CP complements as in (8), when the context requires sluicing, what would otherwise be ambiguous strings are disambiguated in favor of the embedded CP reading, as in (9).

(7)   a   Jack knows Guard Mulligan.
      b   Jill remembers the important announcement from yesterday.

(8)   a   Jack knows which guard was present.
      b   Jill remembers what I told you yesterday.

(9)   a   He claimed one of the guards had been present. Who knows which?
      b   I told you something important yesterday. Which of you remembers what?

In the context given, (9a) for example has only the sluiced CP reading of (10a), not that of a multiple DP question as in (10b). In other words, possible answers to (9a) are those in (11a), not those in (11b).

(10)   a   (9a) = Who knows which guard he claimed had been present?
        b   (9a) ≠ Who knows which guard?

(11)   a   Jack does./Jack knows which.
        b   #Jack knows Guard Mulligan, Bill knows Guard Keeley, etc./#Everyone knows the guard outside his cell.

The difference between a sluicing interpretation of a wh-DP 'object' of one of these predicates, and a regular, true argument interpretation of the same would be completely mysterious under van Riemsdijk's proposal, which collapses the two. Instead, the relevant readings for (9a,b) indicate that we are dealing with a usual CP complement to these verbs.

2.1.2 Number Agreement

A second point made by Ross (1969) is that the agreement on the main verb that appears with a sluiced wh-phrase is the typical agreement seen with CP subjects, and is independent of the number marking on the wh-phrase itself. Just as the CP subject in (12a) requires singular agreement on the verb (see McCloskey 1991*c* and references therein), so does the sluiced plural wh-phrase in (12b).

(12)   a   [$_{CP}$ Which problems are solvable] {is/*are} not obvious.
        b   Some of these problems are solvable, but [which problems] {is/*are} not obvious.

2.1.3 Case

Ross credits George Williams for noting that the 'question-word must . . . agree in case with some NP in a preceding clause' (1969: 253). He illustrates this with the verbs *schmeicheln* 'flatter', which assigns dative to its object, and *loben* 'praise', which assigns accusative, as in (13) and (14):

(13)   Er will   jemandem   schmeicheln, aber sie   wissen nicht,
        he wants someone.DAT flatter   but   they know   not

        {wem   /*wen}.
        who.DAT who.ACC

        'He wants to flatter someone, but they don't know who.'

(14)   Er will   jemanden   loben, aber sie   wissen nicht,
        he wants   someone.ACC praise but   they   know   not
        {*wem /   wen}.
        who.DAT who.ACC

        'He wants to flatter someone, but they don't know who.'

These examples illustrate as well that the case of the sluiced wh-phrase is independent of the case that would be assigned to an object of the embedding predicate, if this predicate can assign case. *Wissen* 'know', when transitive, assigns accusative to its object, as in (15). Nevertheless, the sluiced wh-phrase in the accusative is impossible if a verb like *schmeichlen* is understood, as in (13).

(15)   Sie   wissen   {*der Antwort /   die Antwort}   nicht.
        they know   the answer.DAT the answer.ACC not
        'They don't know the answer.'

The following example from Greek illustrates the same point with respect to the nominative case required by subjects in (16a), which contrasts with the accusative case normally assigned by the verb *ksero* 'know' as in (16b).

(16)   a   Kapjos   irthe,   alla dhe ksero   {pjos /   *pjon}.
             someone came, but not know.1sg   who.NOM   who.ACC
             'Someone came, but I don't know who.'

        b   Dhe ksero   {*i   apantisi   /tin apantisi}.
             not know.1sg   the   answer.NOM the   answer.ACC
             'I don't know the answer.'

Similar facts can be found with English prenominal genitives:

(17)   Somebody's   car   is   parked   on   the   lawn,   but   we   don't   know
        {whose/*who}.

With *whose*, however, it is not possible to be sure that we are dealing only with a case-marked wh-phrase, since it is more likely that we have NP-ellipsis as well, as in *[Whose [NP ~~car~~]] is parked on the lawn?* and *[Ben's [NP ~~car~~]] is parked on the lawn* (see Lobeck 1995). But the basic point is unaffected by such invisible pied-piping: the case of the wh-phrase itself must correspond to that of its antecedent (*somebody's* in (17)), and cannot vary. We will return to these facts in Chapter 3.

But it is not the whole story to state only that the case of the wh-phrase must 'agree' with an antecedent—this is only the case when there *is* an antecedent. When no overt antecedent for the wh-phrase is available, the case properties of the sluiced wh-phrase are nevertheless not free, and, in particular, are completely independent from any case that the embedding predicate may assign to nominal objects of its own. The case found on the sluiced wh-phrase will always correspond to the case its non-elliptical counterpart would have shown in a full CP. I state this correlation in (18).

(18)   The wh-phrase shows only the case-marking from the elliptical IP-internal case position, not that of the embedding predicate.

We can see this in the absence of an antecedent DP in an example like (19):

(19)   A car is parked on the lawn, but we don't know {whose/*who}.

This is also visible in cases where a verb assigns a particular case to its object, but can appear intransitively as well, as German *helfen* 'help', which assigns dative to its object.

(20)   Er meinte, er hätte   geholfen, aber wir wüßten   nicht,
        he thought he had.SUBJ helped   but we knew.SUBJ not
        {wem   /*wen}.
        who.DAT who.ACC
        'He claims he helped, but we wouldn't be able to say who.'

In all of these cases, the sluiced wh-phrase appears in the case assigned by the elliptical predicate or in the case required by its function in the elliptical clause, and not in the case that would be assigned by an embedding predicate.

Another case-related argument against the bare-complement analysis comes from adjectives that allow embedded questions under certain conditions, such as *obvious, clear, certain*, etc. (essentially, these allow CP complements, with the licit illocutionary force of the CP being determined by the matrix clausal characteristics: see Adger and Quer 1997 and references therein). One of these is illustrated in (21):

(21)   Somebody had called, but it wasn't clear who (had called).

It is standardly assumed, however, that these adjectives cannot assign case, accounting for the deviancy of (22a). In fact, even if case considerations could be argued to not play a role, as in a *there*-insertion context like (22b), a DP complement to *clear* is impossible.

(22) a *It wasn't clear his idea(s).
      b *There weren't clear his ideas.

The contrast between the sluiced version of (21) and these sentences militates against the wh-fragment analysis. Even an adjective like *worth*, which can assign case (see van Riemsdijk 1983) but does not license CP complements, cannot license sluicing:

(23) a The watch is worth five dollars.
      b *The watch isn't worth which bonds he cashed in.
      c *He cashed in some bonds, but I don't think the watch is worth which.

All of these cases indicate that the sluiced wh-phrase must receive case from a case-assigner internal to the elliptical IP, and not from the embedding predicate.

2.1.4 Positional Distribution

Another powerful argument that sluices are CPs comes from the positional distribution of sluiced wh-phrases in a variety of languages. The basic generalization is that given in (24):

(24) The positions available to a sluiced wh-remnant are always the same as the positions available to full interrogative CPs, not the positions available to non-moved wh-phrases.

Ross (1969) examines the facts of extraposition in English; his findings are given in the next subsection. I give further arguments of a similar nature from German, Dutch, Irish, and Hindi in §2.1.4.2.

2.1.4.1 *Extraposition in English*

Ross (1969) notes that contrasts like those in (25) and (26) are mysterious if the sluiced wh-phrase is not dominated by a CP. In (25) we see that the adjectival predicate *clear* does not license 'extraposition' of a DP argument.

(25) a The correct approach wasn't clear.
      b *It wasn't clear the correct approach.

Nevertheless, exactly this pattern seems to occur with a sluiced wh-DP, as in
(26b).

(26)   a   One of these approaches is correct, but [which of them] is not
             clear.
        b   One of these approaches is correct, but it's not clear [which of
             them].

Of course, under the CP view, this simply reflects the fact that interrogative
CPs can occur both as subjects and in extraposition contexts:

(27)   a   [$_{CP}$ Which of these approaches is correct] is not clear.
        b   It's not clear [$_{CP}$ which of these approaches is correct].

   Ross also gives examples with wh-PPs and adverbials phrases, which cannot
occur as arguments of *clear* in any case:

(28)   a   *{With Bob/Quickly} wasn't clear.
        b   *It wasn't clear {with Bob/quickly}.

But of course wh-phrases of these categories can appear in sluicing:

(29)   a   We know that he was eating, but {with whom/how rapidly} isn't
             clear.
        b   We know that he was eating, but it isn't clear {with whom/how
             rapidly}.

These patterns would be mysterious if the wh-phrase were somehow generated
directly as an argument of *clear*.

2.1.4.2 $SO_{DP}VO_{CP}$ *Languages*

Another argument from positional distribution comes from languages in
which nominal arguments (including wh-phrases) occur on one side of the
predicate, while sentential arguments (including interrogative CPs) occur on
the other. German, Dutch, Hindi, and Irish are languages with this property:
all are SOV with respect to nominal arguments under some circumstances
(German and Dutch only in embedded clauses; Irish only in non-finite
clauses), but in general require CP arguments to appear to the right of the verb
(or topicalized, as we will see). The varying predictions of the two analyses
under consideration are clear: if sluiced wh-phrases are just base-generated wh-

fragments in the clause like other non-sentential arguments, they should appear to the left of the verb (in the Mittelfeld). If the CP analysis is correct, sluiced wh-phrases should appear to the right of the verb (in the Nachfeld). I concentrate here on German to begin with, though the facts in Dutch are parallel. Hindi and Irish enter the discussion at the end.

In German, wh-phrases can occur clause-internally in multiple wh-questions, as in (30):

(30)   Wann hat Elke gestern   {was/   welches Auto} repariert?
        when   has Elke yesterday what/   which   car *repaired*
        'When did Elke fix {what/which car} yesterday?'

These wh-phrases are generally assumed not to be able to scramble like other DPs (Fanselow 1990; Müller and Sternefeld 1993), giving rise to the contrasts in (31). In (31a) we see that an object DP can scramble to precede the subject and an adverbial, yet in (31b) the corresponding wh-phrase cannot.[1]

(31)   a   Wann hat [das Auto]$_i$ Elke gestern t_i repariert?
            when   has the car   Elke yesterday   repaired
            'When did Elke repair the car yesterday?'

        b   *Wann hat [{was/ welches Auto}]$_2$ Elke gestern t_2 repariert?
            when   has   what/which   car   Elke yesterday   repaired
            ('When did Elke fix {what/which car} yesterday?')

The data in (32) show that DPs to the right of the final verb (in the Nachfeld) are degraded: wh-phrases, if anything, are worse here than definites like *das Auto* (cf. similar restrictions on Heavy XP Shift in English).

(32)   a   *Wann hat Elke gestern t_i repariert [das Auto]$_i$?
            when   has Elke yesterday   repaired   the car
            ('When did Elke fix the car yesterday?')

---

[1] This picture is somewhat simplified: wh-phrases seem to behave like indefinites with respect to scrambling. See (i) for an attested example (from *Die Zeit*, 12 Oct. 2000, p. 47).

(i)   ... gründlicher   ist wissenschaftlich notiert worden, wer wann was wie
           more.rigorously is scientifically   noted   been   who when what how
           lange sieht.
           long watches

       '... it has been more rigorously scientifically recorded who watches what when for how long [on TV].'

See Beck (1996) for further examples.

b *Wer hat gestern *t₂* repariert [welches Auto]₂?
   who has yesterday repaired which car
   ('Who fixed which car yesterday?')

Full embedded interrogative CPs, on the other hand, cannot appear clause-internally—they must either be extraposed as in (33a), or in SpecCP (the Vorfeld) as in (33d) (see Büring 1995 and Müller 1995 for evidence that CPs are generated clause-internally and reach their observed positions by movement):[2]

(33) a Wir haben nicht gewußt, [welches Auto Elke repariert hat].
         we have not known, which car Elke repaired has

      b *Wir haben [welches Auto Elke repariert hat] nicht gewußt.

      c *Wir haben nicht [welches Auto Elke repariert hat] gewußt.

      d [Welches Auto Elke repariert hat] haben wir nicht gewußt.

         'We didn't know which car Elke repaired.'

The same holds for Hindi (thanks to R. Bhatt for discussion and data):

(34) a Mujhe nahīī pataa   [ki   Gautam ne kis se   baat
         I.DAT NEG knowledge that Gautam ERG who with talk
         kii   thii].
         do.PFV PAST

      b *Mujhe nahīī [ki Gautam ne kis se baat kii thii] pataa.

      c *Mujhe [ki Gautam ne kis se baat kii thii] nahīī pataa.

      d [Gautam ne kis se   baat kii   thii], mujhe (yeh)
         Gautam ERG who with talk do.PFV PAST I.DAT itₐₚ
         nahīī pataa.[3]
         NEG knowledge

         'I don't know who Gautam talked to.'

Crucially, sluiced wh-phrases in German and Hindi appear in the same positions as embedded [+wh]CPs, and not clause-internally as wh-phrases in situ do:

---

[2] Note that, in this respect, embedded questions behave differently from embedded propositions, whose positional possibilities are a function of the embedding predicate (see Webelhuth 1992 and Büring 1995).

[3] For independent reasons, the complementizer *ki* cannot appear in fronted finite clauses:

(i) *[ki   Gautam ne kis se   baat kii   thii], mujhe (yeh) nahīī pataa.
     that Gautam ERG who with talk do.PFV PAST I.DAT itₐₚ NEG knowledge
     ('Who Gautam talked to, I don't know.')

(35)   [Daß Elke ein Auto repariert hat] haben wir gewußt, aber . . .
        that Elke a   car   repaired has have we known but

        'We knew that Elke repaired a car, but . . .'

   a   wir haben nicht geahnt, [welches].
        we have not suspected which

   b   *wir haben [welches] nicht geahnt.

   c   *wir haben nicht [welches] geahnt.

   d   [welches] haben wir nicht geahnt.

        'we had no idea which.'

(36)   Gautam ne   kisi   se   baat kii   thii, lekin
        Gautam ERG someone with talk do.PFV PAST but

        'Gautam talked with someone, but . . .'

   a   mujhe nahĩĩ pataa   [kis se].
        I.DAT NEG knowledge who with

   b   *mujhe [kis se] nahĩĩ pataa.

   c   *mujhe nahĩĩ [kis se] pataa.

   d   [kis se] (yeh) mujhe nahĩĩ pataa.

        'I don't know with who.'

The data in (35) and (36) are entirely expected under the hypothesis that the sluiced wh-phrase occupies the specifier of a full CP, but not if the wh-phrase is simply base-generated in the matrix clause.

Exactly the same kind of argument comes from Irish, which, while lacking the full range of possibilites seen in German and Hindi, also exhibits a difference in the positions occupied by CP versus DP complements in some environments. (Thanks to J. McCloskey for these data.) In non-finite clauses, a DP object must precede the verb, as in (37).

(37)   Rinne sé socrú   le   duine den   dís,
        made he arrangement with person of.the two

   a   . . . ach níl   sé sásta   [rud ar bith] a inseacht dúinn.
        but not.is he willing anything   tell[-FIN] to.us

   b   . . . *ach níl sé sásta a inseacht dúinn [rud ar bith].

        'He made an arrangement with one of the two people, but he won't tell us anything.'

Embedded CPs, however, must appear clause-finally:

(38)   a . . . *ach níl   sé sásta   [caidé a tá ar bun]
           but not.is he willing   what C is going-on

           a inseacht dúinn.
           tell[-FIN]   to.us

        b . . . ach níl sé sásta a inseacht dúinn [caidé a tá ar bun].
           '. . . but he won't tell us what's going on.'

Again, sluiced wh-phrases appear where the CP appears, clause-finally, not
clause-internally as a DP argument would:

(39)   a . . . *ach níl   sé sásta   [céacu ceann] a inseacht dúinn.
           but not.is he willing   which of.them tell[-FIN]   to.us

        b . . . ach níl sé sásta a inseacht dúinn [céacu ceann].
           '. . . but he won't tell us which of them.'

These data again support the identification of sluiced wh-phrases with
CPs.[4] Note also that these data show that whatever regulates the clause-
peripherality of CPs in these languages, simply appealing to phonological
weight as measured by number of syllables or the like will not suffice.
Instead, these data clearly indicate that, if such positioning is driven by
prosodic considerations as is often assumed, these prosodic rules must be
sensitive to higher prosodic structure, and not necessarily to the (say, syllabic)
content. In other words, if, say, intonational phrases (IntP) must extrapose,
but not perhaps smaller prosodic phrases, then the syntactic category CP
must itself directly project IntP by virtue of its syntactic structure. This
conclusion seems to me a welcome one, though I will not pursue the algorithms necessary for deriving the prosodic exponence from syntactic categories
here.

---

    [4] Judith Aissen (p.c) informs me that it should be possible to make a similar argument on the
basis of the distribution of certain enclitic elements in Tzotzil, which attach to the right edge of
an intonational phrase. CPs, but not DPs, can extrapose, giving rise to the order . . . *enclitic
CP* but not * . . . *enclitic DP*. In this regard, sluiced wh-phrases should behave just like full, extraposed clauses, not like DPs, as in the following hypothetical data she provided:

    (i)   [Someone left . . .]
          a pero mu sna'   li Xun-e   buch'u (ibat).
             but NEG he.knows the Juan-ENC who   left

          b *pero mu sna'   li Xun buch'u-e.
             but NEG he.knows the Juan who-ENC

          'but Juan doesn't know who (left).'

If these data are correct, they also indicate that the sluiced wh-phrase is internal to a CP. See
Aissen (1992) for more discussion of these enclitics.

2.1.5 German Wh-Stress Shift

My last argument is based on the contrast in stress possibilities for wh-phrases in German noticed by Höhle (1983) and discussed in Reis (1985). These authors point out that certain multisyllabic wh-words can have variable stress in SpecCP of a matrix clause, as in (40) and (41); stress can fall either on the operator part of the wh-word (*wV–*) or the non-operator part (the 'incorporating' preposition, essentially). In an embedded clause, however, these wh-words permit stress only on their non-operator portion, as in (42) and (43). My concern here will not be to account for this contrast, but simply to point out that sluiced wh-phrases pattern with wh-phrases in embedded contexts.

(40) a Warúm ist Elke gekommen?
      b Wárum ist Elke gekommen?
      why   is Elke come
      'Why did Elke come?'

(41) a Worán hat Elke gedacht?
      b Wóran hat Elke gedacht?
      what-on has Elke thought
      'What was Elke thinking about?'

(42) a   Wir haben nicht gewußt, [warúm Elke gekommen ist].
      b *Wir haben nicht gewußt, [wárum Elke gekommen ist].
       we   have   not   known   why   Elke come   is
      'We didn't know why Elke came.'

(43) a   Wir wollten gerne wissen, [worán Elke gedacht hat].
      b *Wir wollten gerne wissen, [wóran Elke gedacht hat].
       we   would   gladly know   what-on Elke thought has
      'We'd love to know what Elke was thinking about.'

Note that this stress contrast is sensitive to depth of embedding, not simply sentence-initial position, since a wh-phrase in the specifier of a topicalized CP still cannot take initial stress:

(44) a   [Warúm Elke gekommen ist] haben wir nicht gewußt.
      b *[Wárum Elke gekommen ist] haben wir nicht gewußt.
        why Elke   come   is   have we not   known
      'Why Elke came, we didn't know.'

(45)   a   [Worán   Elke gedacht hat] wollten wir gerne wissen.
       b   *[Wóran Elke gedacht hat] wollten wir gerne wissen.
           what-on Elke thought has would we gladly know

       'What Elke was thinking about, we'd love to know.'

Initial stress can also sometimes occur in wh-phrases in clause-internal positions (*pace* Reis 1985); this stress pattern is found, for example, in echoic multiple wh-questions:

(46)   a   Wer will   wohín   fahren?
       b   Wer will   wóhin   fahren?
           who wants where.to to.drive

       'Who wants to go where?'

(47)   a   Wer ist warúm gestorben?
       b   Wer ist wárum gestorben?
           who is why   died

       'Who died for what reason?'

Note that even in wh-expletive constructions[5] (see McDaniel 1989 and Müller 1995), wh-words that presumably are in the initial SpecCP at LF but not at Spell-Out cannot take initial stress:

---

  [5] Sluicing over a wh-expletive itself is impossible, even when the corresponding question would be well formed, as in (ii):

  (i)   *Du hast mir gesagt, ich sollte dich an jemanden erinnern, aber ich weiß
         you have me told   I should you on someone   remind   but I know

         nicht mehr, [was^x [~~du mir gesagt hast, an wen^x ich dich erinnern sollte~~]]
         not   longer what you me told   have on who I you remind should

         ('You told me to remind you about someone, but I can't remember who.')

  (ii)   Was^x hast du mir gesagt, an wen^x ich dich erinnern sollte?
         what have you me told   on who I   you remind should

         'Who did you tell me to remind you about?'

  This is presumably the result of the fact that the remnant wh-phrase in the sluice would have to be focused, but wh-expletives, and expletives in general, cannot be; cf. the examples in (iii).

  (iii) a   *IT was raining.
         b   *THERE are prisoners in the yard.
         c   *IT is obvious that I'm right.
         d   *WAS hast du gesagt, an wen ich dich erinnern sollte?
             what have you said   on who I   you remind should

             ('Who did you say I should remind you about?')

(48) a   Was hast du nochmal gesagt, worán   ich dich
     b   *Was hast du nochmal gesagt, wóran   ich dich
         what have you again   said   what-on I   you

     erinnern sollte?
     erinnern sollte?
     remind   should

     'What did you say again that I was supposed to remind you about?'

Crucially, the wh-phrase in a sluice has only the final stress found in embedded clauses ((49) and (51)), even when fronted ((50) and (52)):

(49)   Elke ist gekommen, aber wir haben nicht gewußt
       Elke is come   but we have   not   known

       a   [warúm].
       b *[wárum].
          why

       'Elke came, but we didn't know why.'

(50)   Elke ist gekommen, aber
       Elke is come   but

       a   [warúm] haben wir nicht gewußt.
       b *[wárum] haben wir nicht gewußt.
          why   have we not   known

       'Elke came, but we didn't know why.'

(51)   Elke hat an etwas   gedacht, und wir würden gerne wissen,
       Elke has on something thought and we would PRT know

       a   [worán].
       b *[wóran].
          what.on

       'Elke was thinking of something, and we'd love to know what.'

(52)   Elke hat an etwas   gedacht, und
       Elke has on something thought and

       a   [worán] würden wir gerne wissen.
       b *[wóran] würden wir gerne wissen.
          what.on would we PRT   know

       'Elke was thinking of something, and what, we'd love to know.'

Again, this is entirely expected if the wh-phrase in a sluice is in the specifier of an embedded CP, but quite mysterious otherwise.

2.1.6 Summary

We have seen five reasons to believe that sluiced wh-phrases are the audible part
of a CP whose sentential domain is elliptical, and that these sluiced XPs are not
simply fragment XPs generated by the grammar and inserted in place of CPs as
proposed by van Riemsdijk (1978). For the remainder of this book, then, we
can take it that sluices have at least the structure in (53). This structure supposes
that the wh-XP occurs in SpecCP, which I take to be the null hypothesis based
on the overt manifestations of interrogative structures in the languages examined above. The question whether such movement must be overt will briefly re-
engage our attention later when we examine data from wh-in-situ languages,
but in general I will proceed on the assumption that the wh-remnant is immediately dominated by CP.

(53)

Having established what the external syntax of the sluice is, let us turn now
to the more difficult question of its internal syntax.

2.2 INTERNAL SYNTAX:
THE HIDDEN STRUCTURE OF THE SLUICE

Discerning the internal syntax of the sluice means investigating the structure of
silence: attempting to determine what structure must be present in order to
generate the perceived interpetation of elliptical phrases. I take it for granted
that the primary desideratum of any theory of the interpretation of ellipsis
is providing the appropriate material for interpretation. Within the theory
assumed here, this means providing appropriate structures to LF, though of
course these will be supplemented by interpretational mechanisms that do not
rely on structural conditions.

For sluicing in particular, this means that the missing IP must be supplied by
the syntax, either by being present throughout the syntactic derivation with the
ellipsis being deletion at PF or by copying of phrase-markers at LF. This point
cannot be emphasized enough—the data presented in this book are significant
in how clearly they show that ellipsis is *structural*—that is, that an ellipsis site
contains syntactic structures of the kind familiar from overt syntax.

This is not a trivial basis to start from, of course, and some researchers have
sought to do without it (see e.g. Ginzburg 1992, in preparation). But doing

without it entails complicating the syntax–semantics interface in ways that, while clearly needed for the interpretation of certain elements that take parts of their meaning from the context (indexicals, deictics, gradable adjectives, and so on), are not so clearly needed for the interpretation of ellipsis. Sluicing in particular, in contrast to the more often studied VP-ellipsis, clearly shows syntactic dependencies that require that certain structures that are not audible nevertheless be present in the syntax. The alternative would be to burden the semantics with information about idiosyncratic case assignment and whether or not a language allows preposition stranding, as we will see in detail in the next chapter. I take it that it is desirable to construct a theory in which such information is not available to the semantics *sensu stricto*, and is available in the derivation only as late as LF, a syntactic structural level.

This brings us back to the point made above—if ellipsis is indeed structurally represented, we have two choices: either the structure is provided by the syntax as usual, and the grammar does something unusual to it (that is, it issues instructions not to pronounce any of it), or the structure that provides the input to phonology itself contains no phonologically relevant material in the ellipsis site, requiring that structure be provided after Spell-Out on the LF-side of the derivation. As has been noted in the literature (see Lobeck 1995 for discussion and references), the former view requires a kind of communication between the distinct levels of PF and LF that might seem problematic. But this kind of 'communication' is necessary in any case, to account for the distribution of deaccenting phenomena, where appeal to copying procedures is irrelevant in principle.[6] In much of what follows, whether one adopts a copy or deletion approach will not be crucial, the evidence being compatible with either approach. In later sections, however, anticipating the data and conclusions of later chapters, I will phrase the analytical options in terms that implement the generalizations using deletion at PF.

2.2.1 Licensing Conditions on IP-Ellipsis

The elliptical IP in sluicing is licensed only in certain environments, as has long been noted in the literature, going back to Ross (1969). It is not generally the case that IPs can be elided, as the examples in (54) show for IP complements to the complementizer *that*.[7]

---

[6] This 'communication' is also required to account for semantic focus and pitch correlations, and indeed for the fact of sound–meaning correspondence in general.

[7] This holds, of course, for the complementizer *that* in (54b), not for the demonstrative *that*. In languages such as Greek where there is no homophony between these elements, the relevant

(54)   a   She was there, but Ben didn't know [CP that [IP she was there]].
        b   *She was there, but Ben didn't know [CP that [IP e]].

   The embedded IP in example (54a), for instance, is preferably pronounced
with the 'low-flat' intonation characteristic of repeated material in English.
This deaccented intonation is often taken to be in essentially free variation with
complete phonological reduction—that is, deletion. But, while deaccenting is
possible here, ellipsis is not. This means that we must postulate some additional, grammatical requirement on this kind of ellipsis that goes beyond simply allowing the phonology to interpret given structures either as 'deaccented'
or 'unpronounced' *ad libitum*.
   Exactly the same holds for *that* in all other environments as well:

(55)   a   It was painted, but it wasn't obvious [CP that [IP it was painted]].
        b   *It was painted, but it wasn't obvious [CP that [IP e]].

(56)   a   It was painted, but [CP that [IP it was painted]] wasn't obvious to the
            casual observer.
        b   *It was painted, but [CP that [IP e]] wasn't obvious to the casual
            observer.

(57)   a   She had arrived, but [CP that [IP she had arrived]], they didn't tell us.
        b   *She had arrived, but [CP that [IP e]], they didn't tell us.

As noted by Ross (1969), the complementizers *whether* and *if* also fail to license
null IP complements:

(58)   *The Pentagon leaked that it would close the Presidio, but no-one
        knew for sure [CP {whether / if} [IP e]].

The same holds for the complementizer *for*, as pointed out by Lobeck
(1995: 46):

(59)   *Sue asked Bill to leave, but [CP for [IP e]] would be unexpected.

   Lobeck, adapting the CP projection of Chomsky (1986a), gives the structure
in (60) for sluicing:

examples are unambiguously ungrammatical (*oti* is the complementizer 'that', while *afto* is the
demonstrative):

(i)   a   *Itan ekei, alla o Petros dhen iksere [CP oti [IP e]].
        b   Itan ekei, alla o Petros dhen iksere [CP oti [IP   itan ekei]].
            was there but the Petros not   knew   that   was there
        'She was there, but Peter didn't know she was there.'

(60)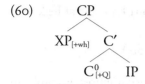

Lobeck (1995) further discusses a number of cases that indicate that the null IP in sluicing is subject to quite strict licensing and identification requirements. To begin, null IPs do not occur when lexically governed, as in (61) and (62) (Lobeck 1995: 56):

(61) a *Even though Mary doesn't believe [$_{IP}$ *e*], Sue expects Hortense to be crazy.
      b *John appears to be smart, and Mary also seems [$_{IP}$ *e*].
      c *Mary doesn't expect Bill to win, but she wants [$_{IP}$ *e*].

(62) a *John talked to Bill, but before [$_{IP}$ *e*], Mary called.
      b *Mary ate peanuts during the game, and while [$_{IP}$ *e*], the home team made four runs.

Lobeck proposes that the null IP must be properly head-governed by an agreeing head, here C^0, which must be specified [+wh]. This correctly rules out cases of 'partial' sluicing, as in (63) (her (54), p. 56), since the embedded C^0 is not [+wh].

(63) I know someone likes Mary, but
      a *who do you think [$_{CP}$ *t* [C^0 [$_{IP}$ *e*]]]?
      b who do you think [$_{CP}$ *t* [C^0 [$_{IP}$ *t* likes her]]]?

However, even if the embedded complementizer is [+wh], such partial sluicing is still impossible:

(64) *They wondered if Marsha would invite someone, but I don't remember who they wondered whether [$_{IP}$ *e*].
      (cf. ?Who did they wonder whether Marsha would invite?)

Lobeck's system rules this out as well, by stipulating that the licensing C^0 must be coindexed with a lexical wh-phrase in SpecCP. However, even if this condition is met, embedded sluicing may still be impossible, as in Williams's (1986) example:[8]

---

[8] I will not go into Williams's account of the ungrammaticality of this example, since it relies on the incorrect assumption that distinct operators may not bind into an ellipsis site, from

(65)   *John knows how to do something, but I don't know what he knows how [$_{IP}$ *e*].

(i.e. . . . I don't know what he knows how to do.)

What seems to be causing the degradation of the 'partial' ellipsis examples in (64)–(65) is a prohibition on eliding less than possible: partial ellipsis as in (64)–(65) requires that redundant material be destressed adjacent to an ellipsis site. It is this constraint,[9] whatever its ultimate source may be, that seems to play a role in the unexpected oddness of examples like (66b,d):

(66)   a   Ben knows who she invited, but Charlie doesn't.
        b   ??Ben knows who she invited, but Charlie doesn't *know who.*
        c   Ben knows who she invited, but Charlie doesn't *know who she invited.*
        d   ??Ben knows who she invited, but Charlie doesn't *know who she did.*

To return to the conditions on the C-system in sluicing: simple agreement with a [+wh] operator in SpecCP is not enough to license the null IP, since sluicing is not possible in relative clauses ((67c) is Lobeck's (57b), p. 57).

Williams (1977) and Sag (1976*a*). Such a restriction on alphabetic variance incorrectly rules out examples like (i):

(i)   I know what I like and what I don't.

[9] This restriction on 'partial' deletions, or mixing ellipsis with wh-operators and deaccenting, also extends to the problematic example discussed by Tancredi (1992: 123) (see Hirschbühler 1978, 1981 for the original observations and discussion; Tancredi's example is equivalent to Hirschbühler 1981: 139 (14)).

(i)   A: I wish I knew who brought what to the party.
       B: I wish I did too. I have no IDEA   a   *who did.*
                                                b   *who brought what (to the party).*

Something like Tancredi's stipulation limiting this to interactions involving wh-operators seems necessary, given the well-formedness of the following examples with VP-ellipsis:

(ii)   a   Abby knew that he had quit, but Beth didn't *know that he had.*
        b   Abby asked if he had quit, but Beth didn't *ask if he had.*

These examples contrast for some speakers with examples where the ellipsis site contains, under standard assumptions, the origin site of the fronted adjunct *when*.

(iii)   a   ??Abby knew when he had quit, but Beth didn't *know when he had.*
         b   ??Abby asked when he had quit, but Beth didn't *ask when he had.*

These contrasts raise interesting questions about the interaction between deaccenting, ellipsis, and wh-extraction that I will not go into here. The interested reader should see the discussion in Lobeck (1995: §6.3) and Johnson (1997), as well as Winkler (1997). I will set them aside here, and concentrate on the core data any theory of IP-ellipsis should aim to cover.

(67) a *Somebody stole the car, but they couldn't find the person who.
      b *The judge gave five years each to the adults who participated in
         the riot, but she hasn't yet sentenced the minors who.
      c *Although the place where is unclear, the time when the meeting is
         to be held is posted on the door.

Lobeck assumes that the complementizer that occurs in relative clauses with
overt relative operators is [−wh], citing Rizzi (1990). This allows her to maintain that the 'strong' feature (value) [+wh] is sufficient to license and identify
the null IP. In fact, however, Rizzi's (1990) system makes a slightly different
division from the one Lobeck assumes, though one that can be modified to her
purposes easily enough. For Rizzi, the complementizer in relative clauses can
be either [+wh], co-occuring with overt wh-relative operators, or [−wh], co-
occuring with the null operator. The former is always null in English, while the
latter varies, subject to conditions not of interest here.

Instead of basing the feature-checking mechanism solely on the [±]
value of the feature [wh], we must instead seek to identify uniquely the complementizer that occurs in questions (and hence, in sluicing), and distinguish
it from the complementizer that occurs, for example, in relative clauses with
overt relative pronouns, among others. Fortunately, this is easily done. The
complementizer of interest to us is uniquely specified by the features [+wh,
+Q], assuming as is standard that these two features appear together only on
the complementizer in constituent questions. Adapting this to Lobeck's system, we claim that only the null [+wh, +Q] C^0 of interrogatives will license the
null IP.

Similar reasoning extends to the cleft examples in (68):[10]

(68) a *We thought it was Abby who stole the car, but it was Ben who.
      b *Somebody stole the car, but no one knew that it was Ben who.

---

[10] Interestingly, pseudoclefts seem to allow sluicing to some extent:

(i)   a ?Ben stole something—[what] was a car.
      b ?He left, and when was yesterday.

I use the order [wh-phrase]-[pivot] to avoid the distracting presence of such collocations as the
following:

(ii) a What did Ben steal? A car is what! *What is a car.
      b What's he doing? Dancing a jig is what! *What is dancing a jig.

The availability of sluicing in pseudoclefts is expected if these are 'self-answering' questions, as
proposed in Higgins (1973) and den Dikken *et al.* (1998), and less free-relative-like; free-relatives,
like regular relative clauses, do not license sluicing:

(iii) *He's up to something again, and I don't like [what]!

Lobeck's earlier licensing and identification requirements were meant to have much in common with the Empty Category Principle, and as such relied crucially on the notion of head government. In a more recent approach to these requirements on ellipsis, consonant with the Minimalist Program's program to eliminate government as a theoretical device, Lobeck (1999) has proposed that the null category undergoes movement into the specifier of the licensing head. Her discussion is confined to the case of VP-ellipsis: in this approach, the null VP (a maximal and minimal null element similar to *pro*) moves into SpecTP to check a strong agreement feature, since feature-checking requires a spec-head configuration, by hypothesis. She assumes that SpecTP is free for this VP, the subject being in SpecAgr$_S$P. Whatever the merits of this approach, it is clear that extending it to sluicing is impossible: in sluicing, a wh-phrase occupies SpecCP, blocking movement of the null IP.

It seems instead that, if we are to capture the intuitions behind the government approach to licensing in a Minimalist framework dispensing with government *per se*, we should locate the necessarily local relation between the licensing head C and the elided category IP not in a spec–head relation, but in a head–head relation.[11] We can employ the same conditions on licensing identified by Lobeck, recasting them as featural matching requirements in a head–head relation, the other structural relation available for feature checking.

What is needed is a feature on I that can be checked only by a [+wh, +Q] C head, and that triggers deletion of the IP at PF. Call this feature E. E moves from I to C, along the lines discussed above, being checked in C.[12] E issues an instruction to the PF system to skip its complement for purposes of parsing and production.[13] Here I am assuming a strictly left-to-right algorithm for PF: at each syntactic node, the features on that node trigger operations in the phonological component, whether these be lexical insertion or construction of prosodic categories, or the like. For example, a CP node must be mapped onto some higher level prosodic category (perhaps an intonational phrase) regardless of how many syllables occur inside CP, as discussed in §2.1.4. While some features on nodes may indicate that they are to be prosodically incorporated into their sisters, the E feature will indicate the opposite: its sister is not to be prosodically incorporated into the PF structure at all.

Modulo the resolution of independent questions about how one implements semantic composition for complex heads that I will ignore, we can also

---

[11] Or feature–feature relation, to the extent these differ.

[12] Equivalently, the feature could start on C, not being moved there from I at all. In this case, we would state the checking requirement of E as a feature compatibility requirement.

[13] Another possibility is to have a general constraint on deletion that is sensitive to E, as explored in Kennedy (2000).

give the semantics for E: essentially, E is the feature that imposes the Focus condition defined in Chapter 1. The simplest way of implementing this, assuming that E will combine with IP (how the independent, usual contribution of C is implemented is a separate question, not unique to the current issue), is to assimilate the failure of deletions that do not respect the Focus condition to a kind of presupposition failure. Under this approach, we would have a partial identity function for the meaning of E (following the implementation of Heim and Kratzer (1998: 244) for φ-features):

(69) $\llbracket E \rrbracket = \lambda p : p$ is e-GIVEN . p

By giving a semantics for E, the licensing (the local featural requirements of E) and identification (the semantic condition E imposes on its complement) requirements on ellipsis can for the first time be directly linked.

This view of the mechanism of ellipsis retains the advantage of the government approach in requiring a very local relation to hold between the head that checks the E feature ('licensing' the ellipsis, in traditional terms) and the category affected by E, while at the same time integrating this with a more restrictive view of the possible relations employed in the syntax. Note that this particular implementation leaves open the exact nature and number of the checking features, and the requirements of E to be checked, allowing for cross-linguistic variation in this domain if necessary. This seems to me to be a promising line of attack, opening the way to a reformulation of Lobeck's notion of 'strong agreement'.

At this point, however, we still have little in the way of concrete empirical evidence which of the general approaches examined here is to be preferred: the data thus far are compatible either with the view that treats ellipsis sites as empty categories in the syntax, or with the view that takes ellipsis as the result of deletion at PF.

2.2.2 The COMP Domain in Sluicing

This section examines that area of structure traditionally known as COMP: material dominated by CP but external to IP, in a structure like (70):

(70) $[_{CP} XP_{[+wh]} \; C^0 \; [_{IP}...]]$

'COMP'

Languages differ widely on what sort of material can appear in the COMP field and under what circumstances. It is not my aim here to give a review of the literature that deals with how languages differ in this respect and how the various patterns are to be accounted for. My aim here will be limited to examining the behavior of the COMP field under sluicing, and in extracting the significance of the data presented for the proper analysis of the syntax of sluicing. The data that I will present can be described in a very simple and surprising generalization, given in (71):

(71)   *Sluicing-COMP generalization*
        In sluicing, no non-operator material may appear in COMP.

    Here, let us understand 'operator' as 'syntactic wh-XP', as in (70) above. By 'material' in (71) is meant simply any pronounced element. This is meant to include complementizers, verbs, clitics, agreement morphemes, and the like. The claim is that only segments directly associated with the syntactic operator—the wh-XP—will be found overtly in sluiced interrogatives.

    The generalization as stated subsumes two separate subcases, which I will examine independently below. The first subcase concerns elements that are usually analyzed as originating within IP and moving into COMP or cliticizing parasitically onto elements base-generated there. These include I^0-to-C^0 verb movement in the Germanic languages, complementizer agreement, Wackernagel clitics in South Slavic and other Balkan languages, and a variety of 'second position' phenomena in general. The second subcase concerns elements that are usually assumed to be base-generated in the COMP system—namely, complementizers themselves (as well as wh-expletives in some languages, see note 5, and wh-operators that bind resumptive pronouns, see §4.3).

    The conclusion reached is that, although the facts from this domain (to the extent they have been discussed at all) have been taken to support the null-category approach to ellipsis over the deletion approach, upon closer inspection these facts are fully compatible with the deletion approach, and may provide the basis for interesting conclusions on the nature of feature-driven movement as well. Finally, the restrictions on elements in sluicing seem best thought of as operative at the PF interface, similar in some respects to the COMP-trace effect.

2.2.2.1 *Non-Operator Foreign Elements in COMP*

I begin with an examination of the facts from English, Dutch, German, and Danish main-clause sluicing (to the best of my knowledge, these facts are identical in the other Scandinavian languages as well). As is well known (see Vikner 1995 for discussion and references), all of these languages exhibit verb-second

(V2) in unembedded interrogatives, as shown in (72). Though they differ in whether they require V2 in non-interrogative main clauses, such structures will not be of interest here, since sluicing is limited to interrogative structures only.

(72)   a   Who   has   Max   invited?   [English]
        b   Wen   hat   Max   eingeladen?   [German]
        c   Wie   heeft   Max   uitgenodigd?   [Dutch]
        d   Hvem   har   Max   inviteret?   [Danish]

This is standardly analyzed as I^0-to-C^0 movement, illustrated in (73) for English (I assume for simplicity that this movement is substitution and not adjunction, the ordering of inflectional elements within a 'complex head' being determined by principles of morphology and not by directionality of adjunction):

(73)

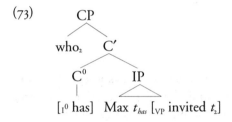

$[_{I^0} \text{ has}]$ Max t_{has} $[_{VP}$ invited $t_2]$

Given the structure in (73), we might expect that main-clause sluices in these languages would consist of the wh-XP followed by some moved verb, especially if the IP-ellipsis in sluicing is simply phonological deletion of the material remaining in the IP at PF. This expectation is not borne out:

(74)   a   A: Max has invited   B: Really? Who   (*has)?   [English]
           someone.
      b   A: Max hat jemand   B: Echt?   Wen   (*hat)?   [German]
           eingeladen.
      c   A: Max heeft iemand   B: Ja?   Wie   (*heeft)?   [Dutch]
           uitgenodigd.
      d   A: Max har inviteret en   B: Ja?   Hvem   (*har)?   [Danish]
           eller anden.

One might wonder whether such structures really consist of sluices at all—after all, fragment questions clearly exist, in echo functions, and indeed need not even display wh-forms, though this is certainly also possible.

(75)   A: Superman tricked Mr Mxyzptlk.
        a   B: Who?
        b   B: Mr who?
        c   B: Superman tricked Mr who?

But it is easy to see that such bare-echo wh-XPs differ considerably from the matrix sluices in (74). First, the intonational contour on the wh-phrase in (75a) is the same intonation that the questions in (75b,c) bear—namely, a rise (L*H; though see Gunlogson in preparation for a much fuller picture). The sluiced wh-phrase in (74a), on the other hand, bears the contour assigned to full questions in this context: a fall, as in *Who did he trick?* As signalled by the differing pitch contours, the status of bare echo wh-XPs like (75a) and that of matrix informational question (sluiced) wh-XPs as in (74) are distinct.

Note also that the illocutionary modifier *really* that precedes the matrix sluice in the examples in (74) is not possible before an echo question:

(76)   A: Superman tricked Mr Mxyzptlk.
                        L*H
        B: #Really?   Who?

This derives from the fact that *really* here indicates that B has accepted the content of A's utterance into the common ground (though perhaps signalling some surprise). This uptake is obviously not possible if B has not understood the content of A's utterance to begin with, as indicated by the use of the rise contour.

A second, syntactic piece of evidence for keeping main-clause sluicing and fragment wh-questions separate comes from the phenomenon of sluiced wh-phrase inversion with prepositions ('swiping') in English, as discussed in detail in Merchant (forthcoming).[14] We can observe that some wh-operators can invert with a governing preposition in English sluicing, as illustrated in (77):

---

[14] Space prevents a full discussion of this phenomenon here, but I note that it is also found in some of the Scandinavian languages (thanks to P. Svenonius for the Norwegian and L. Mikkelsen for the Danish):

(i)   Per har   gått på kino,   men jeg vet ikke hvem med.   [Norwegian]
       Per er   gået i biografen, men jeg ved ikke hvem med.   [Danish]
       Per has/is gone to cinema   but I   know not who with

       'Per went to the movies but I don't know who with.'

In English at least, this inversion is limited to the 'minimal' wh-operators *who, what, where,* and *when*. Despite this, it is not (just) prosodically conditioned, since *which* and *whose* are impossible while—as pointed out to me by J. Itô (p.c.)—compounds with *the hell* are possible (though not generally in sluicing; see §4.2.2 (35)):

(77)   Lois was talking (to someone), but I don't know [who to].

This is of course not possible in non-sluiced interrogatives:

(78)   a   *I don't know [who to] Lois was talking.
        b   *[Who to] was Lois talking?

This inversion can thus be taken as sluicing-specific, for reasons that will not concern us here. Crucially, such inversion appears also in matrix sluicing:

(79)   A: Lois was talking (to someone). B: Really? Who to?

But this inversion is not possible in echo-wh-fragments:

(80)   A: Lois was talking to Mr Mxyzptlk.
                    L*H
        a   B: To who?
                    L*H
        b   B: *Who to?

With inversion, the presence of a moved auxiliary in C is impossible, parallel to (74a) above:

(81)   A: Lois was talking (to someone). B: Really? Who to (*was)?

This brief excursus has been simply to establish the point that sluicing occurs in matrix clauses as well, *pace* Ross (1969) and M. Klein (1977), but in agreement with Bechhofer (1976*a,b*, 1977) (see the latter for further evidence). This establishes that the pattern in (74) requires an explanation.

A similar puzzle comes from the South Slavic languages that have 'Wackernagel' clitics, such as Slovene, Bulgarian, Serbo-Croatian, and Macedonian. In these languages, a certain class of elements—auxiliaries, negation, and certain pronominals—are subject to positional restrictions on their

(ii)   a   He was talking to one of those guys, but I don't know which (*to).
        b   He was talking to somebody's mom, but I don't know whose (*to).
        c   He was talking, but God knows who the hell to.

It seems the most adequate account is to take the wh-words that participate in these to be heads that have raised to P ('minimal maximal' Xs, like clitics, in Chomsky's terms (1995: 249)). Head-to-head movement picks out exactly this class (ruling out *which*, assuming that excorporation is banned). See §4.2.2 for additional data, and see Merchant (forthcoming) for a full discussion of swiping.

distribution, which, in questions, place them adjacent to wh-phrases. Roughly speaking, these elements, like inflected matrix verbs in V2 languages, must occur in 'second' position, where 'second' is defined either prosodically, with respect to the first prosodic word, or structurally, with respect to the first syntactic constituent. (See Rudin (1985) for discussion, and Anderson (1996, 2000) for a recent approach that attempts to bring the V2 facts into consideration as well.) The account of this phenomenon and its variations is tangential here: of interest is only the fact that, under certain circumstances, these elements may appear within or between complex wh-XPs in the CP system. This is illustrated for Slovene in (82), from Marvin (1997), where the element of interest is the aspectual auxiliary *je*, which obligatorily cliticizes onto the embedded wh-phrase as seen (see also Browne 1974 and Bošković 1995 for Serbo-Croatian; and Legendre 1999 for Macedonian and Bulgarian):

(82)   Peter se   je   spraševal, kako₁ je   Špela popravila t₁   [Slovene]
        Peter REFL AUX asked   what AUX Spela fixed.
        'Peter wondered what Spela fixed.'

This also holds for multiple fronted wh-phrases; in such cases, the auxiliary *je* cliticizes onto the first of the wh-phrases:

(83)   a   Nisem   vprašal, kaj₁ je   komu₂ Špela kupila t₁ t₂.
            NEG.AUX.1sg asked   what AUX who.DAT Spela bought
            'I didn't ask what Spela bought for who.'
        b   *Nisem vprašal, kaj₁ komu₂ je Špela kupila t₁ t₂.

Under no circumstances, however, can such a cliticized element survive under sluicing (thanks to T. Marvin for judgments):

(84)   a   Špela je   popravila nekako,   a   nisem   vprašal,
            Špela AUX fixed   something but NEG.AUX.1sg asked
            kako (*je).
            what AUX
            'Spela fixed something, but I didn't ask what.'
        b   Špela je   kupila nekaj   nekomu,   a   nisem
            Špela AUX bought something someone.DAT but NEG.AUX.1sg
            vprašal, kaj   (*je) komu.
            asked   what AUX who.DAT
            (lit.) 'Spela bought something for someone, but I didn't ask what for who.'

Another kind of data that is relevant in this regard comes from the various manifestations of non-wh-agreement in the C-system found in several languages. Such complementizer agreement systems are particularly well attested within the Germanic family. The term 'complementizer agreement', as used in the Germanic literature, refers to manifestations of agreement with certain features of an embedded subject only, and should not be confused with complementizers that agree with wh-phrases, as are found in Irish. The details of Germanic complementizer agreement will not be my concern here (see Zwart 1993: 3.3 for discussion and references); of interest here is only the fact that this agreement appears equally well when there is a wh-phrase in SpecCP, as illustrated in (85) (Luxemburgish, from Zwart 1993: 163) and (86) (Bavarian, from Lobeck 1995: 58).

(85)   . . . mat wiem (datt) s   de spazéiere gangng
        with who   that   2sg you walk   gone

        bas.   [Luxemburgish]
        are.2sg

        '. . . with whom you went for a walk.'

(86)   Du woidd-st   doch kumma, owa mia wissn ned
        you wanted-2sg PRT come   but   we   know   not

        wann-st (du) kumma woidd-st.   [Bavarian]
        when-2sg you come   wanted-2sg

        'You wanted to come, but we don't know when you wanted to come.'

Lobeck (1995: 59) points out that, although complementizer agreement can phonologically cliticize onto a wh-phrase in SpecCP when no overt complementizer is present, and though sluicing is generally possible in these dialects, nevertheless such agreement cannot appear in sluicing (her (65)):

(87)   Du woidd-st   doch kumma, owa mia wissn ned
        you wanted-2sg PRT come   but   we   know   not

        wann(*-st).   [Bavarian]
        when-2sg

        'You wanted to come, but we don't know when.'

She relates this fact to the fact that, when the verb bearing the matching agreement features is not present, as in phrasal comparatives, complementizer agreement is likewise impossible. The data are from Bayer (1984):

(88)   a   Der Hans is gresser (als) wia-st   du bist.   [Bavarian]
            the Hans is taller   than how-2sg you are-2sg

            'Hans is taller than you are.'

        b   Der Hans is gresser (als) wia(*-st) du.
            the Hans is taller   than how-2sg you

            'Hans is taller than you.'

Lobeck makes a similar point based on the distribution of the complementizer *som* in Norwegian, which appears obligatorily in embedded questions
with subject extraction, as in (89a) (modified slightly from Rizzi 1990: 57; see
also Taraldsen 1986 and Vikner 1991; likewise for Danish *der* in spoken registers, if *der* is indeed in C[15]):

(89)   a   Vi   vet   hvem *(som) snakker met   Marit.   [Norwegian]
        b   Vi   ved   hvem ??(der) snakker med   Marit.   [Danish]
            we know who   C°   talks   with Marit

            'We know who is talking with Marit.'

Lobeck points out that this *som* is nevertheless impossible in sluicing, shown in
(90a) (her (68), p. 60); she suggests that this is because *som* must agree with
INFL (in order to license the subject trace), which on her account is missing.
This assumption assimilates the deviancy of (90a) to that of the lack of complementizer agreement seen above. The Danish example in (90b) shows the
same contrast (again, if *der* is in fact in C).

(90)   a   Noen   snakker met Marit, men vi vet   ikke
        b   En eller anden snakker med Marit, men vi ved   ikke
            someone   talks   with Marit but we know not

            hvem (*som).   [Norwegian]
            hvem (*der).   [Danish]
            who   C°

If this assumption regarding the nature of the relation between *som* (and *der*)
and INFL is correct, then, it provides another case of an illicit non-operator
dependency holding between an element in the C-system and a position or element internal to the missing IP.
    All of the data presented in this section have one thing in common: under
usual assumptions, the non-operator elements that appear in the C-system
originate within the clause. Consider the first case discussed above, and the

---

[15] Thanks to L. Mikkelsen for the Danish data.

most familiar one: V2 in matrix questions in the Germanic languages. The standard analysis takes the fronted elements to originate inside IP, either in I^0 itself (for the English modals and pleonastic *do*), or within a lower VP, raising into I^0 (for *have* and *be* in English; in the other languages, almost all verbs can raise). V2 is then triggered in different configurations in the various languages (in all matrix clauses in all the languages besides English; in matrix questions, imperatives, 'negative inversion', and other very restricted contexts for English)—crucial here is only that such fronting is I^0-to-C^0 raising (or into whatever heads the projection whose specifier is the landing site for wh-movement in these languages). Complementizer agreement, too, is usually analyzed as involving movement of a functional head or some of its features (I^0 for Hoekstra and Marácz 1989, Agr_S^0 for Zwart 1993) from within the IP to C^0. (Whether the Norwegian *som* facts fall into this line of analysis is unclear; it could be that the problem here is related to the facts described in the next section.) Finally, for the purposes of the syntax, it is clear that the Wackernagel clitic elements must originate within the IP: the pronominals satisfy selectional restrictions, and the auxiliaries determine the form of their verbal complements. How these clitics come to occupy their observed positions is immaterial, whether via syntactic (presumably head movement, as is sometimes supposed), or via phonological mechanisms.

The fact that none of these elements occurs in sluicing has a number of possible explanations.

The first is to maintain, as Lobeck (1995: 58–60) does for the facts from Norwegian and Bavarian, that these facts support a null IP empty category in the syntax. Her reasoning, which extends equally well to the V2 cases, is straightforward: in the syntax, there is only $[_{IP} e]$, hence these elements, in I^0, will not be present at all to raise in the first place. This reasoning is also applicable to the C-agreement facts, as she points out, if 'morphologically realized agreement in COMP . . . is contingent on agreement with embedded INFL' (p. 60). 'Contingent' here translates directly into those approaches that take V2 and C-agreement to express parallel relations of (head-)movement into C^0. Identical reasoning applies to the Wackernagel clitic placement facts of the South Slavic languages: their origin site is IP-internal, and, if IP is empty, by hypothesis, these elements simply will not be available for either syntactic or phonological operations to manipulate.

While this argument seems reasonable, it rests on an assumption that is difficult to maintain. Recall that, under the empty structure approach, the wh-phrase is base-generated in SpecCP, and binds nothing at S-structure (or, perhaps, binds the IP empty category itself, to extend Haïk's (1987) proposal that the relative operator in antecedent-contained deletions binds the VP empty category: see Kennedy and Merchant (1997, 1999) for discussion). But, if this is the case, what prevents us from base-generating any of the non-operator elements in their landing sites or 'moved' positions external to IP, fully parallel to the case of the wh-phrase? It would seem that we would have to stipulate a difference between operator binding, which can be voided at S-structure (or Haïk-bind a categorially distinct empty category), and head-binding (for V2, complementizer agreement, and possibly the South Slavic Wackernagel clitics).

But such a distinction seems mostly unmotivated. One might argue that the difference is not in the category but in the level of the category: the wh-phrase is an XP, and by hypothesis binds the empty XP (IP), while the heads X^0 cannot do so. If this were so, however, taken in conjunction with an analysis of VP-ellipsis as also consisting of a null VP ($[_{VP}\ e]$), we might expect VP-ellipsis with 'raised' auxiliaries in I^0 to be impossible, if one were to assume that these elements are heads exceptionally base-generated in I^0 (usually, of course, the auxiliaries in question—aspectual *have*, and progressive, passive, and copular *be*—must originate in a lower V^0 projection). This is incorrect:

(91)   a   I've been writing, and Bill has, too.
        b   Frank is learning Swahili because Marsha is.
        c   Max was arrested, but Andy wasn't.
        d   Cathy is a doctor, and so is her husband.

Under such an analysis, these would have the structure in (92):

(92)

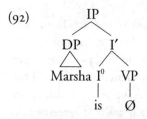

The force of this objection, however, is very little, since it is clear that a structure like that in (92) is incorrect for the sentences in (91). Lobeck (1995) argues convincingly that such sentences instead derive from the following structure (see also especially Potsdam 1996: 83–8):

(93)

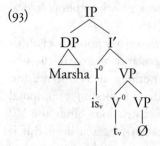

The objection does go through, however, for the Irish data discussed in McCloskey (1991a) (and the Hebrew data in Doron 1990, 1999). McCloskey argues that Irish displays a phenomenon of predicate-ellipsis similar to VP-ellipsis in English; the difference arises from the fact that Irish subjects remain low (not in SpecIP), while Irish verbs raise (say, to I^0). 'VP'-ellipsis applied to such a structure will yield apparently verb-only sentences, as in (94):

(94)   Cheannaigh siad teach?
         bought   they house

         'Did they buy a house?'

         a   Cheannaigh.
              bought

              '(Yes.) They did.'

         b   Níor   cheannaigh.
              NEG.PAST bought

              '(No.) They didn't.'

These elliptical answers, McCloskey argues, have the structure in (95) (updating his 1991a proposal slightly to reflect his 1996 arguments for a (slightly) VP-external subject, though it is unclear whether an elided VP-internal subject might not be able to avoid overt raising in any case, parallel in some respects to *There were rabbits in the garden today, though there weren't yesterday*):

(95)

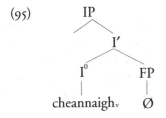

If such 'displaced' heads need to bind an empty element before LF-reconstruction, then head-binding of a maximal (empty) category must be countenanced. If such head-binding is simply not a requirement whatsoever, and if only true operators must bind an empty category at every stage of the derivation (as in Koopman and Sportiche 1982), then the ungrammaticality of the sluicing cases above cannot follow from this line of argument.

Another possible strategy would be to claim that while such head-binding is licit, the problem in the sluicing cases is that more than one element—the wh-phrase and the head-material—must bind the empty IP category simultaneously. Any version of Koopman and Sportiche's Bijection Principle would then rule out such multiple 'displacements'. However, this logic too fails to go through consistently, given the data discussed in Kennedy and Merchant (1997, 1999). There, it is shown that comparative ellipsis is licit with pseudo-gapping, as shown in (96a), with the presumed structure in (96b) (where the order of the remnant and null VP is irrelevant):

(96)   a   Jack read a longer magazine than Abby did a book.
        b   . . . than CP

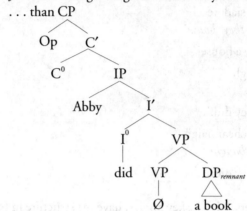

What this entails on the base-generation view of ellipsis is that the VP-external remnant must bind the VP empty category at the same time the DegP operator in SpecCP does (this argument rests upon the idea that 'displaced' remnants would have to 'bind' the ellipsis site like other 'displaced' elements, parallel to the head cases in sluicing above).

In sum, under the standard null IP category approach to sluicing, there seems little reason to believe that whatever mechanism licenses the base-generation of a wh-phrase in SpecCP with concomitant later satisfaction (at LF, under standard assumptions) of its binding requirements would not also license the base-generation of heads, agreement, or Wackernagel clitics in these 'displaced' positions in exactly the same way.[16]

Under the deletion approach pursued here, on the other hand, the data fall out under an ordering solution: if deletion of the IP material precedes the

---

[16] The Wackernagel clitics present a special case, since it seems clear that the mechanisms regulating their ordering are phonological, and not syntactic, so it is possible to give an independent argument ruling them out in sluicing structures, along the following lines. Assume Anderson (2000) and Legendre (2000) are correct: Alignment constraints at PF require these clitics to be as close to the left edge of the clause as possible, with other constraints making sure that 'as close as possible' is realized as either one prosodic word or one XP (perhaps more generally, prosodic phrase) removed from the actual left edge. This prosodic material is supplied by the syntax, but, by assumption, the syntax does not impose any particular order on these elements beyond what is required for auxiliaries, negation, and arguments in general. If this is the case,

(head) movement and prosodic reordering operations responsible for the appearance of IP-internal morphology in the C-system, none of this material will appear. The question to be asked at this point is whether there is a principled way to derive this ordering, beyond simply stipulating it. Some considerations suggest that there is. First, a general remark, pointed out in much of the literature on these phenomena: it seems that such prosodic reordering operations are fairly 'late' processes, fed by syntax but not necessarily generated by syntax (this is most obvious for the case of clitics, though similar remarks apply to I-to-C movement as well).

Theoretically, this state of affairs seems to be a reflection of economy (both of economy of derivation and of representation, to the extent that these are distinguishable). Simply put, if deletion is possible with these elements, it is preferred. Consider the case of I-to-C movement. This movement is usually thought to be driven by some strong feature of C that must be checked by a matching feature on I (see e.g. Holmberg and Platzack 1995). Under normal conditions, movement of I into C can be non-overt (occurring at LF) only if this feature is weak—in this case, only the feature itself need move at LF, since PF pied-piping considerations will not apply. Under this theory, PF requirements force 'pied-piping' when a strong feature is checked. This is usually thought to be because the bare feature would not be able to be spelled out at PF. But it might just as well be the case that the PF crash is caused by the lack of an item corresponding to the feature bundle remaining in I, now lacking the moved feature. There seems no way to decide between these alternatives.

But now consider the case where ellipsis can apply as well. One way to interpret the facts above, consistent with the standard approaches to I-to-C movement, is to assume that it is indeed the remnant feature bundle that is causing the PF crash. Under IP ellipsis, minimal feature movement out of I into C will be possible without pied-piping the rest of I, since the remnant feature bundle left behind in I will not need to be pronounced; this was implicit in the proposal regarding the ellipsis feature E above. Note that this turns Chomsky's (1995) 'feature'-pied-piping convention on its head: it is the partial remnant that triggers the PF-crash, not the bare feature itself, which has no phonological content by itself. This line of analysis is also in line with the general idea that I-to-C movement occurs at PF, as mooted in Chomsky (1995).

Another interpretation of the facts would be to suggest that, contrary to standard analyses, it is a strong feature in I that drives I-to-C movement (in

then, under sluicing, we would have to have exceptional base-generation of these elements (which I will assume are heads, not phrases) external to IP. Given constraints on adjunction, this means that they would have to occur in or adjoined to C^0, since neither CP, IP, nor the wh-phrase in SpecCP, being maximal projections, is a licit adjunction site for a head.

English, presumably only certain kinds of matrix C can check this feature). Since unchecked strong features cause a PF crash, this will force overt I-to-C movement in the regular range of cases. But again an interesting exception emerges under ellipsis: if the IP is deleted, the strong feature on I does not reach the PF interface, avoiding the crash. (This is exactly the logic that will be applied to several cases in Chapter 5.) At this stage, I see no compelling reason to adopt one of the interpretations of the evidence over the other, both appearing equally viable for the case at hand, and will leave the question open.[17] (See also Lasnik 1999, who reaches similar conclusions.)

To summarize, the fact that IP-internal elements that usually appear in the C-system do not appear there under sluicing is compatible with the deletion account pursued here, and do not, as sometimes supposed, support a null-category approach over deletion.

2.2.2.2 *Base-Generated COMP-Internal Elements*

The logic applied to elements moved into the C-system above does not extend to the data to be considered in this section. Here, I will consider material that is usually analyzed as being base-generated in COMP, in the C^0 head. While English will be of no use here, owing to the effects of the Doubly-Filled Comp-Filter, we can examine languages that do not obey this filter, languages that allow an overt complementizer to co-occur with a wh-phrase in SpecCP. Certain varieties of Dutch present one example, as the following examples show ((97a) modified from Bennis (1986: 234), (97b) modified from J. Hoekstra (1993) and Zwart (1993: 169); see also den Besten (1978: 647, 1989)).

(97) a Ik weet niet, wie (of) (dat) hij gezien heeft.
       I   know not who if that he seen has

                              [(esp. Southern) Dutch]

          'I don't know who he has seen.'
       b Ik wit net wa (of) *('t)   jûn   komt.   [Frisian]
          I know not who if that.CL tonight comes
          'I don't know who's coming tonight.'

The example (97a) has the structure given in (98) (whether or not the displaced *wie* has moved through the specifier of *dat* is immaterial, here, though see Zwart (1993: §5.2.2) for evidence that it does not). In this tree, I use recur-

[17] Note that at least the $C^0_{[+wh]}$ must be present to trigger the attested wh-movement; if the [+wh] on C is strong, as usually assumed for English, we have evidence that the deletion targets IP, not C'—if C' were targeted, the offending [+wh] feature would be eliminated without triggering wh-movement into SpecCP.

sive CP labels for simplicity; the different projections have been identified as WhP and TopP (see J. Hoekstra 1993, Müller and Sternefeld 1993, Zwart 1993, Rizzi 1995, and below).

(98)

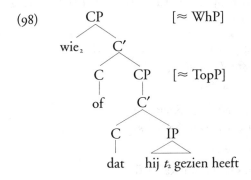

Given this structure, we might expect that either the CP headed by *dat* (TopP) or the IP complement to *dat* might be elidable. If the presence of *of* in (97) is simply the overt counterpart to the null C^0[+wh, +Q] complementizer in English embedded questions, as is usually supposed, then it should bear all the relevant features to license an elliptical complement. Similarly, if *wie* moves through the specifier of *dat*, we might expect that it could bear the relevant agreement features that could license a null IP complement. However, as we see in (99) and (100), neither of these possibilities is attested; the only grammatical sluice is one in which only the wh-phrase itself remains (J. Hoekstra, J. Gerbrandy, p.c.):

(99)   Hij heeft iemand gezien, maar ik weet niet   [Dutch]
    he has someone seen   but I know not

    a wie.
    b *wie of.
    c *wie   dat.
    d *wie of dat.
      who if that

    'He saw someone, but I don't know who.'

(100) Ien   komt jûn,   mar ik wit   net   [Frisian]
    someone comes tonight but I know not

    a wa.
    b *wa   of.
    c *wa   't.
    d *wa of 't.
      *who if that.*CL

    'Someone's coming tonight, but I don't know who.'

A similar case is provided by Slovene, as discussed in Marvin (1997). As in Dutch, Slovene also allows for complementizers to co-occur with fronted wh-phrases; whether the complementizer is the interrogative C *ali* 'whether' or the declarative C *da* 'that' is determined by the matrix predicate. The following examples are from Marvin (1997: 50).

(101) a Rad bi vedel, koga da je Peter videl.
         glad SUBJ know whom C[-wh] AUX Peter seen
         'I would like to know who Peter saw.'

     b Sprašujm se, koga ali Špela ljubi.
         I.ask REFL whom C[+wh] Spela loves
         'I wonder who Spela loves.'

     c Nisem ga vprašal, komu kaj da zameri.
         NEG.AUX.1sg him asked whom what C[-wh] blames
         'I didn't ask him who he blames for what.'

In no case, however, can any of the complementizers co-occur with the remnant wh-phrase(s) in sluicing (T. Marvin, p.c.):

(102) a Peter je videl nekoga in rad bi vedel, koga (*da).
         Peter AUX seen someone and glad SUBJ know who that
         'Peter saw someone and I would like to know who.'

     b Špela ljubi nekoga, a nisem vprašal, koga (*ali).
         Spela loves someone but NEG.AUX.1sg asked who if
         'Spela loves someone, but I didn't ask who.'

     c Nekomu nekaj ocita, a nisem ga
         someone.DAT something he.blames but NEG.AUX.1sg him
         vprašal, komu kaj (*da).
         asked who.DAT what that
         'He blames someone for something, but I didn't ask him who he blames for what.'

Likewise for the various complementizers that can co-occur with operators in Irish (J. McCloskey, p.c.):

(103)   Cheannaigh sé leabhar inteacht ach níl fhios agam
       bought he book some but not.is knowledge at.me
       céacu ceann (*a/ *ar).
       which one C_{trace} C_{pro}
       'He bought a book, but I don't know which.'

And for stacked complementizers in (some registers of) Danish (L. Mikkelsen, p.c.), which I gloss simply as 'C' (see Vikner 1991 and Mikkelsen, forthcoming):

(104)   Vi ved   hvem (som) (at) der snakker med Marit.
        we know who   C   C   C talks with Marit

                                                [(colloq.) Danish]

        'We know who is talking with Marit.'

(105)   En eller anden snakker med Marit, men vi ved   ikke
        someone   talks   with Marit but we know not
        a   hvem.
        b   *hvem som.
        c   *hvem som der.
        d   *hvem at.
        e   *hvem at der.
        f   *hvem som at der.

        'Someone is talking with Marit, but we don't know who.'

In these cases, appealing to an IP-internal origin for the non-operator material, as Lobeck does for the Bavarian and Norwegian cases reviewed above, obviously cannot help.

Given the split CP system, then, two questions arise for a Lobeck-style analysis: first, why can't the IP complement of Top elide leaving Wh^0, Top^0, or both intact, and secondly, why can TopP elide only if C[+wh] is empty?

Under Lobeck's system, the answer to the first question comes from the hypothesis that a head that licenses the null IP-proform must agree with a wh-XP in its specifier position: since the wh-XP in these examples never passes through SpecTopP, the necessary spec-head relationship is never established, and the Top head does not have the appropriate features to license a null complement.

The answer to the second question is more involved. If we assume that the projection of functional structure is uniform across languages (as in Cinque 1999, for example), then what we have been assuming for the structure of sluices has been too simple. Instead, we have two options for the phrase structure of sluices, illustrated in (106) and (107):

(106)   CP   [≈ WhP]

        wh-XP   C′

            C[+wh]   CP   [≈ TopP]
                      |
                      Ø

(107)

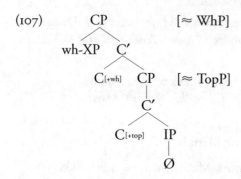

The second structure, in (107), bears more resemblence to the structure traditionally assumed for sluices, as in (2) above, in that it posits an empty IP node.
But, if the wh-XP does not move through SpecTopP, we do not expect such a
null element to be licensed.

An immediate side question arises, of course: could the fronting of a topic-
XP to SpecTopP license such a null complement? Answering this question is
complicated by the fact that, in general, topicalization in the languages that
provide the best evidence for such a phrase structure (the continental West
Germanic varieties) cannot co-occur with a fronted wh-XP:

(108)   a   *Wann   {hast} den Wagen {hast} du gemietet? [German]
         b   *Wanneer {heb} de auto {heb} je gehuurd?   [Dutch]
             when   *have the car*   *have you rented*

         ('When did you rent the car?')

(I use a weak pronoun subject in German here to ensure that the object has not
scrambled over the subject; object-over-subject scrambling is not usually possible in Dutch in any case.) Since overtly filling both SpecWhP and SpecTopP
is impossible in these languages, this subquestion cannot be answered, at least
on the basis of Dutch or German.

Still, the absence of a Doubly-Filled Comp Filter effect in Dutch, Frisian,
and Slovene leaves the ill-formedness of the ungrammatical examples in (99),
(100), and (102), respectively, mysterious. One possibility is that the ill-
formedness of this kind of example is related to, or indeed the same as, classical
COMP-trace effects like those in (109).

(109)   a   *Who did Lex say that __ kidnapped Lois?
         b   *Which guy did Jimmy wonder if __ had tipped Lois off?

If the COMP-trace effect is a PF effect, as several lines of evidence suggest
(see §5.1.2), then sluicing structures will trigger a violation just as examples like

those in (109). For concreteness, let us assume a filter of the form in (110), while recognizing its limitations (in English subject relatives, inapplicability to *pro-drop* languages, etc.; see Perlmutter 1971).[18]

(110)   *$[_C \alpha]$ $[_x \ldots]$, where x is a prosodic constituent containing no phonetic exponence, if α has phonetic exponence

This seems to work at first sight for Dutch and Frisian, where (111) is bad:

(111)   a   *Wie vraag je je   af of __ hem heeft
         b   *Wa fregest   dy ôf oft __ hem
             who ask   you REFL PRT if   him has

         gezien?   [Dutch]
         sjoen hat?   [Frisian]
         seen has

         ('Who were you wondering if __ saw him?')

But unfortunately the deviance of (111) cannot be distinguished from the fact that, in these languages, as in German, argument extraction from any position out of embedded questions leads to greater deviancy than in English:

(112)   a   *Wie vraag je je   af of zij __ heeft
         b   *Wa fregest   dy ôf oft se __
             who ask   you REFL PRT if she has

         gezien?   [Dutch]
         sjoen hat?   [Frisian]
         seen has

         ('Who were you wondering if she saw __?')

In fact, Dutch and Frisian do *not* exhibit the classical case of the COMP-trace effect—namely, with extraction of subjects of non-wh CPs:

---

[18] See also Kayne (1994: 94) for the suggestion that something like the COMP-trace effect applies to rule out overt Cs in relative clauses in Amharic and other languages with N-final relative clauses (which for Kayne have the structure $[_{IP_2} [the [_{CP} [_{NP} picture] [C [_{IP} t_2]]]]]$), with the IP complement to C fronted past the determiner head. Unfortunately, this suggestion runs counter to his analysis of final complementizers on p. 53, where he analyzes $[IP C]$ orders in languages like Japanese as the result of IP movement into SpecCP: $[_{CP} IP_2 [C [_{IP} t_2]]]$. In these latter cases, the C can, and sometimes must, be overt.

(113)   a   Wie denk   je   dat __ komt?   [Dutch]
        b   Wa   tinkst   dat __ komt?   [Frisian]
            who think.2sg you that   comes
            'Who do you think that __ is coming?'

Such an account runs into an identical problem in Slovene, which also lacks the *that*-trace effect (Marvin 1997: 51):

(114)   Kdo je   Peter mislil, da   je   prišel?
        who AUX Peter thought that AUX come
        'Who did Peter think that __ came?'

One can salvage this approach by relativizing the filter to apply only to [+wh] complementizers:

(115)   *$C_{[+wh]}$ [$_x$ . . .], where x is a prosodic constituent containing no pho-
        netic exponence, if $C_{[+wh]}$ has phonetic exponence

This would correctly rule out all the desired cases, while applying superfluously in cases like (111).

Another possibility would be to appeal to inherent cliticization properties of the C^0s in question: if it could be shown that these elements must cliticize onto phonological material to their right, we would have an independent explanation for the ill-formedness of the ungrammatical examples in (99), (100), and (102). It is certainly true that complementizers show a high degree of susceptibility to prosodic incorporation into following domains, at least in right-branching languages (see Shlonsky 1988 and McCloskey 1996 for discussion of rightward dependencies in the C-domain in Hebrew and Irish, respectively).[19]

Note that both of these alternatives locate the ill-formedness of examples with complementizers under sluicing at PF.[20] The first—assimilating these to

---

[19] This also recalls the suggestion sometimes made (see Lightfoot 2000 for a recent version) that reduced auxiliaries in English morphosyntactically cliticize to their right (though prosodically to their left), accounting for their non-occurence before ellipsis and movement sites. But see Pullum and Zwicky (1997) for a serious complication in this picture based on the contrast in (i), among others:

(i)   a   He is SO going!
      b   *He's SO going!

[20] These have the pleasant side effect of perhaps being able to accommodate certain ameliorations to apparent 'if/whether' sluices when these are followed immediately by certain elements,

some kind of generalized COMP-trace effect—might even extend to much of the data discussed in the previous section. Although only further work will determine if these suggestions bear fruit independently of accounting for the data discussed here, they do seem to me to place the problem in the correct arena, even if they do defer formalization until more is known about the processes that operate at the PF interface. These solutions strike me as more likely to be on the right track than, say, a structural solution that would stipulate that sluicing deletes a C′, not an IP, given that it is difficult to identify other instances of rules that target non-maximal projections. Note in addition that these proposals also have the salutory effect of reducing the demands on the nature of the material in the C-system: unlike Lobeck's (1995) proposal, we do not need to stipulate that SpecCP must be overtly filled.

I conclude this section with a brief remark on the only potential counterexample to the sluicing-COMP generalization in (71) known to me, from Hungarian. In wh-questions in Hungarian, the wh-phrase does not move into SpecCP overtly, occurring instead in a 'focus' position immediately preceding the verb (see Puskás 1999 for discussion and references; I consider only non-multiple wh-questions here). This wh-phrase can co-occur with the complementizer *hogy* 'that', as seen in (116) (thanks to D. Farkas and G. Puskás for judgments):

(116) Nem emlékszem, (hogy) kivel   találkoztak a   gyerekek.
       not I.remember that who.with met   the children
       'I don't remember who the kids met.'

Somewhat surprisingly, from the above perspective, the same options appear under sluicing: while the complementizer may be omitted, it may also be retained:

(117) A   gyerekek találkoztak valakivel   de nem emlékszem,
       the children met   someone.with but not I.remember

---

as in (i), modified slightly from Winkler (1997: 30 (33c)) (see also W. Klein 1993)), and in reverse sluicing examples like (ii) as analyzed in Giannakidou and Merchant (1998).

(i)   Bitte laß mich hören, wie Ralf reagiert und ob *(überhaupt).
      please let me hear   how Ralf reacts and if at.all
      'Please let me know how Ralf reacts, if (he reacts) at all.'

(ii) Magdalena worried about whether and how to break the news to her father.
      (Giannakidou and Merchant 1998: 239 (18a))

These facts recall the 'adverb intervention' improvements to COMP-trace effects; see §5.1.2.

(hogy) kivel.
that   who.with

'The kids met someone, but I don't remember who.'

Hungarian, therefore, represents a prima facie counterexample to the generalization in (71)—there seems no reason not to assume that *hogy* in (117) is in its
usual C position. The difference between this case and those discussed above is,
of course, that in (117) the wh-phrase itself is not in COMP, remaining low in
the structure, presumably in the position it occupies in (116). It might seem that
the sluicing-COMP generalization only applies if the wh-phrase itself has
moved to SpecCP. But notice that, if either of the above prosodic approaches
suggested above is correct, this state of affairs is exactly what we expect, since,
in Hungarian, the (sluiced) wh-phrase will follow the complementizer, satisfying either of the above mooted constraints. Especially the ban on complementizers in sluicing seems to be related to the fact that these complementizers
would end up adjacent to the ellipsis site, which is not the case in Hungarian.[21]

2.3 SUMMARY

There are two main results to be taken away from this chapter. First, the wh-
phrase that appears in sluicing is not a floating ghost, a mysterious fragment XP

---

[21] The case of Hindi seems to be slightly more complicated—while it is like Hungarian in
placing wh-phrases in a 'focus' position preverbally, it nonetheless disallows complementizers in
sluicing, as in English, Dutch, etc. A further complication is the fact that the presence of the
complementizer, unlike in Hungarian, is not wholly optional. Embedded CPs in Hindi, as
in German, can occur either 'extraposed', clause-finally, or 'topicalized', clause-initially; see
§2.1.4.2. In final position, the presence of the complementizer *ki* is highly preferred, while in
initial position it is impossible. While it is thus unsurprising that fronted sluiced CPs also disal-
low *ki*, shown in (ib), the fact that final sluices as in (ia) also prohibit *ki* is unexpected:

(i)   a   Gautam ne kisi   se   baat kii   thii lekin mujhe nahĩĩ pataa
          Gautam ERG *someone with   talk do.*PFV *PAST but   I.*DAT NEG   *knowledge*

          [(*ki) kis   se].
           that who   with

      b   Gautam ne kisi   se   baat kii   thii lekin [(*ki) kis   se]
          Gautam ERG *someone with   talk do.*PFV *PAST but   that who   with*

          mujhe nahĩĩ pataa.
          *I.*DAT NEG   *knowledge*

      'Gautam talked with someone, but I don't know who.'

Thanks to R. Bhatt for these data and discussion.

integrated in some strange and novel way into the surrounding syntax. Instead, the sluiced wh-phrase sits in its usual position, in SpecCP, and occurs exactly in those circumstances where we would expect an interrogative CP. This conclusion leads us to the second main result: that there is a missing IP in sluicing and some structure internal to this missing IP—CP must dominate IP, and the wh-phrase must originate somewhere. This second result requires that we develop a theory of the distribution—the licensing—of such null IPs. It was seen that the conditions under which an IP can go missing are sensitive to the kind of features present on the C sister of the IP. Although such a relation has usually been treated in terms of government, an alternative based on local feature distribution (implemented either by base-generation or featural/head movement) is equally up to the task, and allows us to state the theory of ellipsis in terms of deletion at PF, which we will see has very desirable consequences. Happily, stating the licensing conditions in terms of a feature also gives us a hook to hang our semantics on, unifying for the first time the licensing and identification requirements. Finally, a range of new facts were brought to light, embodied in the Sluicing-COMP generalization: in sluicing, no non-operator material may appear in COMP. This surprising fact seemed to fit in best with the view of ellipsis advocated here: that prosodic constraints, acting in league with economy constraints, serve to restrict the kinds of material that can occur outside, adjacent to, the target of deletion.

Appendix: Wh-in-situ Languages

An obvious further question is posed by wh-in-situ languages. Do such languages have sluicing in the form found in languages with wh-movement, the focus of our attention throughout? If so, what mechanisms drive the movement that feeds the deletion? How is it that this movement is seen only with sluicing, and not otherwise (since wh-movement in these languages does not generally occur overtly)? While these questions are interesting and important, it is beyond the scope of the present enquiry to be able to delve deeply into them. The literature on these questions is most extensive for Japanese, where several approaches to the relevant data have been pursued. An example of 'sluicing' in Japanese is given in (A1); data of this sort were apparently first noted in Inoue (1976, 1978).

(A1)   Abby-ga dareka-o   mi-ta   ga, watashi-wa dare ka wakaranai.
       Abby-NOM someone-ACC see-PAST but I-TOP   who Q know.not
       'Abby saw someone, but I don't know who.'

There have been several approaches to this kind of data. Takahashi (1994) proposes that there is, exceptionally, a kind of wh-movement in Japanese ('scrambling' to SpecCP), followed by deletion, giving structures essentially equivalent to their English congeners. His analysis has been widely criticized, however, both from analysts who follow an LF or post-LF copying approach (Nishigauchi 1998; and, for one sort of sluicing, Fukaya 1998 and Hoji and Fukaya 1999) and those who defend an analysis of 'sluicing' as a reduced cleft structure (Shimoyama 1995, Kuwabara 1996, Nishiyama *et al.* 1996, Kizu 1997, and Merchant 1998; and, for another sort of sluicing, Hoji and Fukaya 1999; see §4.2 for reasons why such an approach is not tenable for English).

My own limited exploration of this kind of data in Japanese and Chinese suggests a similar conclusion—namely, that what appears to be sluicing in these languages is the result of operations different from the movement + deletion derivation found in languages with overt wh-movement. This dovetails with the conclusions of Nishiyama *et al.* (1996) and Kizu (1997) for Korean and Chinese as well.

The situation in languages such as Hungarian, Hindi, and Turkish is somewhat less clear. In these languages, wh-phrases occur in a specified position adjacent to the verb; in Hindi and Turkish, which are robust SOV languages, this means that the wh-phrase typically occurs clause-internally, following other sentence-internal elements. Here the limited data available to me are mixed. While Hindi does seem to possess structures that at least superficially resemble sluicing in English (see e.g. the data in §2.1.4.2), Kizu (1997) has claimed that Turkish lacks these, requiring instead some form of the copula.

My own limited informant work has indicated that, while such cleft-like structures are clearly preferable, it is not clear whether more English-like sluicing structures are completely unacceptable. For multiple sluicing, for example (see §4.1 for a brief discussion), the copula can be absent.

One possibility is that Hindi and Turkish, to the extent that sluicing structures pattern with those found in overt SpecCP wh-movement languages like English, are employing a scrambling-type movement to create the input structures for deletion, and not using 'true' wh-movement to SpecCP (for example, by scrambling as adjunction to IP, followed by deletion of the lower IP segment). Another possibility is that whatever constraint prevents overt movement into SpecCP is ameliorated by the deletion itself, however such an idea is implemented (one possibility, following the reasoning concerning I-to-C movement above, would be to argue that the traces of wh-movement in these languages would trigger some kind of PF crash that deletion repairs, for example).

These questions seem to me to be fairly straightforward ones of fact and analysis. Unfortunately, I will not be able to resolve these issues at this point, and leave them to specialists in the relevant languages; important though is that nothing from these languages seems inherently incompatible with the overall approach taken here.

3

Islands and Form-Identity

Having established that sluicing involves a CP and a null IP, I turn now to documenting a wide range of data that bears on the dual questions of where the wh-phrase in SpecCP has its origin site, and, concomitantly, how the null IP comes to be null. This chapter sets the stage for the discussion to come in Chapters 4 and 5 by defining the central novel puzzle of this book: I will present a body of evidence that suggests that the wh-phrase does not come to occupy SpecCP via movement, and an apparently contradictory body of evidence that suggests that the wh-phrase has moved from an origin site internal to the null IP. This evidence can be summarized as follows: sluicing appears not to respect islands, while the wh-phrase remnant in sluicing displays a language-specific regularity in grammatical form. The theoretical import of these empirical findings will be examined in detail in the following two chapters.

3.1 SYNTACTIC ('STRONG') ISLANDS IN SLUICING

Ross (1969) noticed that sluicing has an ameliorating effect on several of the islands he discovered in his 1967 thesis. In particular, he gives the following five examples, reproduced here with his original judgments.

(1)   *Coordinate Structure Constraint*   (Ross 1969 (71b))
      ??Irv and someone were dancing together, but I don't know who.

(2)   *Complex NP Constraint*   (Ross 1969 (72b,d))
 a   ?She kissed a man who bit one of my friends, but Tom doesn't realize which one of my friends.
 b   I believe (??the claim) that he bit someone, but they don't know who.

(3)   *Sentential Subject Constraint*   (Ross 1969 (73b))
 ??That he'll hire someone is possible, but I won't divulge who.

(4)   *Left Branch Condition*   (Ross 1969 (74b))
 *I know that he must be proud of it, but I don't know how.

As pointed out by L. Levin (1982), the marginal degradation associated with the examples in (2b) and (3) is due to irrelevant factors: a pragmatic clash that can be repaired easily (see below for better examples). A similar point holds of (2a): there is a slight redundancy associated with the repetition of *one of my friends* in the wh-phrase; if this material is removed, the example is perfect. I will return in Chapter 5 to the status of (1) and (4), where the judgments in part do hold up to closer examination ((4) in particular is completely robust).

Besides these examples, it seems that sluicing can violate a much wider range of Ross's islands, and other islands discovered since. The remainder of this brief section lays out the relevant data, which will be discussed at length in the following chapters.

I will limit myself to 'strong' islands here, reserving 'weak' islands for Chapter 5. The 'strong' islands I will assume to be syntactic in nature; that is, the deviancy found with extraction from these islands does not derive from a purely interpretative effect, as is the case for 'weak' islands. The illustrations here are all from English, though some relevant cross-linguistic data will be introduced in later sections as well.

The first case is the relative clause island, as we saw above. The grammaticality of the sluiced version contrasts with the interpretively equivalent overt question following.

(5)   *Relative clause island*
 They want to hire someone who speaks a Balkan language, but I don't remember which.
 (cf. *I don't remember which *(Balkan language) they want to hire someone who speaks.*)

The same contrast is found in adjunct islands.

(6)   *Adjuncts*
    a Ben will be mad if Abby talks to one of the teachers, but she could-
      n't remember which.
      cf. *Ben will be mad if Abby talks to one of the teachers, but she
      couldn't remember which *(of the teachers) Ben will be mad if she
      talks to.*
    b Ben left the party because one of the guests insulted him, but he
      wouldn't tell me which.

In the following cases, mostly taken from Chung *et al.* (1995) (henceforth
CLM), I refrain from supplying the control case of illicit extraction, relying on
the reader to supply these well-known facts.

(7)   *Complement to nouns*   (CLM (94c))
    The administration has issued a statement that it is willing to meet
    with one of the student groups, but I'm not sure which one.

(8)   *Sentential subject*   (CLM (94b))
    That certain countries would vote against the resolution has been
    widely reported, but I'm not sure which ones.

(9)   *Embedded question*   (CLM (94a))
    Sandy was trying to work out which students would be able to solve a
    certain problem, but she wouldn't tell us which one.

(10)   *Coordinate structure constraint*
    a ?They persuaded Kennedy and some other Senator to jointly spon-
      sor the legislation, but I can't remember which one.   (CLM (83b))
    b Bob ate dinner and saw a movie that night, but he didn't say which
      (movie).

(11)   *COMP-trace effects*   (CLM (85), (86a))
    a It has been determined that somebody will be appointed; it's just
      not clear yet who.
    b Sally asked if somebody was going to fail Syntax One, but I can't
      remember who.

(12)   *Left-branch* (attributive adjective case)
    They hired a tall forward for the team—guess how tall!

(13)   *Derived position islands (topicalizations, subjects)*
    a A: A biography of one of the Marx brothers, she refused to read.
      B: Which one?
    b A biography of one of the Marx brothers {is going to be pub-
      lished/will appear} this year—guess which!

Many other kinds of islands have been documented in the literature (see Postal 1996 for an overview), though I will refrain from demonstrating their effects here. The above list is, I believe, comprehensively representative for our purposes, in that the analysis I will propose to deal with these extends without modification to the other kinds of islands not illustrated here.

These data, taken at face value, strongly suggest that the wh-phrase in sluicing did not reach SpecCP from an IP-internal position by the usual mechanisms of movement.

3.2 THE FORM-IDENTITY GENERALIZATIONS

The goal of this section is to establish the validity of two closely related generalizations, one having to do with the case of the sluiced wh-phrase, and the other with prepositional pied-piping in sluicing. These generalizations will be crucial in constraining the theoretical options in the chapters that follow.

3.2.1 Case-Matching

Part of the first generalization was noted in §2.1.3, and goes back, as do so many of the observations regarding sluicing, to Ross (1969). Those data are repeated here in (14) and (15), with the addition of the nominative form *wer* for completeness:

(14)   Er will   jemandem   schmeicheln, aber sie   wissen nicht,
        he wants someone.DAT flatter   but they know   not
        {*wer   /*wen   /wem}.
        who.NOM   who.ACC   who.DAT
        'He wants to flatter someone, but they don't know who.'

(15)   Er will   jemanden   loben, aber sie   wissen nicht, {*wer
        he wants someone.ACC praise but they know   not   who.NOM
        /wen   /*wem}.
        who.ACC   who.DAT
        'He wants to flatter someone, but they don't know who.'

Recall that the verb *schmeicheln* 'flatter' assigns dative to its object, and *loben* 'praise', accusative. The sluiced wh-phrases in (14) and (15) exhibit the case of their counterparts in non-elliptical embedded questions, as in (16) and (17):

(16)   Sie   wissen   nicht,   {*wer   / *wen   /wem}   er
       they   know   not   who.NOM   who.ACC   who.DAT   he

       schmeicheln   will.
       flatter   wants

       'They don't know who he wants to flatter.'

(17)   Sie   wissen   nicht,   {*wer   / wen   /*wem}   er
       they   know   not   who.NOM   who.ACC   who.DAT   he

       loben   will.
       praise   wants

       'They don't know who he wants to praise.'

These data establish that, at least in monoclausal domains, the case of the sluiced wh-phrase must be the same as the case of its correlate, if there is one. Since the literature on sluicing has been mostly concerned with English, nothing more has been said about such case properties. In fact, this case-matching property holds in every language with overt case-marking on wh-phrases that I have examined (German, Greek, Russian, Polish, Czech, Slovene, Finnish, Hindi, Hungarian, Basque; the situation in Japanese is somewhat more complicated—see the references in the appendix to Chapter 2). Such data seem to be prima facie evidence for a deletion approach, since under the deletion approach, (14) and (15) are derived from (16) and (17), respectively.

An obvious question is whether such case-matching holds across islands as well. While this question has never been investigated to my knowledge, it is easy to show that indeed the same case-matching requirement does hold across islands. I illustrate this here in German with sluicing into a relative clause island.[1] In these data, the verbs *helfen* 'help' and *sehen* 'see' assign dative and accusative to their respective objects.

---

[1] Here and below, I will often illustrate islands only with relative clauses and *if*-clauses, since these are two of the most robust islands cross-linguistically, and speakers are usually more sure of their judgments on these than on other kinds of islands. The choice of a *de dicto* object with a relative clause under an intensional verb like *want* also makes it possible for us to be sure that the island is indeed being interpreted in the ellipsis site: there seems to be no smaller propositional domain than the matrix clause that could be used to resolve the ellipsis coherently here. For this reason, I will often use such examples, and protases of conditionals (which similarly seem to admit of no alternative sensible interpretation under sluicing), since making sure that speakers are judging the appropriate interpretation of otherwise ambiguous sluices would greatly increase the complexity of the judgment task, making the data potentially too noisy to be useful.

(18) Sie will jemanden finden, der einem der Gefangenen
she wants someone find who one.DAT of.the prisoners

geholfen hat, aber ich weiß nicht, {*welcher /*welchen
helped has but I know not which.NOM which.ACC

/welchem}.
which.DAT

'She wants to find someone who helped one of the prisoners, but I don't know which.'

(19) Sie will jemanden finden, der einen der Gefangenen
she wants someone find who one.ACC of.the prisoners

gesehen hat, aber ich weiß nicht, {*welcher /welchen
seen has but I know not which.NOM which.ACC

/*welchem}.
which.DAT

'She wants to find someone who saw one of the prisoners, but I don't know which.'

Although I have illustrated this here with data from German, again, this generalization holds in the nine other case-marking languages I have checked as well (Greek, Russian, Polish, Czech, Slovene, Finnish, Hungarian, Hindi, Basque). This leads to the first form-identity generalization, stated in (20):

(20) *Form-identity generalization I: Case-matching*
The sluiced wh-phrase must bear the case that its correlate bears.

Though this statement of the generalization explicitly mentions a correlate, we saw above in §2.1.3 that the case properties of the sluiced wh-phrase are fully determined by its function in the elided IP, even if a correlate is lacking. I leave such cases out of consideration here for the moment, since, as we will see below, it is extremely difficult for sluiced wh-phrases without correlates to bind 'into' islands, for independent reasons having to do with scope and the Focus requirement. Since this is the case, I leave (20) in its present form, with no mention of intervening islands for perspicuity. The reader should, however, bear this simplification in mind.

3.2.2 Preposition-Stranding

The second generalization concerns the distribution of adpositions with sluiced DPs, and the connection of this distribution to patterns of overt wh-movement.

Broadly speaking, languages appear to choose between two simple options with respect to whether a wh-DP may be displaced from an associated adposition or not: yes or no. In fact, the first option seems hardly attested: Dryer (1997), in his sample of 625 languages, found no language outside the Germanic family that productively allowed such displacement.[2] The facts are simple and very well known: in English, Frisian, and the Scandinavian languages, wh-movement may strand a preposition in all the standard wh-movement environments: interrogatives, topicalization, relativization (including clefts and pseudoclefts), and comparatives. In all other languages, the only productive strategy for displacing a wh-DP governed by an adposition requires the adposition to be displaced along with the DP itself, a phenomenon dubbed 'pied-piping' in Ross (1967).

The second form-identity generalization is easy to state in its simplest form, which I give in (21):

(21)   *Form-identity generalization II: Preposition-stranding*
        A language *L* will allow preposition stranding under sluicing iff *L* allows preposition stranding under regular wh-movement.

The data motivating this generalization is presented in (22)–(45) below. The (a) examples present the sluicing data, and the (b) examples are controls. (In all but one case, the (a) sentence in (23)–(45) is a translation of the English in (22a), and the (b) sentence of (22b), with a stranded preposition.)

The first set includes the preposition-stranding (henceforth *P-stranding*) languages English, Frisian, Swedish, Norwegian, Danish, and Icelandic. The Frisian data I owe to G. de Haan, J. Hoekstra, and O. Vries, the Swedish to K. Sandell and P. Svenonius, and the Norwegian to P. Svenonius, the Danish to L. Mikkelsen, and the Icelandic to H. Thráinsson.

(22)   English
        a   Peter was talking with someone, but I don't know (with) who.[3]
        b   Who was he talking with?

---

[2] P. Hirschbühler (p.c.) informs me that the Nova Scotian dialect of French allows P-stranding productively as well, presumably a result of heavy contact with English.

[3] The English data are in fact somewhat more complicated than the simple picture presented in (22) would lead one to think. A more accurate statement of the facts is given in (i):

(i)   Peter was talking with someone,
        a   but I don't know who.
        b   %but I don't know with whom.
        c   ?but I don't know with who.

(ia) is most natural, and would be preferred in normal speech. (ib) belongs to the formal, primarily written register of English—see discussion below. (ic) is somewhat marked, being essentially a register clash: in the register that pied-pipes the preposition, the form *whom* is strongly proscribed.

(23) Frisian

    a Piet hat mei ien   sprutsen, mar ik wyt net (mei) wa.
        Piet has with someone talked   but I know not with who

    b Wa hat Piet mei sprutsen?
        who has Piet with talked

(24) Swedish

    a Peter har talat   med någon; jag vet   inte (med) vem.
        Peter has talked with someone I know not with who

    b Vem har Peter talat   med?
        who has Peter talked with

(25) Norwegian

    a Per har snakket med noen,   men jeg vet   ikke
        Per has talked   with someone but I   know not

      (med) hvem.
      with who

    b Hvem har Per   snakket med?
        who has Peter talked with

(26) Danish

    a Peter har snakket med en eller anden, men jeg ved
        Peter has talked   with one or   another but I   know

      ikke (med) hvem.
      not with who

    b Hvem har Peter snakket med?
        who has Peter talked with

(27) Icelandic

    a Pétur hefur talað   við einhvern en ég veit   ekki
        Peter has   spoken with someone but I know not

      (við) hvern.
      with who

    b Hvern hefur Pétur talað   við?
        who   has   Peter talked with

The second set of data comes from languages that do not allow P-stranding under regular wh-movement, as indicated by the ungrammaticality of the (b) examples. The data sample is restricted here to those languages that show wh-movement to a clause-initial position; I exclude here languages that place the wh-phrase in a clause-internal focus position, or move wh-phrases only by scrambling, or show no wh-movement at all (see appendix to Chapter 2 for brief discussion). Sluicing data, of course, are absent from traditional grammars, so I have only been able to include data from languages for which I had access to native speaker informants. This has largely skewed the sample pool to the languages spoken in Europe and North Africa, making any strong typological claims impossible. I give here data from eighteen languages. Fifteen of these are Indo-European: Greek (Greek); German, Dutch, Yiddish (W. Germanic); Russian (E. Slavic), Polish, Czech (W. Slavic), Bulgarian, Serbo-Croatian, Slovene (S. Slavic); Persian (Indo-Iranian); Catalan, Spanish, French, Italian (Romance). Two are Afro-Asiatic: Hebrew and Moroccan Arabic (Semitic). The last is Basque (isolate).

The Greek data were checked with Y. Agouraki, A. Alexiadou, E. Anagnostopoulou, K. Danopoulos, A. Giannakidou, and A. Roussou. The judgments were uniform across speakers and sessions.

(28) Greek

    a I   Anna milise me   kapjon, alla dhe ksero *(me) pjon.
       the Anna spoke with someone but not I.know   with who

    b *Pjon milise   me?
       who she.spoke with

The German data were checked with D. Büring, A. Meinunger, A. Mester, H. Rott, and S. Winkler. The judgments were uniform across speakers and sessions.

(29) German[4]

    a Anna hat mit jemandem gesprochen, aber ich weiß nicht,
       Anna has with someone   spoken   but I   know not
       *(mit) wem.
       with who

    b *Wem hat sie mit gesprochen?
       who has she with spoken

---

[4] Similarly for Swiss German, as shown in (i) for the Glarus dialect (due to P. Spaelti: E. Haeberli informs me that the indicated judgments hold for other dialects of Swiss German as well).

(i) a Dr Ruedi hät ds ganz Läbe vumene Land träumt, aber ich wäiss nüd
       the Ruedi has the whole life of.a   land dreamt, but I   know not
       *(vu) welem.
       of which.DAT

       'Ruedi has dreamt his whole life of some country, but I don't know of which.'

    b *Welem Land hät dr Ruedi ds ganz Läbe vu träumt?
       which country has the Ruedi the whole life of dreamt

       ('Which country has Ruedi dreamt of his whole life?')

The Dutch data[5] were checked with N. Corver, J. Gerbrandy, H. Hendriks, P. Hendriks, J. Hoeksema, B. Hollebrandse, I. Mulders, H. van Riemsdijk, R. van Rooy, and E. Ruys.

(30)   Dutch[6]

    a   Anna heeft met iemand gesproken, maar ik weet
        Anna has with someone spoken   but   I   know

        niet ??/?/✓ (met)   wie.
        not   with   who

    b   */??/?Wie heeft zij mee gesproken?
        who has   she with spoken

The Yiddish data are from J. Sadock and E. Steinberg.

---

[5] This is one minor wrinkle worth noting here. Dutch, German, and Swiss German do allow preposition-stranding with a small class of elements, known as R-pronouns (see van Riemsdijk 1978). Nevertheless, these elements do not occur as bare remnants under sluicing, as seen in (i) for Dutch (likewise for German and Swiss German).

(i)   *Hij rekent ergens   op, maar ik weet niet, waar.
     he   counts something on but I know not what

('He is counting on something, but I don't know what.')

This is presumably due to the requirement that the remnant wh-phrase in these environments must be focused, mentioned in Chapter 2, n. 5. This requirement is in conflict with the fact that these elements cannot be accented:

(ii)   a   *Ik weet niet, WAAR hij op rekent. [only constrastive on WAAR]

     b   Ik weet niet, waar hij OP rekent.
        I   know not what he on counts

     'I don't know what he's counting on.'

See Gussenhoven (1983: ch. 5) and J. Hoekstra (1995) for discussion of accent placement in these elements.

[6] The situation in Dutch appears to be the most fluid of the languages examined here, which is reflected in the variety of stigmata used in both in the (a) and (b) examples in (30), representing the variety of responses received from informants. Many informants (6 of 10) accepted the sluiced version without the preposition (all accepted it with the preposition); some informants (2 of 10) also accepted preposition-stranding in the non-elliptical question in (30b), though the correspondence was less than perfect (normative factors perhaps influencing the judgment in non-elliptical test cases).

In general Dutch appears to be a transition case, allowing preposition-stranding in a wider range of cases than German, for example, but in a more restricted set than Frisian. Normatively rejected preposition-stranding under A′-movement is attested even in carefully edited literature; compare the examples in (i) (from Voskuil 1996: 65):

(31)   Yiddish

   a   Zi hot mit emetsn geredt, ober ikh veys nit *(mit) vemen.
       she has with someone spoken but I know not with who

   b   *Vemen hot zi mit geredt?
       who   has she with spoken

The Russian data are from S. Avrutin and D. Krizhanskaya.

(32)   Russian

   a   Anja govorila s   kem-to, no ne znaju *(s)   kem.
       Anja spoke   with someone but not I.know with who

   b   *Kem ona govorila s?
       who she spoke   with

The Polish data are from D. Mokrosinska and A. Przepiórkowski.

(33)   Polish

   a   Anna rozmawiała z   kimś, ale nie wiem *(z)   kim.
       Anna spoke   with someone but not I.know with who

   b   *Kim rozmawiała Anna z?
       who spoke   Anna with

The Czech data are from H. Filip.

(34)   Czech

   a   Anna mluvila s   někým, ale nevím   *(s)   kým.
       Anna spoke   with someone but not.I.know with who

   b   *Kým mluvila Anna s?
       who spoke   Anna with

   (i)   Onrechtvaardigheid wind ik   me over   op.
         injustice   work I REFL about up

         'Injustice, I get worked up about.'

From the same work comes the following bare sluiced wh-phrase whose correlate is in a PP
(Voskuil 1996: 31):

   (ii) De jongen leek   op iemand, maar hij kon niet bedenken wie.
         the boy   seemed on someone but he could not think   who

         'The boy looked like someone, but he couldn't think who.'

   Given the fluidity of the situation in current Dutch usage, the variety of judgments found for
the sluicing examples does not seem entirely unexpected.

The Bulgarian data are from S. Dianova.

(35)   Bulgarian
a   Anna e   govorila s   njakoj, no ne znam   *(s)   koj.
Anna AUX spoken   with someone but not I.know   with who

b   *Koj e   govorila Anna s?
who AUX spoken Anna with

The Serbo-Croatian data are from S. Godjevac.

(36)   Serbo-Croatian
a   Ana je   govorila sa   nekim, ali ne znam   *(sa)   kim.
Ana AUX spoken   with someone but not I.know   with who

b   *Kim je   govorila Ana   sa?
who AUX spoken   Anna with

The Slovene data are from T. Marvin.

(37)   Slovene
a   Anna je   govorila z   nekom, ampak ne vem   *(s)   kom.
Anna AUX spoken   with someone but   not I.know   with who

b   *Kom je   govorila Anna s?
who AUX spoken   Anna with

The Persian data are from B. Aghaei.

(38)   Persian
a   Ali bā   kasi   harf mi-zad,   ʔamā ne-mi-dan-am
Ali with someone talk PROG-hit.3sg but   not-PROG-know-1sg

*(bā)   ki.
with who

b   *Ki   Ali bā   harf mi-zad?
who Ali with talk PROG-hit.3sg

The Catalan data are from J. Quer.

(39)   Catalan
a   L'Anna   va   parlar amb algú,   però no sé   ??(amb) qui.
the-Anna AUX speak   with someone but   not I.know   with who

b   *Qui va   parlar l'Anna   amb?
who AUX speak   the-Anna with

The French data are from C. Féry, P. Hirschbühler, and M. Labelle.[7]

(40)   French
       a   Anne l'a   offert   à   quelqu'un, mais je ne   sais   pas
           Anne it-has offered to someone   but I NEG know   not

           *(à) qui.
           to who

       b   *Qui est-ce qu' elle l'a   offert   à?
           who Q   she it-has offered to

The Spanish data are from R. Gutierrez and J. Quer.[8]

(41)   Spanish
       a   Ana habló con   alguien, pero no sé   ??(con) quién.
           Ana spoke with someone but   not I.know   with who

       b   *¿Quién habló   con?
           who   spoke.3sg with

---

[7] There was some variation in judgment among these speakers. Although all three speakers rejected examples like that in the text, two of the three did not find examples like (ia) too deviant, as indicated. The expected variant in (ib), with the preposition repeated, was perfect for all speakers.

(i)   a   Elle a   parlé   avec quelqu'un, mais je ne sais pas qui.
          she has spoken with someone   but I NEG know not who

          'She spoke with someone, but I don't know who.'
          [2 of 3 speakers judged this '?'; 1 of 3 judged this '*']
      b   Elle a parlé avec quelqu'un, mais je ne sais pas avec qui.

I return to some discussion of the variation in this domain.

[8] R. Gutierrez speaks Mexican, and J. Quer Castilian Spanish. Gutierrez reported the sluicing variant without the preposition as being mostly acceptable, though dispreferred to the one with it. He did find the fronted version without the preposition in (i), however, markedly worse:

(i)   Ana habló con   alguien, pero *(con) quién, no sé.
      Ana spoke with someone but   with who   not I.know

Similarly clear judgments were given for the examples in (ii) by J. Mora:

(ii) a   Me he   bebido la cerveza de alguien, pero no sé   *(de) quién.
          me I.have drunk the beer   of someone but not I.know of   who

          'I drank up someone's beer, but I don't know whose.'
      b   *¿Quién he   bebido la cerveza de?
          who   I.have drunk the beer   of

          ('Whose beer did I drink?')

At this point, I have no explanation for these variabilities in judgment.

The Italian data are from M. Aloni, G. Cocchi, and P. Monachesi. Two of the three speakers found the variant without the preposition almost acceptable.

(42) Italian

    a Pietro ha parlato con qualcuno, ma non so   ?(con) chi.
        Pietro has spoken with someone but not I.know with who

    b *Chi ha parlato Pietro con?
        who has spoken Peter with

The Hebrew data are from E. Doron, D. Fox, and Y. Winter. There was considerable variation across speakers, with one speaker accepting (43a), another rejecting it, and the third finding it intermediate.[9]

(43) Hebrew

    a Adam diber 'im mišehu, aval ani lo yode ?('im) mi.
        Adam spoke with someone but I not know with who

    b *Mi Adam diber 'im?
        who Adam spoke with

The Moroccan Arabic data are from M. Damir and M. Bennani-Meziane.

(44)   Moroccan Arabic

    a Driss   tkəllem mᶜa ši wahəd, walakin ma ᶜraft š
        Driss   talked with someone but not know NEG

        *(mᶜa) mən.
        with who

    b *Mən tkəllem Driss mᶜa?
        who talked Driss with

[9] E. Doron supplied the following example as unambiguously ungrammatical, while accepting (43a); in (i), the 'preposition' *le* is essentially the marker for dative case, and often glossed as such.

    (i) Dani katav le-mišehu, aval ani lo yode'a *(le-)mi.
        Dani wrote to-someone but I not know to-who

        'Dani wrote to someone, but I don't know who.'

Y. Winter pointed out that where the accusative marker *et* is possible (on partitive indefinites, for example), a similar contrast arises:

    (ii) Ra'iti et exad me-ha-yeladim, aval ani lo yode'a ??(et) mi.
        I.saw ACC one of-the-children but I not know ACC which

        'I saw one of the children, but I don't know which.'

The Basque data are due to A. Elordieta.

(45)   Basque

        a   Ana-k   norbait-ekin   hitzegin   zuen,   baina   ez
            Ana-ERG   someone-with   talk.to   AUX   but   not

            dakit   nor-*(ekin).
            know   who- with

        b   *Nor   hitzegin   zuen   -ekin?
            who   talk.to   AUX   with

These data represent the simplest and clearest cases—monoclausal domains with argument PPs. Speakers' judgments on such examples are the most secure, and I will take it as a working assumption that this core of data should be explained by core grammatical principles. This is not to ignore or deny variations in the data when the database is extended to other kinds of prepositions, and other uses of prepositions (roughly, the distinction usually drawn between 'argument' and 'adjunct' uses). In some cases and in some languages, it seems that speakers are willing to accept a bare wh-phrase in place of the PP, though I have not yet determined with sufficient clarity under what conditions this is possible, or whether or not this is a systematic property of a class of prepositions or languages; this variability across speakers is represented by the occasional use of ?? or ? in the (a) examples, averaged across informants. Most variability of this kind was found in those languages with poor overt case systems, while the judgments were completely uniform and robust in the highly case-marked languages (German, Greek, Russian, Czech, Polish, Serbo-Croatian, and Slovene).[10] For this reason, I will primarily concentrate on these latter cases, since the judgments are clearest. The variability in judgments in the other cases probably comes from one of two sources.

First, I believe that in many cases, because we dealing with an elliptical structure to begin with, particularly accommodating speakers are willing to

---

[10] This also holds in Hindi, though I have omitted this language from discussion in the main text, since the placement of wh-phrases in Hindi is not clause-peripheral as in the above languages (it patterns with Turkish and Hungarian in perferring a placement of the wh-XP in a 'focus' position before the verb). The form identity effect is shown in (i) (thanks to R. Bhatt for this datum).

(i)   Gautam-ne   kisi   se   baat   kii   thii,   lekin   mujhe   pataa   nahĩĩ
      Gautam-ERG   someone   with   talk   do.PFV   PAST   but   I.DAT   knowledge   NEG

      kis   *(se).
      who   with

      'Gautam spoke with someone, but I don't know with who.'

interpret the ellipsis as desired, and judge a particular example as 'acceptable'. Because of the ellipsis, 'acceptable' comes often to mean 'interpretable', in the following sense. In eliciting these judgments, I have often found speakers hesitant about necessarily making the relevant connection: after all, in all cases, the sentence 'I don't know who', with a bare wh-phrase instead of the PP is perfectly well formed and interpretable.[11] The point of the exercise, of course, is that it is not well formed if the antecedent sentence, the source for the elliptical material, is the immediately preceding sentence, and only that sentence. This is not the case, for example, in judging simple P-stranding extractions: no interference from string-identical grammatical sentences is found in such cases. Judgments about sluicing thus require the kind of subtlety and control that judgments about possible binding relations and scope do—notoriously difficult areas to gather clear cross-linguistic data on from naive informants. Even among linguistically sophisticated informants, however, care is required, since sluicing is not a commonly studied area, and accommodation is a real source of noise in the data. Particularly for elliptical structures, determining the intended reading goes hand in hand with judging a particular example grammatical, and it is clear that quite often informants will consider a particular example until the interpretation is clear, at which point they will pronounce the example 'acceptable', on the strength of their understanding it (of course, it is never possible to declare a sentence grammatical before its interpretation is clear, but grammaticality goes beyond and is distinct from simple interpretability). This is true as far as it goes, but it cannot be the whole picture, since in some languages judgments are without variation. This brings me to the second probable source of variation.

It is difficult to believe that the correlation between overt morphological case and clarity in judging the P-stranding examples could be entirely due to chance. More likely is that sluicing might be able to give us a window into the mechanisms at work in controlling P-stranding across languages, with the non-variation in certain languages indicating a strong(er) connection between case and P-marking than in other languages. Although I will have nothing to say about the account of P-stranding (a notoriously open problem for cross-linguistic syntax: see van Riemsdijk 1978, Takami 1992, and J. Hoekstra 1995 for data and references), it seems unlikely that the most productive way to view P-stranding is in terms of some absolute notion of P as a proper governor or not

[11] In particular, in those languages without overt morphological case, we may be dealing with a truncation of something like '. . . who it is', as suggested to me by several speakers, who could give only a non-elliptical form of the target sentence with such a continuation. Presumably this is possible in these languages but not in the more explicit case-marking languages, because of the underdetermination of case on the wh-word in the former; in the latter, the nominative marking on the wh-phrase would be required.

(Kayne 1981) or incorporability into the verb (Hornstein and Weinberg 1981; see especially Takami 1992 and Baltin and Postal 1996 for arguments against this). Instead, it seems most reasonable to take up traditional intuitions about the role of prepositions as grammatical function markers like cases (cf. the common historical connections between these two, and the difficulty in separating them in many languages, such as Finnish, Hungarian, and Lezgian).

The basic idea is that languages vary with respect to the analyticity of the means they use to mark grammatical relations: English, Frisian, and the Scandinavian languages, where prepositions are separable from their notional objects, are at the extreme end of this scale of analyticity, while highly fusional systems like Lezgian might be at the other end, not allowing much of any distinction between 'prepositions' and other morphemes that attach to arguments and indicate grammatical role. This view requires us to give up a uniform scale of 'analyticity' along which an entire language can be ordered, and decompose this as a function of analyticity in several domains. How and whether these should relate is an interesting question, of course, but an independent one.

These remarks are meant only to give some context to the variation in judgment seen above: it may be that the variation of apparent P-stranding under sluicing in languages that otherwise prohibit P-stranding is telling us something about the mechanisms of analyticity in those languages. Such languages would be 'less analytic' with respect to prepositions than languages such as German and Greek, where the preposition cannot be stranded under any circumstances. Again, these brief remarks cannot be thought of as standing in as a theory of preposition-stranding, but simply as representing a possible way to frame the facts above.

The interfering factors of these various considerations should serve here only as a cautionary note; within each language, further research and refinements will certainly prove necessary. Nevertheless, for the remainder of this book, I will concentrate on the data presented in this section as forming the core explicanda, bearing this simplification in mind.

Before continuing to an examination of new kinds of data, I present a few more detailed examples of the kind of data just discussed, from languages to which I have had better access, to help fill out the empirical picture. These data supplement the above more schematic kind of data, and address various minor points within the individual languages in question. I will not go deeply into these data here, however, at the risk of getting sidetracked from the main investigation. Nevertheless, I feel it is important to document the data in a bit more detail than that done above, as a starting point for further research.

First, I give data from other kinds of argument PPs in German, Greek, Polish, and Russian: the PP headed by the equivalent of 'about' selected by predicates of information transfer in all four languages, and the PP headed by *für* 'for' idiosyncratically selected by *entscheiden* 'decide' in German. The Polish and Russian data also address a potential objection to the above use of *s/z* 'with' in these languages, namely that *s/z* is so prosodically dependent that it is little different from a case-marker (compare the difficulties in distinguishing these two on principled grounds in languages such as Turkish, Hungarian, Finnish, and Lezgian); here, the preposition *o* 'about' at least forms its own syllable.

(46)   German

    a   Peter hat über jemanden aus deiner Klasse gesprochen—
        Peter has about someone from your class spoken

        rate mal, *(über) wen
        guess PRT about who.

        'Peter was talking about someone from your class—guess who.'

    b   Peter hat sich für ein amerikanisches College entschieden,
        Peter has REFL for a American college decided

        aber er wollte uns nicht sagen, *(für) welches.
        but he wanted us not say for which

        'Peter decided on an American college, but he wouldn't tell us which.'

(47)   Greek
       I gonis tou pedhiou malosan gia kati, alla
       the parents of.the child argued.3pl about something, but

       arnite na mas pi *(gia) ti.
       refused.3sg SUBJ us tell about what

       'The child's parents were arguing about something, but she refused to tell us what.'

(48)   Polish
       Anna rozmawiała o czymś, ale nie wiem *(o) czym.
       Anna talked about something but not I.know about what

       'Anna was talking about something, but I don't know what.'

(49)   Russian
       Anna govorila o čём-to, no ja ne pomnju *(o) čём.
       Anna talked about something but I not remember about what.

       'Anna was talking about something, but I don't know what.'

Secondly, I give data from these four languages concerning PP adjuncts—locative adjuncts in German and Greek, and comitative adjuncts in Polish and Russian.

(50) German
Anke ist in einem Seminar eingeschlafen, aber ich weiß nicht,
Anke is in a   class   fallen.asleep   but I   know not
*(in) welchem.
  in which

'Anke fell asleep in a class, but I don't know which.'

(51) Greek
I   Anna apokimithike s'ena   apo ta mathimata, alla dhe
the Anna fell.asleep   in-one of the classes   but not
ksero *(se) pjo.
I.know   in   which

'Anna fell asleep in one of the classes, but I don't know which.'

(52) Polish
Anna tańczyła   z   kimś,   ale nie wiem *(z)   kim.
Anna was.dancing with someone but not I.know   with who

'Anna was dancing with someone, but I don't know who.'

(53) Russian
Pëtr tanceval   s   kem-to, no ja ne pomnju *(s)   kem.
Pëtr was.dancing with someone but I not remember   with who

'Petr was dancing with someone, but I don't remember who.'

The above data, though representing a considerable expansion of the database for sluicing and never having been considered in the literature on sluicing before, are nonetheless limited in the same way that the initial data in the previous section were: all of the data concern monoclausal domains. Important data to be taken up in the next chapters come from the fact that the P-stranding generalization in (21) seemingly holds *even 'across' islands*. The following data from English, German, Greek, Polish, and Russian demonstrate that, although the sluiced wh-phrase must apparently be associated with a gap 'inside' an island, nevertheless the language-particular constraints on P-stranding must continue to be respected.

In English, of course, P-stranding is allowed, and a sluice dependent on an indefinite antecedent inside a PP need not pied-pipe the associated preposition.

(54) a Ben's mother will get angry if he talks with someone from his class,
         but I don't remember who.
      b Abby wants to interview someone who lived in one of the Balkan
         countries, but I can't remember which.

If anything, pied-piping of the preposition in English is worse than movement of the wh-phrase alone, as is generally the case for pied-piping of prepositions (I return to this briefly in §4.3).

In German, Greek, Polish, and Russian, on the other hand, P-stranding is impossible, as the (b) control examples in (29), (28), (33), and (32), respectively showed. The following data show that the impossibility of P-stranding holds even when the sluiced wh-phrase apparently associates into an island. I illustrate this with a relative-clause island and the protasis of a conditional, as in the English examples in (54).

German

(55) Anke wird sich ärgern, wenn Peter mit einem der Lehrer
      Anke will REFL upset if Peter with one of.the teachers
      spricht, aber ich weiß nicht mehr, *(mit) welchem.
      speaks but I know not more with which
      'Anke will get upset if Peter talks to one of the teachers, but I don't remember which.'

(56) Anke will jemanden heiraten, der in einem bestimmten
      Anke wants someone marry who in a certain
      mittel-europäischen Land gewohnt hat, aber ich erinnere
      central-European country lived has but I remember
      mich nicht, *(in) welchem.
      REFL not in which
      'Anke wants to marry someone who has lived in a certain central European country, but I don't remember which.'

Greek

(57) I mitera tou Gianni tha thimosi an milisi me kapjon
      the mother of Giannis FUT get.angry if he.talks with someone
      apo tin taksi tou, alla dhe thimame *(me) pjon.
      from the class his but not I.remember with who
      'Giannis's mother will get angry if he talks with someone from his class, but I don't remember who.'

(58) I Maria theli na milisi me kapjon pu na exei
      the Maria wants SUBJ talk with someone who SUBJ has
      polemisi s'enan apo tous Valkanikous polemous, ala dhen
      fought in-one from the Balkan wars but not

    ksero   *(se) pjon.
    I.know   in which

'Maria wants to talk to someone who fought in one of the Balkan wars, but I don't know which.'

Polish

(59)   Anna wścieknie się jeśli Piotr zatańczy z   jedną z jej
      Anna angers   REFL if Piotr dances with one of her

      kolezanek i   Piotr chciałby wiedzieć *(z)   którą.
      friends   and Piotr wants   to.know   with which

      'Anna will get mad if Piotr dances with one of her friends, and Piotr wants to know which.'

(60)   Piotr chciałby ozenić się z   kimś,   kto mieszka w
      Piotr wants   to.marry REFL with someone who lives   in

      jednym z krajów   bałkańskich, ale nie wiem   *(w) którym.
      one   of countries Balkan   but not I.know   in which

      'Peter wants to marry someone who has lived in a certain Balkan country, but I don't remember which.'

Russian

(61)   Anna rasserditsja esli Pëtr budet tancevat' s   odnoj iz   eë
      Anna get.angry if Pëtr will   dance   with one from her

      podrug, no on ne pomnit   *(s)   kakoj.
      friends but he not remembers with which

      'Anna will get mad if Pëtr dances with one of her friends, but he doesn't remember which.'

(62)   Pëtr xočet ženit'sja na ženščine kotoraja živët v odnoj iz
      Pëtr wants marry on woman who   lives in one from

      balkanskix stran,   no ja zabyl *(v) kakoj.
      Balkan   countries but I forgot in which

      'Pëtr wants to marry a woman who lives in one of the Balkan countries, but I forgot (in) which.'

   These data indicatZe that the second form-identity generalization posited above in (21), and repeated here, holds regardless of whether or not there is apparently an island interior to the ellipsis site (that is, in the interpretation of the elliptical IP).

(63)   *Form-identity generalization II: Preposition-stranding*

A language L will allow preposition-stranding under sluicing iff L allows preposition stranding under regular wh-movement.

The data presented in §§3.2.1 and 3.2.2 show that there is an intimate connection between the form of the wh-phrase in SpecCP in sluicing and the form of the wh-phrase that would appear under wh-movement with no IP ellipsis. Both the case facts, and especially the P-stranding facts, seem to indicate that the usual mechanisms for case-assignment and determination of targets of wh-movement that operate in a given language to regulate the shape of wh-phrases in non-elliptical questions operate in identical ways under sluicing as well. All of these facts strongly suggest that wh-movement of the usual sort has taken place, displacing an IP-internal wh-phrase to SpecCP.[12]

This conclusion stands in direct conflict to the conclusion reached at the end of §3.1, where the apparent lack of island sensitivity suggested that no movement had taken place. The remainder of this book is devoted to resolving this conflict.

The data presented in this chapter will be instrumental in testing the hypotheses about the nature of islands and ellipsis to come. Having documented the data that support the two form-identity generalizations, I turn now to an exploration of their theoretical significance.

---

[12] Similar considerations suggest a movement approach to a variety of parallel (though to some extent less robust) form-identity effects in stripping, comparatives, fragment answers, the remnants of gapping, and 'elliptic conjunctions' (*except* phrases, etc.), which often show case and P-stranding dependencies like their sluicing cousins.

4

Deletio nata atque mortua

This chapter reviews representative accounts of extant approaches to sluicing, and shows that each of them fails to deal either with the apparent island-insensitivity of sluicing or with the form-identity facts documented in Chapter 3.

This chapter uncovers a richer set of data than the more schematic data presented in the last chapter, and sets the stage for addressing a range of analytic questions that will be taken up in detail in the next chapter.

4.1 ROSS (1969): DELETION AND THE PROBLEM OF ISLANDS

Ross (1969) proposes a simple deletion account, where deletion of the sentential part of an embedded question is licensed by phrase-marker identity with a preceding sentence. The particular formulation he gives will not concern us (even at the time, Ross recognized its shortcomings), but rather its overall approach, translated into our current understanding of PF-deletion.

For Ross, the great advantage of the deletion account, contrasted with a purely interpretative account, was that it could account directly for the case-matching effects. Although he did not give an actual derivation of his German examples (because his particular formulation of sluicing stumbled on them, owing to the V2/V-final alternations involved), we can see how such a derivation would proceed, provided that the condition regulating identity is not, as assumed by Ross, a condition on S-structure phrase-marker identity, but rather the condition proposed in Chapter 1. Under this conception, the sluice in (1) simply derives from the corresponding embedded question (where deletion is indicated by struck-through text). Since the verb *schmeicheln* assigns dative case, this will be the only possibility for the case of the remnant wh-phrase.

(1)   Er will   jemandem   schmeicheln, aber sie   wissen nicht,
       he wants someone.DAT flatter   but they know   not

       {*wer   /*wen   /wem}   er *t*ₗₑₘ schmeicheln will.
       who.NOM who.ACC who.DAT he   flatter   wants

       'He wants to flatter someone, but they don't know who.'

Although Ross did not note this consequence of the deletion approach, it straightforwardly predicts the P-stranding facts as well. In languages like German, which lack P-stranding, the only well-formed output of wh-movement will have the preposition pied-piped. It is the resulting structure that is subject to deletion, correctly yielding (2) as the only possible grammatical sluice.

(2)   Anna hat mit jemandem gesprochen, aber ich weiß nicht,
       Anna has with someone   spoken   but I   know not

       [mit wem] sie *t*ₚₚ gesprochen hat.
       with who she   spoken   has

       'Anna spoke with someone, but I don't know who.'

This simple fact is the single strongest possible argument for the deletion approach. As we will see, it is a major stumbling block for most other approaches.

Another fact that a deletion approach correctly predicts is that in languages with multiple wh-fronting, sluicing with more than one wh-XP remnant should be possible. One language that has multiple wh-fronting is Bulgarian, as the data in (3) and (4) show, for matrix and embedded questions, respectively (see Rudin 1985: 82 ff., 1988; thanks to L. Schürcks-Grozeva and S. Dianova for judgments on the Bulgarian examples in this section).

(3)   a   [CP Koj kogo [IP e   vidjal]]?
            who whom   AUX seen

            'Who saw who?'

       b   *Koj e vidjal kogo?

(4)   a   Ne znam [$_{CP}$ koj   kogo [$_{IP}$ e   vidjal]].
          not I.know   who whom   AUX seen
          'I don't know who saw who.'

      b   *Ne znam koj e vidjal kogo.

Such a language also allows multiple wh-phrases under sluicing, dubbed 'multiple sluicing' in Takahashi (1994):

(5)   Njakoj e   vidjal njakogo, no ne znam [$_{CP}$ koj
      someone AUX seen   someone   but not I.know   who

      kogo [~~$_{IP}$ e   vidjal~~]].
      whom   AUX seen

      'Someone saw someone, but I don't know who saw who.'

A further consequence of deletion is that if these languages show Superiority effects, and if Superiority is the result of derivational but not representational constraints, then the fact that Superiority effects are attested under sluicing as well argues that wh-movement, constrained by Superiority, has occurred, followed by deletion. The control data that show that Bulgarian exhibits Superiority effects is given in (6), from Rudin (1985: 115). The corresponding sluicing case is in (7), and should be compared to its grammatical counterpart in (5).

(6)   a   Koj kogo e   vidjal?
          who whom AUX seen
          'Who saw who?'

      b   *Kogo koj e vidjal?

(7)   *Njakoj e   vidjal njakogo, no ne znam kogo koj.
      someone AUX seen   someone   but not I.know whom who

      ('Someone saw someone, but I don't know who saw who.')

There is, however, a serious complication in the picture: it appears that not only multiple wh-fronting languages like Bulgarian allow for multiple wh-remnants. The following data, from German, Dutch, Turkish, Greek, and Japanese respectively,[1] show that this phenomenon is attested in other, non-multiple-fronting languages as well.

---

[1] For judgments on these and the following examples, thanks to A. Mester (German), H. Rullmann (Dutch), D. Grate (Turkish), and A. Giannakidou (Greek).

(8) a Jemand hat was   gesehen, aber ich weiß nicht,
        someone has something seen   but I know not

        wer was.
        who what

        (lit.) 'Someone saw something, but I don't know who what.'

     b Iemand heeft iets   gezien, maar ik weet niet wie wat.
        someone has   something seen   but I know not who what

        (lit.) 'Someone saw something, but I don't know who what.'

     c Biri   bir şey   gördü ama, kim   ne
        someone something saw but who.NOM what.ACC

        bil-mi-yor-um.[2]
        know-NEG-PROG-1sg

        (lit.) 'Someone saw something, but I don't know who what.'

     d Kapjos   idhe kapjon,   alla dhe ksero
        someone.NOM saw someone.ACC but not I.know

        pjos   pjon.
        who.NOM who.ACC

        (lit.) 'Someone saw someone, but I don't know who whom.'

[2] The Turkish case raises numerous interesting questions that deserve further examination. Most interesting is the fact that the non-elliptical version, given in (i), requires the genitive on the embedded subject (embedded clauses in Turkish being very similar to nominalizations in many respects).

(i)   Biri   bir şey   gördü ama, kim-*(in) ne   gör-düğ-ünü bil-mi-yor-um.
      someone something saw but who-GEN what see-DIK-ACC know-NEG-PROG-1sg

      'Someone saw something, but I don't know who saw what.'

This case-marking cannot appear in the 'sluiced' version, however; nominative is required, as in (8c).

(ii) *Biri   bir şey   gördü ama, kim-in ne   bil-mi-yor-um.
      someone something saw but who-GEN what know-NEG-PROG-1sg

      ('Someone saw something, but I don't know who what.')

These contrasts indicate that multiple 'sluicing' in Turkish may not be as directly related to its apparent cousins in other languages as first inspection might suggest. One possibility is that the multiple sluice is actually some kind of reduced coordination. This suspicion is supported by the fact that a strong pause is required between *kim* and *ne* in (8c), and that (iii) is a possible, perhaps more natural, variant.

(iii) Biri   bir şey   gördü ama, kim {ve/ veya} ne   bil-mi-yor-um.
      someone something saw but who and/or what know-NEG-PROG-1sg

      (lit.) 'Someone saw something, but I don't know who and/or what.'

Cf. Lewis's (1967: 73) example *neyi ve ne zaman yaptın* (lit.) 'What and when have you done?' (i.e. 'What have you done, and when?'). See Browne (1972), Bechhofer (1976*b*), Giannakidou and Merchant (1998), and Merchant (1999*a*) for related discussion.

e   Sono toki, dareka-ga   nanika-o   mise-ta.
    that time someone-NOM something-ACC showed

Sikasi, dare-ga   nani-o   ka
but   who-NOM what-ACC Q

omoidase-nai. (Nishigauchi 1998: 146 (70))
remember-not

'At that moment, someone showed something (to me). (lit.) But I
can't remember who what.'

Even in English, although the relevant construction is already somewhat
marginal (though noted in e.g. Bolinger 1978[3]), we do find instances of
apparent 'multiple sluicing':

(9)   (?)Everyone brought something (different) to the potluck, but I
      couldn't tell you who what.

In the English case, though not in the languages in (8), this multiple sluicing
seems restricted to environments where an appropriate pair-list reading can be
generated (see the discussion in Nishigauchi 1998)—that is, one of the quantifiers in the antecedent IP must be a generator. When we have two indefinites,
for example, a multiple sluice parallel to the examples in (8) is impossible:
Someone said something, but I couldn't tell you who what. (This is not to imply
that examples parallel to (9) are ruled out in German, Dutch, Greek, Turkish,
and Japanese—on the contrary, such examples are to my knowledge possible,
and show interpretational restrictions reminiscent of the English facts, as noted
in Nishigauchi (1998) for Japanese.)

Thus no interesting implication of the form 'multiple sluicing iff overt
multiple fronting' holds. Though I cannot go into the syntax of this phenomenon in detail here, one interpretation that suggests itself in a Minimalist context is that Procrastinate can be overridden if deletion applies. (Suggesting an
implementation of Procrastinate not as a global evaluation metric, but as a local
one, encoded by some feature of traces that is repaired by the deletion, along
the lines discussed in Chapter 2.) Another possibility is suggested by Ackema
and Neeleman's (1998) account of wh-movement options attested across languages: if the constraint against movement (STAY) penalizes PF occurrences of
traces, the deletion of a containing structure (here the IP) would allow perfect

---

[3] Cf. also the following attested example, from a letter by Paul Postal (20 Oct. 1975), quoted
in Pullum (1991: 149).

(i)   'In French, we have noticed that some intransitive V permit Extraposition of Indefinite,
       while others permit Impersonal Passive. Which which?'

satisfaction of the lower-ranked contraints favoring multiple movements. The logic here is parallel to that employed in a number of cases in the next chapter: deletion converts an otherwise suboptimal candidate to an optimal one. See Kennedy (2000) for an insightful application of this logic also to comparatives and subcomparatives.[4]

In any case, the prediction with respect to Superiority can be tested in those languages that exhibit Superiority effects. The situation in German and Dutch is the subject of certain complications, making these languages less than ideal as test cases. In English and Greek, however, Superiority effects are clearly attested in the relevant simple monoclausal structures:

(10) a *I couldn't tell you what who brought to the potluck.
      b *Dhen ksero   pjon   pjos
         not   I.know who.ACC who.NOM

         idhe. (on non-echo reading for *pjos*)
         saw

         ('I don't know whom who saw.')

Crucially, these effects are equally attested in the corresponding multiple-sluicing structures:

(11) a *Everyone brought something (different) to the potluck, but I couldn't tell you what who.
      b *Kapjos   idhe kapjon,   alla dhe ksero
         someone. NOM saw someone.ACC but not I.know

         pjon   pjos.
         who.ACC who.NOM

         (lit.) 'Someone saw someone, but I don't know whom who.'

---

[4] One caveat is in order: it is not entirely clear whether the movement of the non-initial remnant is the result of usual wh-movement, and not of some other, similar movement operation, such as the one that is responsible for the rescuing of the non-initial remnant in gapping, or pseudogapping, for instance. One striking fact about multiple sluices in the languages above is that they tend not to be separated by a tensed clause boundary (as pointed out in Takahashi 1994), though this is not, as sometimes supposed, an absolute. As in gapping, cross-tensed-clausal examples are possible just in case the embedded subject is bound by the matrix one:

(i)   [Everybody₁ said he₁'d bring something different to the potluck.] Jack₁ said he₁'d bring wine, Bob₂ ⟨said he₂'d bring⟩ beer, and Sam₃ ⟨said he₃'d bring⟩ whiskey.
(ii) [Everybody₁ said he₁'d bring something different to the potluck.] But I can't remember who what.

See Nishigauchi (1998) in particular for relevant considerations, and Johnson (1997) for discussion with respect to gapping; cf. also Romero (1997*a*) for discussion of some of the differences between multiple sluicing and gapping (embeddability, non-coordinativity, etc.).

This patterning in the data is expected if Superiority is the result of a derivational constraint on wh-movement (for example, a result of the Minimal Link Condition as in Chomsky 1995; see also Hornstein 1995, Grohmann 1998, 2000, and Pesetsky 1998*b* for recent discussion), and if the remnant wh-phrases reach their surface position in sluicing by the application of the usual processes that drive overt wh-movement. Since they undergo wh-movement, the Superiority condition will apply, with the desired results.

Despite these successes, a serious problem remains for the deletion approach. The problem, as Ross (1969) recognized, is the apparent violation of the islands. Under his approach, examples like (12a) and (13a) have the derivations in (12b) and (13b), where wh-movement has violated the island, hidden by deletion.

(12)   a   They want to hire someone who speaks a Balkan language, but I
           don't remember which.
       b   *I don't remember which ~~(Balkan language) they want to hire
           someone [who speaks]~~.

(13)   a   Ben will be mad if Abby talks to one of the teachers, but she
           couldn't remember which.
       b   *Ben will be mad if Abby talks to one of the teachers, but she
           couldn't remember which ~~(of the teachers) Ben will be mad [if she
           talks to]~~.

Ross's solution to this problem was to conclude that ungrammaticality was calculated across the derivation—that is, that global rules were necessary that could inspect island violations and determine whether they had been 'repaired' by deletion (whether 'the island-forming node does not appear in surface structure' (p. 277)), in which case a lesser mark of deviance would be assigned. This conclusion is repeated in Lakoff (1970, 1972).

Besides the murkiness of such an evaluation metric—see the rebuttal in Baker and Brame (1972)—there is good reason to reject this approach to the island facts on empirical grounds. As pointed out in the Introduction, VP-deletion does not repair island violations, though the Ross approach (or an updated congener) would expect them to.

(14)   [Everyone wants to hire someone who speaks a different Balkan
       language]
       *Abby wants to hire someone who speaks Greek, but I don't
       remember which (language) Ben does ~~want to hire someone [who
       speaks]~~.

(15)   *Ben will be mad if Abby talks to Mr Ryberg, and guess who Chuck will be ~~mad [if she talks to]~~.

These examples indicate that, for at least these islands, the effect is due to the crossing of an island boundary by wh-movement, regardless of whether the island-inducing node surfaces at PF. The reanalysis of these facts suggested by Chomsky (1972) and reiterated in Baker and Brame (1972)—namely that crossing an island-node marks that node with some feature (Lakoff 1972 calls it '[+bad]'), and that this feature, if not deleted, causes the ungrammaticality—fails for the same reason.[5]

4.2 PSEUDOSLUICING

Faced with these difficulties, it was not long before the suggestion was made to reanalyze Ross's sluicing facts as the result not of island-insensitive wh-movement, but rather as related to an entirely different, non-island-containing structure. This suggestion was made independently in both Erteschik-Shir (1977) and Pollmann (1975).

   In the last footnote on the last page of her dissertation (Erteschik-Shir 1977: 107–8, n. 4), Erteschik-Shir mooted an 'interesting alternative to sluicing [that] might be worth investigating', in which a sluice like (16a) would be derived from the underlying structure in (16b) by deletion of the subject *it* and the copula:

---

[5] It might be suggested that the examples in the text are less than ideal test candidates, since, for reasons still mostly unclear, wh-extraction out of VP-ellipsis sites is best when the extraction is parallel to an extraction in the antecedent, as in (i):

(i)   We need to know which languages₁ Abby speaks t_1, and which₂ Ben does ⟨~~speak t_2~~⟩.

However, it remains a fact that wh-extraction out of a VP-ellipsis site is possible when the correlate to the extractee is heavily focused, as discussed in Hardt (1993, 1999); cf. (ii).

(ii)   We know that Abby *does* speak [Greek, Albanian, and Serbian]_F—we need to find out which languages₂ she *doesn't* ⟨~~speak t_2~~⟩!

The examples in (14) and (15) remain much worse than examples such as (ii) that do not contain islands and that do not instantiate parallel extraction. Further, the potential objection does not apply to comparative structures, where such 'parallel' extraction is not required:

(iii)   Abby speaks more Balkan languages Op_2 than Ben does ⟨~~speak t_2~~⟩.

Nonetheless, embedding such ellipsis sites in islands remains ungrammatical:

(iv)   *The University of Chicago hired a professor who speaks more Balkan languages Op_2 than Northwestern did ⟨~~hire a professor who speaks t_2~~⟩.

In such cases, the potential objection based on 'parellelism of extraction' loses much of its force.

(16)   a   Someone just left—guess who.
        b   Someone just left—guess who ~~it was~~.

She was concerned exactly with the island-ameliorating examples that we
have been discussing, and supposed that the question of such island effects
becomes irrelevant if the structure of such an example (her (iii)) contains only
matrix elements (*it will be*).

(17)   That he'll hire someone is possible, but I won't divulge who
        ?(it will be).

Precisely the same suggestion is made in Pollmann (1975), who formulates
an optional transformation that deletes '[+pro, +def]$_{NP}$ + copula',[6] though he
does not recognize the solution it provides to the island problem.

Neither author explicitly identifies the reduced structures posited as
underlying sluices as related to the structure found in clefts, but it seems reasonable to make this identification, and in fact what appears to be sluicing
in Japanese has been claimed by a number of authors to derive exactly from
a cleft (see Merchant 1998 for discussion and references). In other words, (16b)
is itself most likely a reduced form of a cleft whose pivot is an extracted
wh-phrase, as in (18a). This type of ellipsis I will call 'pseudosluicing', as it
gives rise to structures seemingly indistinguishable from 'true' sluicing (wh-
fragments, derived, by hypothesis, from more usual interrogative structures,
as in (18b)).

(18)   a   Guess who [~~it was~~ — ~~that just left~~].   *pseudosluice*
        b   Guess who [— ~~just left~~].   *sluice*

Both derivations, in other words, potentially give rise to the attested data.
In the following sections, I develop a number of diagnostics to distinguish
the two, and conclude that it is at best highly unlikely that 'sluicing' can be
reduced to pseudosluicing in any interestingly general way. These sections
recapitulate many of the arguments presented in Merchant (1998), though
several are new.

---

[6] Pollmann's formulation is meant to include *dat* 'that' as well as *het* 'it'. This incorrectly
allows for potential reductions of the kind in (i), as pointed out by M. Klein (1977: 71 (his (84)));
similarly for the English translation.

(i)   We hebben gisteren Pollini horen spelen. Raad eens wie *(dat is).
       we have   yesterday Pollini hear   play   guess PRT who that is
       'We heard Pollini play yesterday. Guess who *(that is).'

4.2.1 Initial Considerations

Let us begin by considering the CP portion of the pseudosluice. If the suggested reduction of 'it be XP' structures to 'it be XP that . . .' cleft structures is essentially correct, we might wonder whether there is reason to believe that the presuppositional (relative-clause-like) part of a cleft could be omitted to begin with. Such 'ellipsis' would seem to be available in English as well, if the short forms of the answers below are indeed transformationally related to their non-elliptical apparent counterparts. Compare the following pairs of questions and answers.

(19)   a   Q: Who knocked?
            A: It was {Alex/me} (who knocked).
       b   Q: What did they steal?
            A: It was the TV and stereo (that they stole).
       c   Q: Why is the bus late?
            A: It's because of the traffic (that it's late).

In fact, sometimes the presuppositional part *must* be missing:

(20)   Q: Who's that?
        A: It's me (*that is that).

But even if these structures are somehow related, the nature of this 'ellipsis' is quite different from the head-licensed ellipsis generally discussed in the literature (NP-ellipsis, VP-ellipsis, IP-ellipsis), consisting as it does of a CP. There is in fact good reason to doubt that CP-ellipsis in this form exists. Let us examine the two likeliest candidates.

There are two other kinds of environments that would seem to involve missing CPs in English. The first is in comparative clauses such as (21).

(21)   a   More people came than we thought (would come).
       b   He's sicker than the doctor {thought/expected/realized/admitted}
            (that he was).

Given the perceived interpretation, and the fact that these verbs do not in general allow null complements (cf. *I didn't expect *(that)*), it seems reasonable to assume that their CP complements have been elided (perhaps via some generalized comparative deletion) in (21). But, as Kennedy and Merchant (2000*b*) show, this assumption is wrong. In fact, there is good reason to believe that the embedded verbs in (21) take DP, not CP, complements.

Several pieces of evidence point to this conclusion: here I will mention only one, relating to the fact that DPs, but not CPs, need Case. Observe that if the verbs in (21) are passivized, the examples become ungrammatical.

(22)   a   *More people came than it was thought.
        b   *He's sicker than it was {thought/expected/realized/admitted}.

This effect extends as well to adjectives that take CP complements:

(23)   *Sally had a more serious problem than it was {evident/apparent}.

The ungrammaticality of these examples would be surprising if it were simply a matter of a CP being missing, all the more so given that, when a CP *is* present, the examples are fine.

(24)   a   More people came than it was thought would come.
        b   He's sicker than it was {thought/expected/realized/admitted} that he was.
        c   Sally had a more serious problem than it was {evident/apparent} that she had.

The contrast between the examples in (22) and (23) and those in (24) is completely surprising if the former are simply elliptical versions of the latter. Instead, Kennedy and Merchant (2000*b*) propose that what is missing in (22) and (23) is a DP, not a CP, and that this DP, like all argument DPs, requires Case. Support for this approach is given by the fact that (22) and (23) improve if the expletive subject is omitted: this allows the DP to move into subject position, getting Case there.

(25)   a   More people came than was thought.
        b   He's sicker than was {thought/expected/realized/admitted}.
        c   Sally had a more serious problem than was {evident/apparent}.

We can thus conclude that what appeared to be a form of CP ellipsis in comparatives does not in fact involve a CP at all.

The second environment in which a CP complement appears to be missing is as the complement to certain verbs, as in (26):

(26)   a   A: They're late again. B: I know (that they're late again).
        b   A: Will she come? B: I don't know (if she'll come).

But here again it is highly unlikely that a syntactic operation of CP-ellipsis is at work. The fact that certain verbs, such as *know*, *insist*, and *wonder*, can appear without a complement seems to be an idiosyncratic fact about these verbs (generally called 'Null complement anaphora', cf. Hankamer and Sag 1976, Fillmore 1986, and others) that requires some other explanation. Note that, if deletion of a complement CP were in general possible, we would need some way to prevent it from applying in cases like those in (27):

(27)　a　I {regret/asserted} *(that we bought the charcoal grill).
　　　　b　I {proposed/demanded} *(that we buy the charcoal grill).

There therefore seems to be no reason to believe that English has an independent operation of CP-ellipsis, and that, contrary to first appearances, structures of the form *It's Bob* do not represent syntactically reduced clefts.

But even if, for the sake of the argument, English *did* license ellipsis of CP, it is equally highly implausible to assume that the expletive *it* present in clefts and the copula (with concomitant modals, if present) could be missing, since these are not properties found independently in English (that is, English is neither a *pro*-drop nor a null copula language). This difficulty was noted by Erteschik-Shir (1977), who admits that '[the deletion transformation that deletes "it + be (tensed)"] cannot occur equally well in all environments, and an investigation of the conditions on this deletion transformation is necessary' (p. 108).

What is at stake, of course, is wild overgeneration. A proponent of such an approach would have to answer why 'it + be' deletion could not apply in the cases in (28), for example.

(28)　a　Q: Who knocked?
　　　　　　A: *(It was) {Alex/me} who knocked.
　　　　b　Q: What did they steal?
　　　　　　A: *(It was) the TV and stereo that they stole.
　　　　c　Q: Why is the bus late?
　　　　　　A: *(It's) because of the traffic that it's late.

In general, in fact, fragment answers do not have the same properties as pivots of clefts: they do not enforce exhausitivity the way the pivot of a cleft does, for example, nor do they have the same presuppositional properties. A cleft is generally assumed to have a true existential presupposition (though see Prince 1978 and Delin 1992 for some caveats to this blanket claim: new information can sometimes appear in the 'presuppositional' part, especially in performatives in clefts), whereas a question is typically assumed to have a conversational implicature of existence of something that satisfies the kernel of the question (see the series of papers culminating in Karttunen and Peters 1979). This difference is illustrated here with negative quantifiers in answers, which are well formed, while negative quantifiers in the pivot of clefts are not (since the assertion contradicts the presupposition).

(29)   a   Q: What did the burglar take?
           A: Nothing.
       b   #It was nothing that the burglar took.

(30)   a   Q: What did he do to help you?
           A: Nothing at all.
       b   #It was nothing at all that he did to help us.

These initial considerations cast serious doubt on the plausibility of the operations necessary to produce the posited ellipsis. In the next section, I present a number of other differences that make any attempt to reduce sluicing to pseudosluicing seem unlikely, differences that would remain mysterious under such a reduction.

4.2.2 Contra the Equation 'Sluicing = Pseudosluicing'

There are at least ten differences between sluicing and cleft questions with wh-XP pivots. My goal here is not to offer explanations or analyses of these differences—my point is served simply by showing that they exist, since their very existence makes any assimilation of sluicing to elliptical clefts problematic. These differences concern the distinct behavior of sluices and wh-pivot clefts with respect to adjuncts and implicit arguments, prosody, aggressively non-D-linked wh-phrases, 'mention-some' modifiers, 'mention-all' modifiers, *else*-modification, swiping (wh-preposition inversion), languages with limited or no cleft strategies, languages with nominative pivots of clefts, and left-branch sluices.

1 *Adjuncts and implicit arguments*

The first reason to keep sluicing and clefting distinct is provided by a simple comparison of the behavior of adjuncts and implicit arguments in these two constructions. As the data in (31) for adjuncts (similar to the data given by M. Klein 1977: 70) and that in (32) for implicit arguments show, sluicing with these is grammatical, but a wh-adjunct or implicit argument is highly degraded as the pivot of a bare cleft in English. (The cleft versions improve substantially if the presuppositional part of the cleft is retained, at the risk of prolixity. The

significance of this fact is difficult to assess, however, lacking a better understanding of what makes wh-adjuncts and implicit arguments ungrammatical
pivots in the first place.)

(31)   a   He fixed the car, but I don't know how (*it was).
        b   He fixed the car, but I don't know why (*it was).
        c   He fixed the car, but I don't know when (*it was).
        d   He's hidden the jewels, but I don't know where (*it is).
        e   He served time in prison, but I don't know how long (*it was).

(32)   a   They served the guests, but I don't know what (*it was).
        b   He said they had already eaten, but I don't know what (*it was).
        c   They were arguing, but I don't know about what (*it was).

2 Prosody

The second difference comes from the intonational contour associated with
sluicing. Standard cases of sluicing require that the greatest pitch accent fall on
the wh-phrase. In wh-pivot clefts, on the other hand, the pitch accent must fall
on the copula, as the following contrasts show.

(33)   Someone gave me a valentine, but
        a   I don't know WHO.
        b   I don't know who it WAS.
        c   *I don't know WHO it was.

(34)   a   Someone KISSED you, and you can't remember WHO?!?
        b   Someone KISSED you, and you can't remember who it WAS?!?
        c   *Someone KISSED you, and you can't remember WHO it was?!?

This is actually somewhat surprising, given that in general the pivot of a cleft
must contain the pitch accent. Note that the above contrasts cannot be simply
reduced to the effects of some general preference for the nuclear accent to fall
at the (absolute) end of the utterance, since exactly the same judgments obtain
if the embedded CP is left-dislocated, for example.

3 Aggressively non-D-linked wh-phrases

Aggressively non-D-linked wh-phrases (as in Pesetsky 1987) generally cannot
occur in sluicing,[7] though they are unobjectionable as pivots of a cleft:

---

[7] The one exception to this rule being in swiping cases (sluices with inverted prepositions), as
discussed in Ch. 2 n. 14 and in Merchant (forthcoming).

(35)   Someone dented my car last night—
        a   I wish I knew who!
        b   I wish I knew who the hell it was!
        c   *I wish I knew who the hell!

The problem in (35c) is not with emphasis on *who the hell*, as the well-formedness of (36) demonstrates:

(36)   Who the HELL do you think you are?!?

4 'Mention-some' modification

Because of the exhaustivity entailed by the pivot (see Kiss 1998), only a 'mention-all' interpretation (see Groenendijk and Stokhof 1997: §6.2.3 for discussion) will be compatible with a wh-phrase in the pivot (thanks to S. Tomioka for suggesting this test). Thus wh-pivots will be incompatible with modifiers like *for example*, which explicitly requires the 'mention-some' interpretation, in contrast to sluicing, which allows such modification. Example (37a) illustrates the contrast in embedded sluicing, and (37b) does so for a matrix sluice.

(37)   A: You should talk to somebody in the legal department for help
        with that.
        a   B1: Could you tell me who (*it is), for example?
        b   B2: Who (*is it), for example?

5 'Mention-all' modification

The reverse argument holds for the exhaustivity enforcing wh-modifier 'all' as in *Who all was at the party?* (see McCloskey 2000). Such modification seems degraded in sluicing in some examples; crucially, this degradation does not carry over to the clefted counterpart:

(38)   A bunch of students were protesting, and the FBI is trying to find out
        who all *(it was).

6 Else-*modification*

Likewise, the modifier *else* applied to wh-words can occur in sluicing, but not in clefts.

(39)   Harry was there, but I don't know who else (*it was).

7 *Swiping (sluiced wh-phrase inversion with prepositions)*

A further difference between sluicing and clefts comes from a somewhat intricate set of facts concerning the ability of certain wh-words in English to invert with a selecting preposition under sluicing, a phenomenon I dub 'swiping' (*s*luiced *wh*-phrase *i*nversion with *p*repositions *i*n *N*orthern *G*ermanic) in Merchant (forthcoming) (this phenomenon is also attested in Danish and some varieties of Norwegian, though not in Swedish or Frisian).

As observed in Ross (1969) and Rosen (1976), sluicing allows a seemingly 'stranded' preposition under certain conditions. Examples of swiping are given in (40).

(40) a She bought a robe, but God knows who for.
  b They were arguing, but we couldn't figure out what about.
  c This opera was written by someone in the 19th century, but we're not sure who by.   (Chung *et al.* 1995: (4d))
  d He was shouting to someone, but it was impossible to tell who to.
  e A: She's going to leave her fortune to someone. B: Really? Who to?
  f He'll be at the Red Room, but I don't know when till.
  g She's driving, but God knows where to.

Swiping looks at first glance similar to West Germanic R-pronoun inversion (this identification is made in van Riemsdijk 1978 and Chung *et al.* 1995, for instance): it is well known that certain elements (known as 'R-pronouns') can invert with a preposition, as illustrated in (41a) and (42a) for German and Dutch (the (b) examples give non-inverted controls):

(41) a Wo-r-an denkst du eigentlich?
      where-on think you actually
      'What are you thinking of, anyway?'

  b Du denkst an dein Buch wieder!
      you think on your book again
      'You're thinking of your book again!'

(42) a Waarover   praten zij?
      where-about talk   they
      'What are they talking about?'

  b Zij praten over het boek.
      they talk   about the book
      'They're talking about the book.'

Somewhat like R-pronoun inversion in German and Dutch, swiping is very restricted, though it is more liberal with respect to the wh-words that participate than the continental varieties of R-pronoun inversion (see J. Hoekstra 1995 for a survey of the various continental dialects). In English, only certain 'minimal' wh-operators can invert: *who, what, when,* and *where* (and, for some speakers, *how long, how much,* and possibly *how many*). We can note here that, whatever the correct account of this restriction, it is not simply a prosodic condition on inversion, as the following examples with *which* demonstrate.

(43) a *She bought a robe for one of her nephews, but God knows which (one) for.
      b *They were arguing about animals, but we couldn't figure out what kind about.
      c *This opera was written by an Italian composer in the 19th century, but we're not sure which (one) by.
      d *He was shouting to one of the freshmen Republican senators supporting the bomber program, but it was impossible to tell exactly which (senator) to.
      e *He'll be at the Red Room, but I don't know what time till.
      f *She's driving, but God knows which town to.

Crucially, however, the kind of inversion found in swiping is impossible in wh-pivot clefts:

(44) a It was [for Humphrey] that I voted.
      b [For who] was it that you voted?[8]
      c *[Who for] was it (that you voted)?

(45) a It was [about the election] that they were arguing.
      b [About what] was it that they were arguing?
      c *[What about] was it (that they were arguing)?

Again, this asymmetry between the behavior of wh-words in PPs under sluicing and as pivots of clefts would be unexpected if the former were simply a case of the latter.

[8] Prescriptively, we expect the form [for whom] here, since the register that includes pied-piping also requires the archaic form *whom* after prepositions. This form is not found in swiping, however: *Peter went to the movies, but I don't know who(*m) with.* This is due perhaps to the clash of registers that would be involved in such a case: while *whom* belongs to the most formal register of written (and sometimes spoken) English, swiping characterizes highly informal, colloquial speech, more so even than preposition-stranding in non-elliptical interrogatives.

8 *Languages with limited or no cleft strategy*

The eighth argument comes from the fact that there are languages that either have a very limited cleft strategy, or lack any kind of cleft construction at all, but that nevertheless allow sluicing.

The first kind of language is illustrated by German, which does not allow PP pivots of clefts (among other restrictions; see Grewendorf and Poletto 1990). But, of course, as we have seen above, PP wh-phrases can be remnants of sluicing, even 'into islands'.

(46)   a   *Mit wem war es, daß er gesprochen hat?
          with who was it that he spoken has
          'With whom was it that he spoke?'

    b   Er hat mit jemandem gesprochen—rate mal mit wem!
          he has with someone spoken guess PRT with who
          'He spoke with someone—guess with whom!'

The second kind of language is represented by Romanian and Hungarian. As the following data, given in Grosu (1994: 203–4; see also Dobrovie-Sorin 1993), show, Romanian does not permit structures like the English cleft.

(47)   a   *E Maria (că) vreau să întîlnesc.
          is Maria that want.1sg SUBJ meet.1sg
          ('It's Maria that I want to meet.')

    b   *E Ion {ce / care} a cîştigat premiul întîi.
          is Ion that/ who has won prize.the first
          ('It's Ion that won first prize.')

    c   *E Ion pe care (l-) am întîlnit ieri.
          is Ion ACC who him- have.1sg met yesterday
          ('It's Ion who I met yesterday.')

Whatever the explanation for this fact (Dobrovie-Sorin 1993 suggests that Romanian may lack the appropriate kind of null operator), the lack of cleft structures in this language predicts, if the pseudosluicing hypothesis were correct, that Romanian should lack sluicing structures as well. This, however, is incorrect:

(48)   a   Vrea să întîlnească pe cine-va, dar nu ştiu
          want.3sg SUBJ meet.3sg ACC someone but not I.know
          pe cine.
          ACC who
          'She wants to meet someone, but I don't know who.'

    b   Cine-va a   câştigat premiul întîi—ghici cine!
        someone has won   prize.the first   guess who

        'Someone won first prize—guess who!'

    c   Am   întîlnit pe unul diutre fraţii   tăi, dar nu
        I.have met   ACC one among brothers you but not

        ţin   minte pe care.
        I.have memory ACC which

        'I met one of your brothers yesterday, but I don't remember which.'

A parallel argument comes from Hungarian, which employs a preverbal position for identificational focus, but lacks the cleft construction of English. Thus (49a), modified from Kiss (1998: 249) (her (8a)), corresponds to the English cleft (hence the translation), while (49b) is impossible.[9]

(49)   a   Mari a   kalapot nézte.
          Mary the hat.ACC looked.at

          'It was the hat that Mary was looking at.'

      b   *Volt a   kalap   amit   Mari nézte.
          it.was the hat.NOM which.ACC Mary looked.at

          ('It was the hat that Mary was looking at.')

But Hungarian does allow sluices of the relevant form:

(50)   Mari nézett   valamit,   de nem emlékszem, mit.
          Mary looked.at something.ACC but not I.remember what.ACC

          'Mary was looking at something, but I don't remember what.'

9 Languages with pivots of clefts in the nominative

The ninth argument against assimilating sluicing to cleft or cleft-like structures comes from languages like Greek, which do have both sluicing and clefts, but which also have clearly distinguishable case. In Greek, the pivot of a cleft, including wh-pivots, appears in the nominative in the environments relevant for this discussion. The case of a sluiced wh-phrase, in contrast, must match the case of its correlate (as discussed in §3.2.1 above). This gives rise to the contrasts seen in (51a) and (51b) (thanks to A. Giannakidou for judgments).

---

[9] Structures like (49b) are possible, but receive an existential interpretation; the use of the definite pivot in (49b) rules out this irrelevant possibility. Thanks to G. Puskás for discussion.

(51) I   astinomia anekrine   enan   apo tous Kiprious prota, ala
      the police   interrogated one.ACC from the   Cypriots first but

      dhen ksero
      not I.know

      a   {*pjos   /pjon}.
           which.NOM which.ACC

      b   {pjos   itan   /*pjon   itan}.
           which.NOM it.was   which.ACC it.was

'The police interrogated one of the Cypriots first, but I don't know {which/which it was}.'

A related concern comes from English, where assimilation to clefting would allow ill-formed sluices to be generated such as the following:

(52) The police said that finding someone's car took all morning, but I can't remember who *(it was).

10 Left-branch sluices

Finally, sluices can violate certain instances of the left-branch constraint, illustrated here with an attributive adjective (see §5.1.1 for more discussion of these cases):

(53) He married a rich woman—wait till you hear how rich!

But these have no well-formed cleft counterparts:

(54) a   *How rich is it (that he married [a __ woman])?
      b   *He married a rich woman—wait till you hear how rich it is!

4.2.3 Summary

This section has presented a number of reasons to be skeptical of any attempt to reduce sluicing in English to a kind of pseudosluicing. In addition to syntactic difficulties in accounting for the missing copula, expletive *it*, and CP, I provided evidence from adjuncts and implicit arguments, prosody, aggressively non-D-linked wh-phrases, 'mention-some', 'mention-all', and *else* modifications, swiping, languages with limited clefts, languages with nominative cleft pivots, and left-branch sluices to support the conclusion that wh-pivot clefts and sluices should be kept distinct.

4.3 SLUICING ≠ WH-OP + RESUMPTIVE

This section explores the possibility of reducing the cases of sluicing that violate strong islands to cases in which a resumption strategy is employed to rescue what would otherwise be an illicit movement configuration. This approach would allow us to maintain the standard account of islands as arising through illict (syntactic) *movement* operations, since wh-operators can bind resumptive pronouns in configurations in which movement is impossible (see McCloskey 1990 for an overview). A closer inspection of the relevant data, however, will show that this approach is untenable.

Let us first examine why a reduction of sluicing into strong islands to the mechanism used to form the operator-variable chain with resumptive elements might be attractive. Though this approach has never been explored in much detail in the literature,[10] it is nevertheless suggestive, based on certain distributional parallels. Compare the following examples—the examples in (55) are standard cases of strong extraction islands, while in (56), the initial wh-operator can associate with a resumptive pronoun inside the island. For terminological ease, I will call a wh-operator that binds a resumptive pronoun a *resumptive-binding operator* (I will show below that resumptive-binding operators have a number of peculiar properties cross-linguistically that distinguish them from their more familiar trace-binding counterparts). In (57), a sluiced wh-operator seemingly binds a variable in those very positions.

(55) a *Who$_1$ did the Brazilian team improve after t_1 started playing for them?

 b *What play$_2$ does he want to interview the woman who wrote t_2?

(56) a Who$_1$ did the Brazilian team improve after he$_1$ started playing for them?

 b What play$_2$ does he want to interview the woman who wrote it$_2$?

(57) a The Brazilian team improved after somebody from Ajax started playing for them, but I can't remember who.

 b He wants to interview the woman who wrote some play, but I can't remember what play.

The basic idea is that the sluicing examples derive not from movement variants in (55) but rather from their resumptive counterparts in (56). Since the grammar makes this strategy available in any case, the logic would go, there is no reason not to employ it here. For the deletion to proceed, the parallelism

---

[10] It was suggested in passing in Sauerland (1996: 307–8).

condition must simply allow (the variable bound by) the indefinite in the antecedent clause to be equivalent to the resumptive pronoun in the elided IP, instead of to a trace of wh-movement. As we saw in Chapter 1, such a move is harmless, and necessary in any case (see §5.2); such equivalencies are pervasive under ellipsis, and have been known to hold since the beginning of research on this topic, going under various names ('sloppy identity' in Ross 1967 and Bouton 1970; 'vehicle change' in Fiengo and May 1994).

The table below lays out this parallelism:

(58)   *Three types of Op-variable association*

	Is such an association possible across a strong island?
wh-Op and gap (trace)	No
wh-Op and resumptive pronoun	Yes
sluiced wh-Op and 'variable'	(Apparently) yes

This parallelism, while initially attractive, unfortunately breaks down in a number of places, ultimately proving only superficial. It is the purpose of the following sections to brings these failings to light.

4.3.1 Initial Considerations

To begin with, there are a number of possible wh-remnants that do not seem to have readily available resumptive strategies: *when*, *where*, and amount/degree *how*.[11] Though *then*, *there*, and *that* are in English the demonstrative equiva-

---

[11] I leave out of consideration manner *how* and *why*, since there are no simple demonstrative elements corresponding to these; this is related to the fact, often noted in the literature, that *how* and especially *why* are non-D-linked, and do not admit of an ordering relation easily (see Szabolcsi and Zwarts 1993). So, while it is possible to specify a manner or reason with a wide-scope indefinite, sluicing over these indefinites requires the DPs *in what way* or *what reason*, and still does not allow *why* or, to a lesser extent, *how*, for reasons that remain unclear at present.

(i)   a   She's practicing her serve so that she'll be able to hit the ball in a certain deadly way, but her trainer won't tell us {in what way/??how}.

     b   He wants to interview someone who works at the soup kitchen for a certain reason, but he won't reveal yet {?what reason/*why}.

Note of course that, though the expressions *(in) that way* and *for that reason* might be thought to be able to stand in as resumptives for *how* and *why* in extraction dependencies, this is impossible:

(ii)   a   *How$_4$ did she practice her serve so much that she could hit the ball (that way$_4$)?

     b   *Why$_5$ did you interview someone who quit the Red Cross (for that reason$_5$)?

Of course, 'non-island-violating' sluices with *how* and *why* are fine.

lents to *when, where,* and amount/degree *how,* these elements do not generally function as resumptives (see McCloskey 1990: 243 and Finer 1997: 717 for recent discussion and references):

(59)   a   *Where₁ does he want to find a person [who camped (there₁)]?
        b   *When₂ is she looking for journal entries [that describe a battle (then₂)]?
        c   ??How much (weight)₃ did he promise to work out [until he lost (that much₃)]?

Nevertheless, if the correlate makes a wide-scope place, time, or amount variable available, as in (60), 'island-insensitive' *when, where,* and *how much* are possible:

(60)   a   He wants to find a person who has lived somewhere specific in the Pacific, but I can't remember where.
        b   She is looking for journal entries that describe a battle {at a certain time/in a certain year}, but I don't remember when.
        c   He promised to work out until he lost a certain number of pounds, but I don't remember how much.

This line of reasoning is corroborated by Irish, which, although it has available an extremely productive resumptive strategy, nevertheless lacks resumptives corresponding to *then* and *there* (McCloskey 1990: 243 n.10). If such elements are generally absent from the repertoire of resumptive elements (presumably for type reasons: resumptive elements seem only to be of type $\langle e \rangle$), it would be surprising to imagine that they are in fact possible, but only as null resumptives in sluicing.[12]

Irish would also be a natural language to examine in general to see whether or not sluicing (at the very least the apparently island-insensitive variety) makes use of a resumptive strategy, since it marks the presence of the resumptive not

---

[12] There are some instances of locative resumptives cited in the literature: Suñer (1998) gives examples from Spanish and Australian English in restrictive relatives, and Prince (1990) gives examples in such relatives as well (see also Bissell 1999). Wahba (1984: 13–14) gives examples of resumptive locatives in topicalizations in Egyptian Arabic, and discusses the fact that, although these resumptives are impossible in non-island contexts (only a gap may appear), one may appear in an island. Crucially, none of these involves wh-questions (in Egyptian Arabic, questioning locatives out of islands involves the wh-in-situ strategy; see Wahba 1984: 118–26), which would be required if the sluicing examples were to be reduced to resumptives. Interestingly, temporal resumptives seem to be absent even from restrictive relatives.

only in the base-position, as in English, but also on the complementizer (see McCloskey 1979, 1990). Unfortunately for the purposes of conducting this test, as discussed in §2.2.2.2, sluicing never allows for the presence of a complementizer co-occuring with the wh-remnant, as in (61), repeated from Chapter 2 (103). Here, the relevant data would come from the (affirmative) past tense, since in the present the mutation on the verb following the complementizer (lenition for the complementizer that co-occurs with traces, glossed as C_{trace}, nasalization for the resumptive complementizer, glossed as C_{pro}) is the only signal of which complementizer we are dealing with, and of course, in sluicing, the relevant verb is not pronounced. In the past, however, the resumptive complementizer is realized as *ar*, while the trace complementizer is *a* (see McCloskey 1979: 11).

(61)   Cheannaigh sé leabhar inteacht ach níl   fhios   agam
        bought   he book   some   but not.is knowledge at.me

        céacu ceann (*a   /*ar).
        which one C_{trace} C_{pro}

        'He bought a book, but I don't know which.'

Irish does, however, provide an argument against assimilating all kinds of sluicing to resumptive behavior. This argument is based on the fact that no resumptive element can occur as the highest subject in the clause (McCloskey 1979, 1990: 210) (the same restriction holds in Hebrew and Arabic, and the sluicing data in those languages are parallel to that given here for Irish).

(62)   *an fear a   raibh   sé breoite
        the man C_{pro} be.PAST he ill

        (lit.) 'the man that he was ill'

If sluicing structures were only the result of resumptive strategies, we would expect Irish not to allow sluices over the highest subject. But such sluices are perfectly well formed (J. McCloskey, p.c.):

(63)   Tá   duine inteacht breoite, ach níl   fhios
        be-PRES person some   ill   but not.is knowledge

        agam cé.
        at.me who

        'Somebody is ill, but I don't know who.'

4.3.2 Resumptivity and Case

Another important argument against the resumptive strategy comes from
case-marking languages. I will illustrate here with examples from the genitive
case in English, and other cases below in German, Russian, Polish, Czech,
and Greek. The basic point of the argument is simple: while moved wh-phrases
always take their case from their base position, wh-phrases linked to resumptives need not do so, and in general cannot, appearing instead in some
default case if possible. If the remnant wh-phrase in sluicing were binding
a resumptive element, we would expect the case of this wh-phrase to be the
default case associated with resumptive-binding wh-phrases in general. If,
on the other hand, the wh-phrase were actually the product of movement
as in regular trace-binding configurations, the contextually appropriate
case is to be expected. As I will show, the facts show the latter to be the case.
In fact, some of these languages make the point even more clearly: it
appears that, with a wide variety of wh-phrases, there is simply no resumptivity strategy available at all. These same wh-phrases can, however, perfectly
well appear in sluicing. Whether this lack of resumptivity is a systemic
property of the languages in question or not (which is a separate question,
addressed briefly in the following section), even a single non-equivalency
between the range of wh-operators available to sluicing and those available as
resumptive-binding operators makes a reduction of the former to the latter
dubious.

It has been known since Ross (1969) that case-matching effects hold in
sluicing, as we saw above in Chapters 2 and 3. But the cases discussed in
Chapter 2, and throughout the literature, represent examples where the
case-marked wh-phrase does not originate in a strong island (indeed, only
monoclausal examples have ever been discussed for case-marking languages),
and hence might be argued not to bear on the point at hand. Since in none
of these cases do we have a strong island interior to the sluice, an advocate
of the deletion + resumptivity approach might reasonably argue that
these non-island cases involve simple movement followed by deletion,
with no resumptive strategy necessary. It is only for the cases where the
sluiced wh-phrase must apparently originate within a strong island that the
resumptivity strategy must be called upon to save the deletion analysis,
assuming that island constraints hold of movement in general. That is,
we wish to reduce island-violating cases of sluicing to base-generation of the
wh-phrase in SpecCP and concomitant deletion of the IP that contains
both the island and the resumptive element bound by the base-generated
wh-operator.

4.3.2.1 *English*

In order to test this hypothesis against the case-marking facts, we must look at sluicing out of strong islands, as we saw in §3.2.1. For ease of illustration, I begin with the one remnant of case left in the English wh-system, the genitive *whose*.[13] Sluicing of *whose* out of an island is possible, as shown in (64) for the subject island (in addition to being a left-branch violation):[14]

(64)   The police said that finding someone's car took all morning, but I can't remember
      a   whose.
      b   *who.

Crucially, when a resumptive strategy is used, only the bare wh-operator *who* is possible, as in (65a), not the case-marked *whose*, which agrees in case with the genitive resumptive pronoun *his* that it binds in (65b). (The example in (65b) is equally bad without the resumptive *his*, being additionally a left-branch violation.)

(65)   a   Who$_1$ did the police say that finding his$_1$ car took all morning?
      b   *Whose$_1$ did the police say that finding (his$_1$) car took all morning?

This is precisely the opposite of the data in (64), of course. If the grammaticality of the sluice in (64a) were to be reduced to a resumptive source, we would

[13] I disregard the form *whom*, which has been completely lost from (at least) my American English dialect—this form is extremely prescriptive and must be thought of on a par with such extra-grammatical epiphenomena as the injunction not to 'split infinitives', i.e. not to insert adverbials between *to* and following verb, as in *to boldly go*, etc. Such prescriptive elements show vanishingly little about the underlying structure of the system; rather, they reflect conscious modifications of the system that can be brought about, similar to deliberately speaking with a lisp or the like. While such modifications are presumably constrained in a general way by underlying grammatical principles, I doubt that any judgments about such data are reliable, and will henceforth avoid them in what follows.

[14] I am ignoring the question of whether *whose* is truly the morphologically case-marked genitive of *who*, or simply *who* with the *'s* in D°. The evidence bearing on this question is equivocal; the question essentially reduces to the question whether *whose* should be assimilated to other case-marked pronouns such as *his*, *its*, etc., or to possibly phrasal genitives like *who the hell's* (as J. McCloskey points out). If the latter, then the examples in the text illustrate the lack of pied-piping with resumptive-binding operators; if the former, then they show the lack of case-marking on resumptive-binding operators (if this does not in fact reduce to the ban on pied-piping). None of these questions arises with the data from the variety of other languages discussed below.

expect just the opposite judgments, parallel to the judgments on the resumptives themselves in (65).[15]

These data are made slightly less transparent by the fact that *whose* in English licenses an elliptical NP complement, as in (66):

(66)   Abby's car is parked in the driveway, but whose is parked on the lawn?

We can assume that this *whose* has the structure $[_{DP}$ whose $[_{NP}$ e]], without going into details of the NP-ellipsis involved (see Lobeck 1995 and Kester 1996). It is quite possible, in fact, that the sluicing in (64a) hides an elliptical NP, and does not in fact represent a true left-branch extraction at all (see Chapter 5 for the case of attributive adjective sluices). Even if this is the case, however, it does not affect the force of the comparison between (64) and (65): the fact that (64b) is impossible while (65a) is fine already destroys any biconditional relationship between the availability of a resumptive strategy and the possibility of sluicing. This pair shows that there are cases where a resumptive strategy is available to void a strong island, yet the corresponding sluice remains ungrammatical. In fact, a resumptive strategy utilizing a complex operator like *whose car* or, to make the parallel complete, $[_{DP}$ whose $[_{NP}$ e]], is itself ungrammatical:

(67)   a   *?[Whose car]₂ did the police say that finding it₂ took all morning?
        b   *I know that the police said they found Ben's car right away, but [whose e]₂ did they say that finding it₂ took all morning?

Thus no objection to the contrasts in (64) and (65) can be constructed on the basis of the elliptical form $[_{DP}$ whose $[_{NP}$ e]]. If such a form were all that is responsible for the grammaticality of (64a), the fact that the resumptive strategies in (67) are not possible would remain completely mysterious.

This discussion of the differences between *whose* and *who* in sluicing over genitives, and of the contrasts in (67), has raised another interesting point—namely, that complex operators cannot bind resumptive pronouns. For

---

[15] Similar facts were noted in Grosu (1981: 25), who gives the following example, in arguing against a copying (movement) analysis for 'non-standard relative clause constructions':

(i)   The man {who/*whom/*whose} I told you that his pants are always wet has been arrested by the police.

He proposes to account for this in relative clauses by analyzing 'who' in (i) not as a relative pronoun but as a base-generated complementizer. While such an account may work in relative clauses, it is unclear how it would extend to the parallel data in interrogatives discussed in the text.

example, resumptive-binding operators in English may not pied-pipe prepositional phrases—the resumptive-binding operator must be bare.[16]

(68)   a   (*For) which candidate$_2$ did they receive reports that more than 60 per cent of eligible voters were planning to vote for him$_2$?

        b   Lincoln was the candidate {who$_2$/Op$_2$ that/*for whom$_2$} they received reports that more than 60 per cent of eligible voters were planning to vote for him$_2$.

(69)   a   (*Against) what measure$_3$ did they elect a candidate who made it clear that she was against it$_3$?

        b   Proposition 209 was the measure {?which$_3$/Op$_3$ that/*against which$_3$} they elected a candidate who had made it clear that she was against it$_3$.

In contrast, sluicing with prepositional phrases, either with or without an island intervening, seems odd only to the general extent that pied-piping of prepositions in standard American English is odd across the board (see discussion in McDaniel *et al.* 1998). I mark such forms with ® to indicate that they are restricted to a formal register.

(70)   a   ®For which candidate were more than 60 per cent of eligible voters planning to vote?

        b   More than 60 per cent of eligible voters were planning to vote for one of the Red candidates, but I don't remember (®for) which.

        c   They received reports that more than 60 per cent of eligible voters were planning to vote for one of the Red candidates, but I don't remember (®for) which.

[16] The inability of resumptive-binding operators to pied-pipe (both specifier and P-pied-piping) seems to be a quite general property across languages; see discussion below and in Merchant (1999c). Indeed, complex operators of any type are disallowed with resumptives; since pied-piping in questions (and hence in sluicing) is quite limited, this will not be a point of divergence here, but it can be clearly seen in relative clauses, where, although pied-piping is more free, such pied-piping is impossible with resumptives:

(i)   a   the president, a biography of whom she wrote __ last year

      b   *the president, a biography of whom he's married to the professor who wrote (it) last year

This may be accounted for if all resumptives are in fact bound by null operators. Such null operators will have to be identified (à la *pro*; see Browning 1987 and Grosu 1994) but, when the wh-phrase with the identifying phi-features is embedded, the null operator will fail to be licensed. Exactly how this would extend to questions in English must be left open at this point.

We can avoid the vagaries of case and prepositional phrase pied-piping in English by turning our attention to languages with robust case systems such as German, Russian, Polish, Czech, and Greek.

4.3.2.2 *German*

German has four cases: nominative, accusative, dative, and genitive, which it marks in various ways throughout all nominal and adjectival categories, in particular on interrogative pronouns and the interrogative determiner, which will be relevant to us here for sluicing (thanks to H. Rott and especially S. Winkler for patient judgments on the many examples in this section). The paradigm for the first of these is given below (the paradigm for the determiner *welcher* 'which' is similar, though it also inflects for number and gender):

(71)   Declension of German interrogative pronoun *wer* 'who'
    nom   wer
    acc   wen
    dat   wem
    gen   wessen

Recall from §3.2.1 that the case of a sluiced wh-phrase in German, even across a strong island, must bear the case that its antecedent bears, if it has one. This fact led to the formulation of the first form-identity generalization, repeated here as (72):

(72)   *Form-identity generalization I: Case-matching*
    The sluiced wh-phrase must bear the case that its correlate bears.

The account that reduces sluicing to resumptivity makes a direct prediction from this generalization: the case of the resumptive-binding operator should match the case of the resumptive pronoun it binds. This, presumably, is because the ellipsis is sensitive to the equivalency between the (case of the) correlate in the source clause and the (case of the) resumptive pronoun in the target (elliptical) clause.

This prediction, however, is false:

(73)   *{Welchem Gefangenen₁ /wem₁}   will   sie jemanden finden,
     which.DAT prisoner   *who.DAT wants she someone   find*

    der ihm₁   geholfen hat?
    who him.DAT helped   has

    ('{Which prisoner/who} does she want to find someone who helped him?')

(74)   *{Welchen Gefangenen₂ /wen₂}   will   sie jemanden finden,
       which.ACC prisoner   who.ACC wants she someone   find

       der ihn₂   gesehen hat?
       who him.ACC seen   has

       ('{Which prisoner/who} does she want to find someone who saw
       him?')

In these examples, although the case of the resumptive-binding operator
matches the case of the resumptive pronoun, the sentences are ungrammatical.[17] Compare, on the other hand, the grammatical sluices from Chapter 3, (18)
and (19), repeated here:

(75)   Sie will   jemanden finden, der   einem   der   Gefangenen
       she wants someone find   who one.DAT of.the prisoners

       geholfen hat, aber ich weiß nicht, {*welcher
       helped   has but I   know not   which.NOM

       /*welchen /welchem}.
       which.ACC which.DAT

       'She wants to find someone who helped one of the prisoners, but I
       don't know which.'

(76)   Sie will   jemanden finden, der   einen   der   Gefangenen
       she wants someone find   who one.ACC of.the prisoners

       gesehen hat, aber ich weiß nicht, {*welcher
       seen   has but I   know not   which.NOM

       /welchen /*welchem}.
       which.ACC which.DAT

       'She wants to find someone who saw one of the prisoners, but I don't
       know which.'

[17] Similarly in relative clauses, though these are less important for our present purposes.
German has no null operator (i.e. 'that'-) relatives, allowing only the case-marked relative
pronoun (*der, das, die, die*, etc.). With these, no resumptive is possible:

   (i)   *Peter ist der Gefangene, dem₁   sie jemanden finden will, der ihm₁
         Peter is the prisoner   who.DAT she someone find wants who him.DAT

         geholfen hat.
         helped   has

         ('Peter is the prisoner that she wants to find someone who helped him.')

   (ii) *Peter ist der Gefangene, den₁   sie jemanden finden will, der ihn₁
         Peter is the prisoner   who.ACC she someone find wants who him.ACC

         gesehen hat.
         seen   has

         ('Peter is the prisoner that she wants to find someone who saw him.')

The contrasts between these two sets of data—the ungrammatical resumptive strategies in (73) and (74) on the one hand, and the grammatical sluices of (75) and (76) on the other—are an insurmountable problem for the resumptivity approach to sluicing.

The following data illustrate this restriction on case-matching on the resumptive-binding operator in adjunct islands as well.

(77)   a   *Mit welchem Lehrer$_i$ wird Anke sich ärgern, wenn
            with which.DAT teacher will Anke REFL upset   if

           Peter mit ihm$_i$,[18]   spricht?
           Peter with him.DAT speaks

       b   *Welchem Lehrer$_i$ wird Anke sich ärgern, wenn Peter mit
           which.DAT teacher will Anke REFL upset   if   Peter with

           ihm$_i$ spricht?
           him.DAT speaks

           ('Which teacher will Anke get upset if Peter talks to him?')

(78)   *Wen$_2$ glaubst du, daß Italien besser spielt, seitdem sie
       who.ACC think   you that Italy   better plays   since   they

       ihn$_2$ in der Mannschaft haben?
       him.ACC in the team   have

       ('Who do you think that Italy has been playing better since they have
       him on their team?')

---

[18] I use the regular dative pronoun *ihm* here, taken from the set of unreduced frontable pronouns in German. There is also a set of demonstrative ('deictic') pronouns in German, whose forms coincide with those of the relative operator, and which are known in the literature as 'd-pronouns'. Though these are often fronted, they can occur in situ, and in particular in contexts like the one discussed in the text, as in (i).

(i)   Anke wird sich ärgern, wenn Peter mit dem   spricht.
       Anke will REFL upset   if   Peter with demonstrative.DAT speaks

       'Anke will get upset, if Peter talks to that {one/guy}.'

Though these might be thought to make better resumptive elements than the simple pronoun series, this is not the case—(iia,b) have the same status as (77):

(ii)   a   *Welchem Lehrer$_i$ wird Anke sich ärgern, wenn Peter mit dem$_i$ spricht?
       b   *Mit welchem Lehrer$_i$ wird Anke sich ärgern, wenn Peter mit dem$_i$ spricht?

       ('Which teacher will Anke get upset if Peter talks to that {one/guy}?')

I have systematically tested d-pronouns as resumptives alongside their simple counterparts, though the data given in the text are limited to the latter. Because reporting all of these additional data would not add to the argument and would make for tiresome reading, I omit them here, since they pattern without exception with their simple pronominal brethren.

Again, though, parallel sluicing examples are possible (modulo the necessary PP in (79), as discussed in §3.2.2 above):

(79) Anke wird sich ärgern, wenn Peter mit einem der Lehrer
Anke will REFL upset if Peter with one.DAT of.the teachers
spricht, aber ich weiß nicht mehr, mit welchem.
speaks but I know no longer with which.DAT
'Anke will get upset if Peter talks to one of the teachers, but I don't remember which.'

(80) Er glaubt, daß Italien besser spielt, seitdem sie einen von
he thinks that Italy better plays since they one.ACC from
Ajax in der Mannschaft haben, aber ich weiß nicht
Ajax in the team have but I know no
mehr, wen.
longer who.ACC
'He thinks that Italy is playing better now that they have someone from Ajax on their team, but I don't remember who.'

These non-parallels show that an account that reduces sluicing out of islands to resumptivity fails: such a reduction cannot generate the grammatical case-matching wh-operators in the grammatical sluices. In fact, standard German seems not to possess the kind of resumptive strategy familiar from English ('intrusive' resumptives) at all, regardless of the case of the resumptive-binding operator. In particular, no 'default' case strategy appears to be available, taking nominative to be the default (as appears in hanging topic left dislocation structures, for example; see Vat 1981 and van Riemsdijk 1997, and cf. Maling and Sprouse's (1995) discussion). This is illustrated in the following examples, for relative clause islands in (81) and (82), and for adjunct islands in (83) and (84).

(81) *{Welcher Gefangene /wer} will sie jemanden finden,
which.NOM prisoner who.NOM wants she someone find
der ihm geholfen hat?
who him.DAT helped has
('{Which prisoner/who} does she want to find someone who helped him?')

(82) *{Welcher Gefangene /wer} will sie jemanden finden,
which.NOM prisoner who.NOM wants she someone find
der ihn gesehen hat?
who him.ACC seen has
('{Which prisoner/who} does she want to find someone who saw him?')

(83)   *{Welcher   Lehrer /wer}   wird Anke sich ärgern, wenn
         which.NOM teacher who.NOM will Anke REFL upset   if

       Peter mit ihm   spricht?
       Peter with him.DAT speaks

       ('{Which teacher/who} will Anke get upset if Peter talks to him?')

(84)   *Wer   glaubst du, daß Italien besser spielt, seitdem sie
         who.NOM think   you that Italy   better plays   since   they

       ihn   in der Mannschaft haben?
       him.ACC in the team   have

       ('Who do you think that Italy has been playing better since they got
       him on their team?')

For completeness, I should note that resumptivity is equally impossible if
the resumptive pronoun is nominative, making case-matching requirements
and 'default' case indistinguishable in any case:

(85)   *{Welcher   Gefangene /wer}   will   sie jemanden finden,
         which.NOM prisoner   who.NOM wants she someone   find

       dem er   geholfen hat?
       who he.NOM helped   has

       ('{Which prisoner₂/who₂} does she want to find someone who he₂
       helped?')

(86)   *Wer   glaubst du, daß Italien besser spielt, seitdem er
         who.NOM think   you that Italy   better plays   since   he.NOM

       in der Mannschaft ist?
       in the team   is

       ('Who do you think that Italy has been playing better since he's been
       on the team?')

Particularly striking is the ungrammaticality of the following examples,
where the resumptive-binding operator is the R-pronoun wh-operator *wo*
(here glossed 'what' for convenience), which has sometimes been argued not
to need any case at all (as an adverbial: see Trissler 1993 and Müller 1995). In
(87a) the (attempted) resumptive element is the [-wh] R-pronoun *da*, glossed
'that'.

(87)   a *Wo₁ glaubst du, wären   alle   glücklich, wenn Peter
             what think   you would.be everyone happy   if   Peter

da₁mit   aufhörte?
that-with stopped

('What do you think that everybody would be happy if Peter stopped doing it?')

b   *Wo₂ glaubst du, wären   alle   glücklich, wenn Peter
    what think   you would.be everyone happy   if   Peter

das₂ tun würde?
that do would

('What do you think that everybody would be happy if Peter would do it?')

Bayer 1996 uses the island-sensitivity of data like these to argue that the operator *wo* in fact orginates in the PP in examples like (87a),[19] a conclusion shared by J. Hoekstra (1995). Crucially, Bayer argues (citing Wiltschko 1993, contra Müller and Trissler), that the elements *wo* and *da* must have case. This seems a reasonable conclusion, and fits in with the picture of resumptivity in German that emerges above.[20]

In short, standard German, while possessing a familiar range of sluicing across strong islands, appears to have no resumptive strategy available at all. Obviously, any account that attempts to reduce the former to the latter is doomed to failure.

---

[19] He actually argues that the combinations *wo . . . da* are impossible, ruled out by a featural mismatch [+wh] *wo* vs. [-wh] *da*. While doubling is certainly better with *da . . . da*, and much rarer with *wo . . . da*, the latter is at least marginally possible, at least with the reduced *d(r)*; Oppenrieder (1991) gives several examples, as well as Trissler (1993: 265): *Wo hast du dich den ganzen Tag drauf gefreut?* (lit. 'What have you been looking forward to it the whole day?').

[20] Here the standard German *wo* (which is an XP) differs from the Swiss German *wo* found in relatives, which is a realization of C (see also Bayer 1984 for arguments for this from the Bavarian relativizer *wo*). This *wo* can co-occur with resumptives, as the following data, reported in Demirdache (1991: 21 (citing a 1988 unpublished MS by van Riemsdijk)), show:

(i)   de vrund wo ich immer mit em gang go suufle
      the friend that I always with him go go drink
      'the friend that I always go drinking with'

(ii) s auto wo du gsäit häsch das es sich de Peter nod chönti läischte
      the car that you said have that it REFL the Peter not could afford
      'the car that you said that Peter couldn't afford'

This strategy is also found in spoken American English, as in the following attested example:

(iii) I've had dreams where he's been in them. (TV interview, *Entertainment Tonight*, 1 Jan. 1999)

4.3.2.3 *Slavic*

The Slavic languages are another case in point. I begin with Russian, which, like German, possesses a rich case system, having six cases to German's four (thanks to S. Avrutin for judgments on the examples in this section). The paradigm for *kto* 'who' is given in (88); the paradigms for the interrogative *čto* 'what' and the interrogative determiner and relative pronoun *ktoroj* 'which' are similar.

(88)   Declension of Russian interrogative pronoun *kto* 'who'
>   *nom*   kto
>   *acc*   kogo
>   *dat*   komu
>   *gen*   kogo
>   *instr* kem
>   *loc*   kom

Like German, Russian allows for sluicing across strong islands, subject to the first form-identity generalization, given in (72). The third relevant point of similarity is that the operators in (88) cannot bind resumptive pronouns, as the following data illustrate.

(89)   a   *Kogo   ty dumaeš' italjancy stali   lušče posle togo
        who.ACC you think   Italians became better after that

        kak oni vklučili (ego) v komandu?
        how they put   him in team

    b   *Kto   ty dumaeš' italjancy stali   lušče posle togo
        who.NOM you think   Italians became better after that

        kak oni vklučili (ego) v komandu?
        how they put   him in team

        ('Who$_3$ do you think that the Italians became better since they put him$_3$ on the team?')

(90)   a   *Kto   ty dumaeš' italjancy stali   lušče posle togo
        who.NOM you think   Italians became better after that

        kak (on) v komandu?
        how he in team

        ('Who$_3$ do you think that the Italians became better now that he$_3$ is on the team?')

    b   *Čto   ty dumaeš' italjancy stali   lušče posle
        what.NOM/ACC you think   Italians became better after

togo kak oni uvideli (èto)?
that how they saw   it

('What₂ do you think that the Italians became better since they saw it₂?')

c *Kakuju p'esu   Ivan xočet vstretit' ženščinu kotoraja
   which play.ACC Ivan wants meet   woman   who

napisala (eë)?
wrote   it

d *Kakaja p'esa   Ivan xočet vstretit' ženščinu kotoraja
   which play.NOM Ivan wants meet   woman   who

napisala (eë)?
wrote   it

('What play₂ does Ivan want to meet the woman who wrote it₂?')

The same facts hold in Polish, though I will not illustrate them all (thanks to D. Mokrosinska for judgments). Like Russian, Polish has six cases, marks its wh-operators for these cases, allows sluicing across islands with case-matching, but does not permit case-marked wh-operators to function as resumptive-binding operators. Only the final property, of interest here, is illustrated:

(91) a *Która sztucę on chce rozmawiać z kobietą
         which play.ACC he wants to.talk   to woman

ktòra (ją) napisała?
who   it.ACC wrote

b *Która sztuca on chce rozmawiać z kobietą
   which play.NOM he wants to.talk   to woman

ktòra (ją) napisała?
who   it.ACC wrote

('What play₂ does he want to talk to the woman who wrote it₂?')

Like Polish and Russian, Czech also has six cases (thanks to A. Pilátová for judgments). Although case-matched sluices are required, as illustrated in (92), no resumptive strategy is possible, as shown by (93).

(92) Chce   mluvit s   tou ženou, která napsala nějakou
      wants.3sg to.talk with the woman who wrote   some.ACC

hru,   ale nemohu   si   vzpomenout,
play.ACC but NEG.can.1sg REFL recall

{kterou   /*ktera}.
which.ACC   which.NOM

'He wants to talk to the woman who wrote some play, but I can't remember which.'

(93)   *{Kterou   hru   /ktera   hra}   chce   mluvit s
        which.ACC play.ACC which.NOM play.NOM wants.3sg talk   with

tou ženou, která napsala (tu)?
the woman who   wrote   it.ACC

('Which play does he want to talk to the woman who wrote it?')

4.3.2.4 *Greek*

Greek provides yet further evidence along these lines (thanks to A. Giannaki-dou and Y. Agouraki for judgments). It has three cases of interest: nominative, accusative, and genitive (as well as a vocative, which does not occur on wh-operators for obvious reasons). These are marked on the interrogative pro-noun/determiner *pjos* 'who, which' as follows (I give only the masculine form here): nominative *pjos*, accusative *pjon*, genitive *pjanou* or *tinos*. None of these can occur as resumptive-binding operators—neither the case-matching (a) examples are possible, nor the (b) examples with the resumptive-binding operator in the 'default' nominative.

(94)   a   *Pjon$_1$ psaxnun enan giatro pu   na (ton$_1$) voithisi?
             who.ACC they.seek a   doctor that SUBJ him   helps

        b   *Pjos$_2$ psaxnun enan   giatro pu   na   (ton$_2$) voithisi?
             who.NOM they.seek a   doctor that SUBJ him   helps

             ('Who are they looking for a doctor who can help him?')

(95)   a   *{Pjanou$_1$ /tinos$_1$}   ipe i   astonomia oti to   na
             who.GEN   who.GEN said the police   that the SUBJ

             vroune   to aftokinito (tou$_1$) dhiirkese olo to   proi?
             they.find the car   his   took   all the morning

        b   *Pjos$_2$ ipe i   astonomia oti to   na   vroune   to
             who.NOM said the police   that to   na   they.find the

             aftokinito (tou$_2$) dhiirkese olo to proi?
             car   his   took   all the morning

             ('Who did the police say that finding his car took all morning?')

But of course sluices comparable to these do show case-matching effects in accordance with the generalization in (72):

(96) Psaxnun enan giatro pu na voithisi kapjon, alla dhen
they.seek a doctor that SUBJ helps someone.ACC but not

ksero {pjon /*pjos}.
I.know who.ACC who.NOM

'They're looking for a doctor to help someone, but I don't know who.'

(97) I astinomia ipe oti to na vroune to aftokinito enos
the police said that the SUBJ they.find the car of.one

apo tous ipoptous dhiirkese olo to proi, alla dhen
from the suspects took all the morning but not

thimame {pjanou /tinos /*pjos}.
I.remember who.GEN who.GEN who.NOM

'The police said that finding the car of one of the suspects took all morning, but I don't remember which one's.'

4.3.3 Conclusions

The collective force of the data from these languages, then, is to put a nail in the coffin of any hope that sluicing could be reduced to a resumptivity strategy in any sufficiently general way. If these languages simply lack resumptives altogether (as proposed, for example, for West Flemish and Dutch by J. Hoekstra 1995), then, by this token, they should lack sluicing, contrary to fact.

In particular, the simple picture of the table in (58) above based on apparent island sensitivity has proven to be inadequate; the full picture is represented by the following table:

(98) *Three types of Op-variable association*

	Association possible across a strong island?	Form-identity effects?
wh-Op and gap (trace)	No	Yes
wh-Op and resumptive pronoun	Yes	No
sluiced wh-Op and 'variable'	(Apparently) yes	Yes

This suffices to establish the main point of this section—namely, that sluicing (especially 'into islands') cannot in general be reduced to the binding of resumptive elements. (This conclusion is supported by the interpretation of the wh-phrase in sluicing—for example, the fact that functional readings are still available, which is not the case with resumptives; see Doron 1982 and Sells 1984.)

The data we have examined here, as well as additional data from ten other languages, discussed in Merchant (1999*b,c*), lead to the formulation of a very general principle, stated in (99):

(99)   *Case and resumptive-binding operator generalization*
         No resumptive-binding operator can be case-marked.

This follows directly if resumptive-binding operators are base-generated in SpecCP, and can never check their Case features. Note that this is meant to apply especially to operators that are separated from the resumptive pronouns they bind by an island: when no island intervenes, languages differ in whether the resumptive element is actually the spell-out of the trace of movement or not (see Aoun and Benmamoun 1998 for a recent discussion). The fact that (99) holds, at least for binding into islands, supports several strands of evidence that resumptive pronouns inside islands are *not* related to the operators that bind them by movement (*pace* Pesetsky 1998*a*, for example).

The most important point for the purposes of the investigation of sluicing is that the fact that (99) holds rules out using resumptivity as a possible fix for the apparent island-insensitivities documented in Chapter 3.

4.4 CHUNG *ET AL.* (1995): IP COPY, MERGER, AND SPROUTING

To deal with the problem of island insensitivity, Chung *et al.* 1995 (henceforth CLM) propose that the ellipsis in sluicing is not the result of PF-deletion. Instead, following Chao (1987), Lobeck (1995), and others, they posit an empty IP category in the syntax, as in (100), with the wh-XP base-generated in SpecCP:

(100)   Someone called, but I don't know [$_{CP}$ who [$_{IP}$ *e*]]   Spell-out

In order for interpretation to proceed at LF, however, this empty category must be replaced by a syntactic constituent of the appropriate type (namely an IP). This copying operation is a structural isomorphism condition, applied at LF, implemented by copying phrase-markers. As such, almost all the problems noted in Chapter 1 for such a structural isomorphism account will plague CLM's. The one exception is the case of non-overt correlates, for which they propose a novel LF structure-building operation they dub 'sprouting'; we will return to this below. Let us first examine how their account works on the example in (100).

In this example, the first IP can serve as the antecedent to the ellipsis, and can be copied in for *e* in the second clause, yielding (101) (I use bold face to indicate LF-copied material):

(101)   . . . but I don't know know [$_{CP}$ who [$_{IP}$ **someone called**]]

After IP-copy at LF

CLM follow Kamp (1981) and Heim (1982) in assuming that indefinites are not quantificational but rather simply provide a variable (with a descriptive content), which is bound by a separate operation of existential closure that can apply at different points in the structure, deriving the variable scope of indefinites.[21] With this view, the copied indefinite in (101) is free to be bound by the existential operator which binds the variable introduced by the wh-phrase in SpecCP (similarly an indefinite), a process CLM call 'merger'. They represent merger as co-superscripting at LF; the LF output of merger in (102a) will then yield the desired Karttunen-style interpretation for the embedded question in (102b) by standard techniques.

(102)   a . . . [$_{CP}$ who^x [$_{IP}$ **someone^x called**]]   After merger at LF
         b . . .$\lambda p[\exists x.[\textbf{person}(x,w_o) \wedge p(w_o) \wedge p = \lambda w.\textbf{call}(x,w)]]$

In doing this, CLM make the grammaticality of sluicing dependent on the availability of an unbound variable (usually supplied by an indefinite) in the copied IP. If no such variable can be found (for example, if no indefinite is present, or if the indefinite has been existentially closed within the IP, as is the case with narrow-scope indefinites, negative polarity items, etc.), sluicing will fail. CLM thus correctly predict that sluicing will always require a wide-scope reading for the correlate in its own clause, deriving scopal parallelism (since the wh-phrase itself has wide scope over its clause as well).

Since there is no movement of the sluiced wh-phrase, island constraints are not expected to hold. For CLM, the derivation of an example like (103) is straightforward. At Spell-out, the structure is that in (104a),[22] while, after IP-copy and merger, the structure is that given in (104b).

---

[21] The CLM account can also be cast in a theory using choice functions for the interpretation of indefinites, as shown in Reinhart (1995).

[22] The problem of the NP-ellipsis in the *which*-phrase will be ignored here and throughout—presumably similar mechanisms will be used to retrieve the appropriate content of the ellipsis as are used for resolution of 'one' anaphora. This is one aspect of merger that thus seems redundant, since it is clear that such interpretive mechanisms for NP-ellipsis are needed independently of sluicing.

(103)   They want to hire someone who speaks a Balkan language, but I don't
         remember which.

(104)   a   ... [$_{CP}$ which [$_{IP}$ *e*]]
         b   ... [$_{CP}$ which^x [$_{IP}$ **they want to hire someone who speaks [a
              Balkan language]^x**]]

Since sluicing resolved by merger is simply a species of variable-binding,
which is not sensitive to syntactic constraints on A′-movement, no island
sensitivity is expected. Instead, sluicing is sensitive to the scope of the correlate:
if this indefinite has a scope narrower than that required by sluicing, sluicing
will fail. The scopal parallelism enforced by sluicing can be seen in (103), for
example. The indefinite *a Balkan language* in the first clause can only have
scope over *want*, as in (105a), not inside it as in (105b); though the narrow scope
reading in (105b) is certainly available to this sentence in other contexts, when
the clause is meant to serve as the antecedent to the elliptical IP under sluicing,
this reading is excluded. This is because using the LF that generates the reading
in (105b) to resolve the IP-ellipsis in the second clause in (103) would lead to
vacuous quantification of the existential operator in SpecCP, since the necessary variable associated with *a Balkan language* has already been bound by
the lower ∃.

(105)   a   ∃y.[**Balkan-language**(y) ∧ **want**(they, ^[∃x.[**person**(x) ∧
              speak(x,y) ∧ **hire**(they,x)]])]
         b   **want**(they, ^[∃x.[**person**(x) ∧ ∃y.[**Balkan-language**(y) ∧
              speak(x,y) ∧ **hire**(they,x)]]])

When no overt correlate is available, however, some other operation
must be used to supply the bindee for the base-generated wh-phrase in
SpecCP. This is the operation of 'sprouting'. They hypothesize that sprouting
is an instantiation of the syntactic operation of FormChain, and subject
to island constraints, conceived of as constraints on A′-chain formation
(independent of movement, following Cinque 1990). Quite apart from
questions of the theoretical import of this approach, accounting for the
locality restrictions on implicit correlate sluices solely by imposing island
constraints on FormChain overgenerates. There are cases of licit A′-chains as in
(106a) and (107a), which nevertheless do not make good sluices, as in (106b)
and (107b).

(106)   a   When was no nurse on duty?
         b   *No nurse was on duty, but we don't know when.

(107) a When is a nurse rarely on duty?
 b *A nurse is rarely on duty—guess when!

For CLM, the ill-formedness of the (b) examples is unexpected, since, as attested by the (a) examples, the corresponding A′-chains are well formed. Instead, as pointed out by Albert (1993), the 'sprouting' cases are uniformly sensitive to selective islands (Sauerland 1996 makes a related point). This can be reduced again to the requirement for scopal parallelism between the implicit quantifier in the antecedent clause and the quantifier associated with the wh-phrase in the sluicing clause. In the first clause in (106b), for example, the implicitly bound temporal variable has narrow scope with respect to *no nurse*, as in (108a), and does not have the reading expressed in (108b). It is this second reading that would have to be available for the sluice in (106b) to be well formed.

(108) a $\neg\exists x[\mathbf{nurse}(x) \wedge \exists t[\mathbf{on\text{-}duty}(x, \text{at } t)]]$
 b $\exists t \neg \exists x[\mathbf{nurse}(x) \wedge \mathbf{on\text{-}duty}(x, \text{at } t)]$

Thus there is no reason to make an analytical distinction between 'merger' and 'sprouting' cases: both cases can profitably be analyzed as requiring an unbound variable in the antecedent. They differ only in that implicit existentials (whether arguments or adjuncts) always take narrow scope in their clause, and therefore cannot provide the open variable needed in sluicing when certain other operators intervene (as in selective islands). We can, therefore, assume that 'sprouting' as an operation can be dispensed with, and concentrate on examples with overt correlates, as these are the ones that *can* (apparently) violate islands.

When there is an overt correlate as in (103), for example, the possible sluices over that antecedent are constrained only by whether or not the indefinite in question can be bound at a level parallel to that needed for resolution of the ellipsis—that is, external to the IP needed for copying at LF. Since such wide-scoping behavior is found only with (certain kinds of) overt indefinites, island-insensitive sluicing will be found only with these.

While accounting for the scopal parallelism is a significant acheivement of CLM's system, it is not unique to theirs. As Romero (1997*a*) has shown, scopal parallelism also falls out from even the more general focus conditions; indeed, scopal parallelism between quantificational elements in elided or deaccented constituents and those in their antecedents is a quite general property, not limited to sluicing. See Prüst and Scha (1990*a*) and Fox (2000) for discussion relating to VP-ellipsis and Romero (1998) for discussion covering sluicing and IP-deaccenting as well. This being the case, the fact that merger derives scopal parallelism in sluicing is not a particularly overwhelming argument for it.

As CLM acknowledge, their view of the possible interactions between indefinites and wh-phrases leaves the ungrammaticality of examples like the following something of a mystery.

(109)   *Who^x did you see someone^x?

Since their system makes use of just such bindings, they cannot rule this out on principled grounds, suggesting instead that it derives from some additional property holding only of overt wh-chains.

Even if this problem could be overcome, the merger account runs into several other difficulties.

First, merger cannot handle cases where the descriptive content in the sluiced wh-phrase clashes with that of its correlate (the 'contrast'-sluices of §1.4):

(110)   a   She has five CATS, but I don't know how many DOGS.
         b   The channel was 15 feet wide, but I don't know how deep.
         c   Abby knew which of the MEN Peter had invited, but she didn't know which of the WOMEN.
         d   We know which streets are being re-paved, but not which avenues.
         e   Max has five Monets in his collection, and who knows how many van Goghs.
         f   There are nine women in the play, but I don't know how many men.
         g   I know how many women are in the play, but I don't know how many men.
         h   She's an absolute idiot: unaware of who she is, or where.

These are problematic for a merger account, since the variable bound by the wh-operator will incorrectly come to have two restrictions, contrary to intuition. The example in (110a), for example, certainly does not mean that I do not know how many animals she has that are both dogs and cats, since such animals do not exist.

Secondly, the range of possible correlates is not always as predicted (Romero 1997a especially documents a number of counterexamples). To hers, we can add the following, correlates that cannot be analyzed as Heimian indefinites:

(111)   a   More than three of the boys quit, but I can't remember {which/who}.

          b   I counted fewer than six sorts, but I couldn't tell which.

          c   Most of the boys passed, but I don't know exactly how many.

Even pronouns, under the right conditions, can be the correlates to a sluiced wh-phrase, as the following dialog in Dutch attests, where the copied IP would contain the pronoun *er* (Romero 1997*a* also gives some constructed examples in Spanish and Catalan, which for some reason are less felicitous in English, as she points out; see also Fukaya 1998: 11 n. 6 for discussion of the English data):

(112)   'Omdat je   er   nu   gewoon mee kan stoppen?'
          because you it now just   with can stop

          . . . 'Waarmee?' i.e. [Waarmee kan ik nu   gewoon stoppen?]
              what-with   what-with can I   now just   stop

          ' "Because you can call it quits now?"
          . . . "With what?" ' (Zwagerman 1991: 248)

Further, sometimes merger just gives the wrong restriction:

(113)   More than three books were missing, but we didn't know how many.

          a   = we didn't know how many books were missing.

          b   ?we didn't know how many more than three books were missing.

But the biggest problem looming for Chung *et al.*'s (1995) account is the fact that the form-identity effects documented in Chapter 3 remain mysterious. For CLM, it is crucial that the wh-phrase be base-generated in SpecCP—the lack of movement accounts for the lack of island effects. But the form-identity effects seemed to be diagnostic exactly of movement.

First, as concluded in §4.3, it is unclear how the case features of a wh-phrase base-generated in SpecCP could be checked; indeed, there is convincing evidence that such case features cannot be checked, accounting for the distribution of these operators in resumptive structures. But such base-generation is exactly what is posited in the CLM system.

Secondly, the P-stranding generalization comes as a surprise, since there is nothing in the operation of merger that would lead us to expect that 'bare' wh-phrases could not bind indefinites in prepositional phrases in German, for example, as they do in English. Instead, the facts of P-stranding are the best indication we have that wh-movement has occurred. A base-generation analysis like CLM's would have in effect to replicate the constraints on movement out of PPs in the definition of binding relevant to merger. Since merger is supposed to be an interpretative operation, this sensitivity to parochial morphosyntactic facts is surprising. Indeed, it is the *correlation* between P-stranding under overt movement and the form of wh-phrases found under sluicing that makes any such redefinition of merger suspect: since building this condition into merger and then parametrizing it across languages would be independent of the (different) constraint on movement, we might expect to find a random distribution across languages with respect to P-stranding under sluicing and under wh-movement in non-elliptical structures. But this is not what we find: instead, the two go together with a remarkably close fit.

Thus, despite its successes, Chung *et al.*'s (1995) account is beset by serious problems. For a syntactic point of view, the most serious of these is its inability to accommodate the form-identity effects of Chapter 3. One might wonder, however, if there might be some way to retain the advantages of this account over a pure PF-deletion approach. I turn to this question in the next section.

4.5 IP-COPY AND A′-CHAIN UNIFORMITY

In this section, I present a possible alternative to Chung *et al.*'s (1995) LF-copying approach that attempts to capture the form-identity effects, proposed in Merchant (2000*c*). This account, like CLM's, is based on the premise that the identity condition on ellipsis is a fundamentally structural one, implemented by copying of LF phrase-markers. After laying out the basics of the account, I point out its weaknesses, and show why ultimately it does not strike me as a viable alternative.

The data presented in §3.1, showing that islands are voided under sluicing, seemed to show that the PF-deletion approach to islands is inadequate. The preposition pied-piping facts of §3.2, however, showed that Chung *et al.*'s (1995) approach to LF-copying, in which the indefinite is interpreted as a Heimian variable, could not account for the grammatical sensitivities attested.

One difficulty with Chung *et al.*'s approach can be traced to their adoption of the Heimian approach to indefinites. For them, the correlate undergoes no movement, remaining in situ in the target clause, interpreted as an unbound variable. They assume only that the operation of existential closure must apply in the target clause before IP-copy, in order to account for the scope parallelism. It is this reliance on the Heimian theory, then, that precludes any account of the second form-identity generalization above.

Nevertheless, the island-insensitivity facts would seem to favor an LF-copy approach over a PF-deletion. How might one retain the advantages of the movement approach while continuing to make sluicing track the scope of indefinites? One possible answer is suggested by Bayer's (1996) results concerning P-stranding at LF.

On the basis of an investigation of focusing particles and wh-in-situ, Bayer claims that languages differ not only in whether or not they allow P-stranding under overt A'-movement, but also under covert A'-movement, at LF (contra Aoun 1985: 63–9 and references there). His conclusions are based on data like those in (114) and (115), from English and Greek[23] (he does not actually discuss Greek, but this language patterns in the relevant respects exactly like German, his language of illustration). By hypothesis, certain types of focusing particles, like *only*, on their non-scalar readings, require LF movement of their associates. In English, which allows P-stranding, these focus particles can associate directly with a DP inside a PP as in (114b), since the DP can licitly move out of the PP at LF. In Greek, on the other hand, which does not allow P-stranding, the focus particle must attach to the PP, as in (115a). The distribution of the focus particle follows, Bayer argues, if PPs in Greek are islands at LF as well; since the particle+XP must move at LF for scopal reasons, a P-stranding violation will result at LF, correctly ruling out (115b) (assuming for the moment, that overt and covert movement are subject to the same constraints in this domain).

(114)   a   I spoke only to Bill.   LF: [$_{PP}$ only to Bill]$_1$ I spoke t_1
        b   I spoke to only Bill.   LF: [$_{DP}$ only Bill]$_2$ I spoke [$_{PP}$ to t_2]

(115)   a   Milisa mono me   ton Bill. LF: [$_{PP}$ mono me ton Bill]$_1$
            I.spoke only   with the Bill   milisa t_1
            'I spoke only to Bill.'

        b   *Milisa me   mono ton Bill. LF: *[$_{DP}$ mono ton Bill]$_2$ milisa
            I.spoke with only   the Bill   [$_{PP}$ me t_2]
            ('I spoke to only Bill.')

We can use this result to solve the form-identity problem for an LF-copying approach if we give up the assumption that indefinites do not move at LF. Instead, we must adopt the view that indefinites, like other scope-bearing elements, are generalized quantifiers, and as such must move at LF for type-hygienic reasons. After the indefinite has been scoped, the resulting IP can be used to resolve the ellipsis in the sluice. For a simple case like (116a), this will result in the derivation whose parts are given in (116b,c).

[23] Thanks to A. Giannakidou and A. Roussou for judgments on the examples in this section.

(116)   a   Idha kapjon, alla dhen ksero   pjon.
              I.saw someone but not   I.know who

              'I saw someone, but I don't know who.'

         b   kapjon₁ [$_{IP_2}$ idha t_1]
              [[kapjon]] = $\lambda P[\exists x \textbf{ person}(x) \wedge P(x)]$
              [[[$_{IP_2}$ idha t_1]]] = $\lambda y[\textbf{saw}(I, y)]$

         c   [pjon]₁ [$_{IP_2}$ **idha** [$_{DP}$**t**]₁]

The indefinite *kapjon,* 'someone' in the antecedent clause raises at LF (by whatever version of QR is appropriate for indefinites), adjoining to IP, whose lower segment is labelled here IP₂. IP₂ can then be copied in for the missing IP under the sluiced *pjon* 'who', yielding the LF in (116c), after A′-chain formation, represented by the syntactic subscripts.

This approach will also derive the scopal parallelism of Chung *et al.'s* account. If the indefinite scopes too low—namely, inside the copied IP—the existential quantifier of the wh-phrase will vacuously quantify in its second argument (lambda-conversion will not be able to occur, hence the second conjunct will not be type ⟨t⟩ as required). Only if the indefinite scopes outside the IP used to resolve the ellipsis will an appropriate variable be made available. This purely mechanical approach to the syntactic resolution of the missing IP of course does not rule out other elements scoping out and providing a variable. Though in some cases, such IPs may indeed be able to provide a syntactically appropriate IP,[24] we might imagine that other factors may intervene to make the resulting interpretation infelicitous (namely, constraints on focus alternatives; see Romero 1997*a*). For the purposes of exploring this account, we will here be concerned only with the narrower requirement for the structural resolution of the ellipsis (Rooth's (1992*a*) 'redundancy relation 1'; Fiengo and May's (1994) 'reconstruction'). As a structural account, of course, this approach inherits all the problems discussed in Chapter 1; we might assume for the sake of argument, though, that these could be put aside.

We are now in a position to see how to derive the preposition-matching effect under sluicing. Again, the result is general, though I use Greek for exemplification. Indefinites, like other DPs, must pied-pipe a governing preposition at LF, if Bayer is correct. This entails that the derivation of a well-formed example like (117a) will proceed in the steps given in (117b) and (117c). First the QRed indefinite along with the preposition raises in the antecedent clause to its scope-taking position outside IP₂ as in (117b). The resulting IP₂ is then used to resolve the ellipsis as in (117c).

---

[24] Though even this is not obvious—according to Beghelli and Stowell (1997), non-indefinite quantifiers scope to hierarchically different, and lower, positions than wide-scope indefinites.

(117)   a   I   Anna milouse me   kapjon, alla dhen ksero
          the Anna spoke   *with someone but not*   *I.know*

          me   pjon.
          with who

          'Anna was speaking with someone, but I don't know with who.'

   b   [me kapjon]$_i$ [$_{IP_2}$ i Anna milouse [$_{PP}$ t_i]]

   c   [me pjon]$_i$ [$_{IP_2}$ **i Anna milouse** [$_{PP}$ t_i]]

In the representation in (117c), the base-generated wh-PP A′-binds a syntactic variable of the same category—namely, PP. What is needed now is to subject the resulting A′-chain to a condition that requires every link in the chain to share certain basic features, here category features. But, as we saw above, such uniformity among the links of an A′-chain is not limited to category features, but rather extends to case (and φ-features) as well. We can state this in the following condition on A′-chains:

(118)   **A′-chain uniformity**

      $\forall\alpha\forall\beta\,[\,[(\alpha \in C\,) \wedge (\beta \in C\,)] \rightarrow (F(\alpha) = F(\beta))\,]$

      where

   a C = the maximal co-indexed sequence $\langle\alpha_1, \ldots, \alpha_n\rangle$, such that α_1 is in an A′-position and α_n is a trace, *and*

   b $F(x) = \{F|F \text{ a feature of } x\}$ (let *feature* here range over at least category, case, and φ-features)

The constraint in (118) states that the features of every link in an A′-chain must match the features of every other link of the chain (including, of course, self-matching). This is simply one of many conceivable ways of stating the condition; we could have enforced uniformity to any arbitrarily chosen link of the chain (α_1 or α_n, for example) with the same results.

Let us now examine what goes wrong in an ill-formed example like (119).

(119)   *I   Anna milouse me   kapjon, alla dhen ksero   pjon.
          the Anna spoke   *with someone but not*   *I.know who*

          ('Anna spoke with someone, but I don't know who.')

There are two possible derivations to consider. First, parallel to its grammatical English counterpart, we might attempt to provide an appropriate IP for copying into the ellipsis site by scoping the correlate DP *kapjon* 'someone' directly, as in (120).

(120)   *[kapjon]$_1$ [$_{IP_2}$ i Anna milouse [$_{PP}$ me [$_{DP}$ t_1]]]

While the resulting IP$_2$ would be able to resolve the ellipsis, the movement of *kapjon* out of its governing PP is illicit, violating the PP island which holds at LF; cf. (115b) above.

   The second derivation to consider satisfies LF-movement constraints by pied-piping the PP as in (117b) above, yielding (121) as the LF for the antecedent clause.

(121)   [me kapjon]$_1$ [$_{IP_2}$ i Anna milouse [$_{PP}$ t_1]]

IP$_2$ is now the only structural antecedent available to resolve the ellipsis under *pjon*; copying this IP in yields (122).

(122)   [pjon]$_1$ [$_{IP_2}$ **i Anna milouse [$_{PP}$ t_1]**]

Pjon must form an A′-chain with a trace inside the IP; the only trace available here is [$_{PP}$ t_1], and the chain formed is ⟨[$_{DP}$ *pjon*], [$_{PP}$ t]⟩, as indicated by the indexing in (122). But this chain violates the A′-Chain Uniformity condition in (118)—since *pjon* is a DP but *t* is a PP, their category features do not match as required by (118).

   Since neither of the possible derivations for (119) is licit, the example is ruled out. This reasoning applies to all cases of correlates inside PPs. Note that this account places the ungrammaticality of such sluicing examples not on some violation concerning the sluiced wh-phrase itself—DP sluices can be perfectly well formed. Instead, the ungrammaticality arises through an inability of the grammar of Greek (or German, etc.) to provide an appropriate IP antecedent to resolve the ellipsis; since PPs are islands to LF-movement, no DP trace inside a PP can be provided as required by A′-Chain Uniformity.

   We have now seen how A′-Chain Uniformity, combined with Bayer's hypothesis, can derive the form-identity effects documented in Chapter 3. This account rests on treating indefinites as regular generalized quantifiers that reach their scopal positions at LF via some kind of movement operation. Since indefinites can take scope out of islands (see especially Farkas 1981), licit IP antecedents will be able to be generated to resolve the ellipsis in sluicing out of islands as well. Recall for Example (103), repeated here as (123).

(123)   They want to hire someone who speaks a Balkan language, but I don't
          remember which.

Fixing the scope of the indefinite *someone who . . .* under *want*, the first clause has two possible interpretations, corresponding to the scopal possibilities of the embedded indefinite *a Balkan language*. These two possibilities are represented by the LFs in (124a,b), and correspond in essentials to the formulas in (105a,b) discussed above.

(124) a [a Balkan language]$_1$ [$_{IP}$ they want to hire someone who speaks t_1]

  b [$_{IP_1}$ they want [[a Balkan language]$_1$ [$_{IP_2}$ to hire someone who speaks t_1]]]

Only the LF in (124a) provides an IP with an appropriate trace for the sluiced *which* in (123) to bind. In (124b), neither IP$_1$ nor IP$_2$ suffices: IP$_1$ does not contain an unbound trace (since t_1 is still bound within IP$_1$ by *[a Balkan language]$_1$*), while IP$_2$, if it yields an appropriate interpretation at all, does not generate the desired meaning for (123) (in particular, it loses the subordination of *someone who . . . to want*).

As in the non-island cases, the present LF-copying approach correctly derives the observed scopal parallelism. Since the mechanisms for resolving sluicing inside islands as in (123) are the same as discussed for simple cases like (116a), the account of the form-identity effects will persist.

But this account of the form-identity effects 'across' islands requires that indefinites must move at LF out of islands. This is a very dubious conclusion, one that many have sought to avoid for very good reasons (see especially Winter 1997 and Reinhart 1997, whose best argument comes from Eddy Ruys's observation that distributed readings of plural indefinites are indeed island restricted).

In other words, this account leaves it a mystery why only indefinites can move out of islands, and leaves it up to a yet-unspecified theory of islands to allow just such invisible scopal movements. Again, the prospects for a successful development of such a theory strike me as slim. But once such a syntactic approach to the wide-scoping of indefinites is abandoned, we are left with the paradox that has plagued us throughout this chapter.

A further serious objection is that the effects of the uniformity condition in (118) are usually derived from the definition of the operation Move; Move copies an element whole, and does not alter any of its features, thereby ensuring chain uniformity. In other words, such uniformity should be a *derived* property of chains, not a *stipulated* one. Note that such a uniformity condition is actually quite problematic: it has to include a non-trivial exception clause stipulating that it *not* apply to A′-chains terminating in resumptive pronouns inside islands; operators that bind resumptive pronouns have a number of properties that distinguish them from the operators in sluicing, as we saw above in §4.3, one of which is that they *cannot* bear case or occur inside a PP, just the opposite of the effect of imposing a uniformity condition like (118). At this point, I see no way to make the necessary distinction in a non-stipulative way.

Finally, it is up for debate whether the fundamental assumption that this account relies on—namely Bayer's analysis of LF-movement based on the distribution of focus particles—is correct (see Büring and Hartmann 1999 for a competing approach to the restrictions on the placement of these particles). As Bayer himself notes, there are languages with overt P-stranding that seem not to have P-stranding under LF movement, and languages that lack overt P-stranding but which for him must have P-stranding at LF, at least as diagnosed by association with focus particles. This kind of discrepancy between overt and covert movements is not found for the form-identity effects under sluicing.

4.6 SUMMARY

This chapter has examined five different proposals for the structure of sluices. I have shown that each proposal suffers from serious empirical shortcomings, mostly related to a failure to be able to deal with the core data laid out in Chapter 3. This is an important result, because it will force us into accepting what might otherwise be considered a too radical departure from conventional wisdom. In demonstrating the inadequacies of the sometimes quite plausible seeming analyses above, I have eliminated the competitors for what is to come, and have drastically limited our theoretical options, laying the groundwork for the proposals in the following chapter. We have, in effect, been painted into a corner, a corner into which we might otherwise have been loath to go. It is the purpose of the next chapter to explore the nature of this corner, and to bring to light what its properties require us to believe about the nature of islands.

5

Deletio redux

We are now in a position of apparent contradiction: how can the form-identity effects be reconciled with the island-insensitivity? In this chapter, I will propose a two-pronged approach to this conundrum: some islands are indeed PF-phenonema, with the deviancy repaired by PF-deletion, while other cases of apparent insensitivity to islands are illusory on closer inspection.

At the core of my analysis rest two ideas: first, that the condition on identity that deletion is sensitive to is a fundamentally semantic one, not a structural one, as proposed in Chapter 1, and second, that ellipsis in sluicing is the result of PF-deletion.

This combination of semantic conditions with deletion will strike some as odd: generally, the proponents of deletion have been identified with those who claim that the conditions on deletion are indeed structural, while the semantic theories of conditioning have tended to leave the syntactic side underinvestigated. But there is no inherent incompatibility in the claim that I am making here. Rather, it simply states that while ellipsis sites contain syntactic structure (unpronounced due to PF-operations of deletion, triggered by the E feature of Chapter 2), the fact that they *are* ellipsis sites is due to semantic considerations (ideally also implemented by means of E, as proposed in Chapter 2).

This is not to say, of course, that the syntactic structure of the ellipsis site and its antecedent play no role: since the meaning of an expression is a function of its LF structural properties, it will be constrained in certain direct ways by the structure. The novel claim here is simply that there is no *additional*

LF-structural identity condition that must be met, contrary to widespread assumptions in the literature (represented by, but not limited to, Rooth 1992*a*, Fiengo and May 1994, and Romero 1998). In fact, as we have seen especially for sluicing, it is far from clear how such an LF identity condition could ever be met. The researchers who have used such conditions (most prominently, Fiengo and May 1994, who claim that an LF-identity condition is *all* that is needed) have concentrated on VP-ellipsis, where relevant evidence is very hard to come by ('vehicle change' effects being the most prominent). Sluicing, on the other hand, provides more direct evidence bearing on the question: assuming an LF-identity condition forces one to posit otherwise unmotivated structural ambiguities at LF, or to introduce LF-repair operations whose sole purpose is to satisfy the condition. Instead, as shown in Chapter 1, nothing is lost in giving up the LF-identity condition in favor of a purely semantic condition.

The second idea is in one sense a rehabilitation of the earliest approaches to ellipsis, and in particular of Ross's (1969) approach to sluicing. But the tradition behind this idea should not be mistaken for wide acceptance. Instead, such approaches have fallen into disfavor since the early 1980s, and many researchers assume—tacitly or explicitly—that ellipsis does not involve deletion. As we have seen, there are two main competitors to the deletion approach: first, that in the overt syntax there is a null pronominal-like element, and that this empty category is replaced at LF by syntactic structure copied from some appropriate linguistic antecedent. Proponents of this approach include Williams (1977) (under some interpretations), Chao (1987), Lobeck (1991, 1995), and possibly Fiengo and May (1994). The second competitor is the purely 'semantic' approach, such as that advocated by Dalrymple *et al.* (1991), Jacobson (1992), Hardt (1993, 1999), and Shieber *et al.* (1996). Although these authors are not uniformly explicit in what they do assume the syntax of elliptical constructions to be, it is clear that they conceive of ellipsis as something that should be handled primarily by abstract semantic mechanisms, where syntax internal to the ellipsis site has no role to play.

The difficulty these approaches face is accounting for the form-identity facts. The preposition-stranding generalization especially seems mysterious under these approaches, if P-stranding is a syntactic property, an assumption to which I know of no serious challenge. On the deletion approach, of course, nothing special need be said to account for the data: whatever theory one adopts for P-stranding (assuming this theory to be morpho-syntactic) will account for the distribution of pied-piping attested under sluicing as under non-elliptical wh-movement. This is the main motivation for pursuing the deletion account of ellipsis, and one that has not before received attention.

Given its importance, let us briefly review the relevant data from the P-stranding generalization, forming the major empirical problem faced by non-deletion accounts. This is illustrated in German with the following examples, repeated from §3.2.

(1)   German
       a   Anna hat mit jemandem gesprochen, aber ich weiß nicht,
            Anna has with someone   spoken   but I know not

            *(mit) wem.
            with who

            'Anna spoke with someone, but I don't know (with) who.'

       b   *Wem hat sie mit gesprochen?
            who has she with spoken

            ('Who did she speak with?')

The proposed deletion analysis handles such data straightforwardly, and predicts the attested correlation. Under this analysis, the structure of the sluice in (1a) will be that in (2):

(2)   . . . ich weiß nicht, [mit wem]₂ [Anna t₂ gesprochen hat]
           I   know not   with who   Anna   spoken   has

The A′-movement in the syntax feeds the PF representation, where the IP is subject to deletion as in (2). Whatever accounts for overt data like (1b) will apply without modification to the sluicing data. Since we have seen that the LF-copying alternatives fail on this domain, this is the strongest argument for deletion.[1]

This leaves us with the problem of the apparent island-insensitivity of the wh-movement that feeds deletion in sluicing. In this chapter, I propose that this problem has two subparts, requiring two different kinds of solution, depending on the kind of island involved. The following is a list of the islands that will concern us here (see Postal 1996 for a fuller list: most

---

[1] One consequence for the proper analysis of prepositional pied-piping can be drawn from this set of facts, however. Whatever is going wrong in the derivation that gives us (1b) cannot be caused simply by a constraint that applies at PF. Otherwise, it too would be repaired by ellipsis, and the correlation with sluicing, under any possible approach to ellipsis, would be completely mysterious. This rules out assimilating canonical pied-piping to the kind of generalized pied-piping proposed in Chomsky (1995).

of the others he gives will fall into my class C; see also the papers in Goodluck
and Rochemont 1992 and Culicover and McNally 1998):

(3)   Island classes
        A   1 selective ('weak') islands
        B   2 left-branches
             3 COMP-trace effects
             4 derived positions (topicalizations, subjects)
             5 coordinate structures
                 (i)   extraction of conjuncts
        C   (ii) extraction out of conjuncts
             6 complex noun phrases
                 (i)   relative clauses
                 (ii) sentential complements to head nouns
             7 adjuncts

As indicated by the labels A, B, and C in (3), I am (provisionally) making a
division among these islands into three sorts. The first, class A, consists of the
so-called weak islands; a superior name for these is 'selective', which I will adopt
here. I assume that Rizzi (1990, 1994) and Manzini (1998) are incorrect in
attempting to give a structural explanation for these; instead, I will follow
Szabolcsi and Zwarts (1993), Rullmann (1995), Kuno and Takami (1997),
Honcoop (1998), and others in analyzing these as essentially semantic/prag-
matic. The interaction of sluicing and selective islands has been investigated by
Albert (1993), Sauerland (1996), Romero (1998), and Merchant (2000*c*); since
the consensus is that these islands are not in any case syntactic, the 'island'
effects we see under sluicing will not provide us with a testing ground for the
deletion question. I will thus leave them out of consideration for the moment,
returning to them only briefly in §5.4.
    The second class, B, consists of islands whose effects I will argue are indeed
undone by PF-deletion (with the possible exception of 5(i), which seems to
have both LF and PF effects). I will show in §5.1 that this result is compatible
with the amelioration effect sluicing has on these.
    The final class, C, is distinguished by having one thing in common: all
of them involve extraction out of a propositional domain. I will show that
wh-movement out of these islands under sluicing is only illusory, and that
in fact the embedded propositional domain is being used to satisfy the identity
condition on ellipsis. The interpretative effects that led earlier researchers to
assume that an island was present can be accounted for using independently
needed mechanisms of modal subordination and E-type anaphora. Thus the

sluicing facts will not be useful in determining whether these islands are PF phenomena or not (indeed, other evidence suggests that they are not).[2]

The conclusion, then, is that a deletion approach to sluicing is compatible with the apparent immunity to islands that sluicing confers.

5.1 PF-ISLANDS

5.1.1 Left-Branch Extractions

I will begin with one of the least commonly discussed of the islands, but one for which I believe the evidence is strongest that its effects arise at PF—the left-branch condition (LBC). I start by examining a range of previously discussed cases, and introducing a crucial new one that shows that the LBC is not obeyed by sluicing. I then outline the PF-theory of the LBC developed in Kennedy and Merchant (2000*a*), discussing the evidence that the LBC's effects should be located at PF, and show that this theory also makes the correct predictions for a number of novel facts from Dutch. I then demonstrate how the range of intricate facts can be accounted for under the theory developed in Chapter 1. I conclude with a set of new facts that show that illicit subextractions from attributive DegPs that do not follow from the PF-account given here continue to give rise to ungrammaticality under sluicing, indicating that sluicing is not a universal panacea to islands.

Ross's (1967) Left Branch Condition, stated in (4), conflated a number of different illicit extractions, which Grosu (1974) showed to cover more ground than is desirable.

(4)   *The Left Branch Condition* (Ross 1967 (4.181) (1986: 127))
       No NP which is the leftmost constituent of a larger NP can be reordered out of this NP by a transformational rule.

Since Grosu's work, the LBC is generally taken to govern the ill-formedness of extractions like those in (5)–(7); see especially the detailed investigation in Corver (1990). In (5), we have the attempted extraction of a prenominal genitive, an amount phrase, and the degree word.

[2] One kind of island that I do not examine in detail is wh-islands: these pattern with the other propositional islands, though certain complications make the data with them more involved, and less perspicuous for explaining the theory developed here.

(5)   a   *Whose did he see [___ car]?
        b   *How many inches is the monitor [___ wide]?
        c   *How is the monitor [___ wide]?

The examples in (6) represent extractions of attributive adjectival and amount modifiers of singular count nouns, plural count nouns, mass nouns, and predicate nominals.

(6)   a   *How detailed does he want [a ___ list]?
        b   *How {expensive/fast/big} did she buy [a ___ car]?
        c   *How thorough does she write [___ reports]?
        d   *How expensive did he buy [___ {toys/jewelry}]?
        e   *How smart is your brother [a ___ doctor]?
        f   *How good is she [a ___ carpenter]?
        g   *How many did she buy [___ cars]?
        h   *How much did she find [___ gold]?

The cases in (7) exemplify one kind of attempted subextraction from a left branch.

(7)   a   *How does he want [a [___ detailed] list]?
        b   *How did she buy [a [___ {expensive/fast/big}] car]?
        c   *How does she write [___thorough reports]?
        d   *How did he buy [___expensive {toys/jewelry}]?
        e   *How is your brother [a [___ smart] doctor]?
        f   *How is she [a [___ good] carpenter]?
        g   *How did she buy [___ many cars]?
        h   *How did she find [___ much gold]?

These contrast with their (mostly) grammatical pied-piping counterparts, given in (8) and (9); the one exception here is attributive pied-piping of plurals and mass nouns, in the examples in (9c,d) (a mysterious restriction that has never been satisfactorily explained: see Bolinger 1972 for discussion, and note 5 below).

(8)   a   Whose car did he see?
        b   How many inches wide is the monitor?
        c   How wide is the monitor?

(9)   a   How detailed a list does he want?
        b   How {expensive/fast/big} a car did she buy?

c *How thorough reports does she write?
d *How expensive {toys/jewelry} did he buy?
e How smart a doctor is your brother?
f How good a carpenter is she?
g How many cars did she buy?
h How much gold did she find?

Whether sluicing obeys the LBC is a question that has been touched on only briefly in the literature. L. Levin (1982: 605) contrasts the following examples (her (43)), building on Ross (1969: 277 (74)):

(10)   a *I know he must be proud of it, but I don't know how.
        b I know he must be proud of it, but I don't know how proud (of it).

These authors conclude on the basis of these examples that sluicing obeys the left-branch constraint. They do note, however, that examples like (11) are grammatical (specifically, those like (11a): cf. Ross (1969: 284 n. 21) and L. Levin (1982: 653 n. 10)).

(11)   a Someone's car is parked on the lawn—find out whose!
        b I should buy some peppers for the dinner, but I don't know how many.
        c She found gold, but won't say how much.

But these, as they also point out, are irrelevant to the point at hand, since English independently licenses NP-ellipsis in these contexts; cf. *Bob's (car) is on the lawn* and *Several (peppers) were missing*. There is, therefore, no way to be sure that examples like (11) represent left-branch extractions, and are not simply derived from well-formed questions such as *Whose is parked on the lawn?* and *How many should I buy?*, exhibiting NP-ellipsis.[3]

To Ross's example of *how*-extraction from a predicate adjective we can add the following examples, with extraction of *how* from attributive position within a noun phrase as well.

(12)   a *He wants a detailed list, but I don't know how.
        b *She bought an {expensive/fast/big} car, but I don't know how.
        c *She writes thorough reports, and wait till you see how!

---

[3] The fact that *how many* licenses NP-ellipsis, but *how AP* does not also argues against the common assumption that the former should be assimilated to the latter. This conclusion is reached on independent grounds in Kennedy and Merchant (2000*a*) as well.

d   *He bought expensive {toys/jewelry}, but he wouldn't say how.
e   *Your brother is a smart doctor, but it's not clear how.
f   *She is a good carpenter, but it's not clear how.
g   *She bought many cars but it's not clear how.
h   *She found much gold, but she wouldn't say how.

These examples might be taken, as Ross and Levin take them, to show that sluicing does obey the LBC. This conclusion, however, would be premature. Corver (1990) has convincingly argued that the kind of deviance found in (4c) and (6) is due simply to the restrictions on head movement. He argues for the extended adjectival projection proposed in Abney (1987), given in (13):

(13)

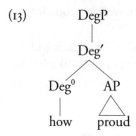

Given this phrase structure, the relevant examples only illustrate the impossibility of extracting a head from these environments:

(14)   *[$_{Deg^0}$ How]$_2$ is he [$_{DegP}$ [$_{Deg^0}$ t_2] [$_{AP}$ proud of it]]?

Since *how* is a head, not a phrase, there is no expectation that it should be able to move into SpecCP. Independently, as pointed out by Lobeck (1995: 62 ff.), Deg^0 heads do not license the ellipsis of their complements. This rules out a structure like (15), which would be parallel to the kind of ellipsis we saw above after *whose* and *how many*.

(15)   *[$_{DegP}$ how [$_{AP}$ *e*]]

This being the case, we do not expect sluices like those in (10a) or (12) to be well formed, in accordance with the data. Note that this result is expected both under the movement analysis advocated here (since a head cannot move into a specifier), and under a base-generation analysis (since a head cannot be generated in a specifier, and since *how* does not permit its complement to be null).

This discussion thus dispatches the kinds of left-branch violations found in examples (5) and (7). But this is not the whole story.

5.1.1.1 *LBC Violations under Sluicing*

What has gone unnoticed in the literature is that it is possible to find examples of true LBC-violating sluices, corresponding to the examples in (6). These are given in (16).

(16) a He wants a detailed list, but I don't know how detailed.
  b She bought an {expensive/fast/big} car, but I don't know how {expensive/fast/big}.
  c She writes thorough reports, and wait till you see how thorough!
  d He bought expensive {toys/jewelry}, but he wouldn't say how expensive.
  e Your brother is a smart doctor, but it's not clear how smart.
  f She is a good carpenter, but it's not clear how good.

Note that these cannot be reduced to any kind of DP-internal ellipsis, since English does not license ellipses of the necessary kind:[4]

(17) a *He turned in a sketchy list, but we need a detailed.
  b *A thorough report is better than a hasty.
  c *Not only is she a carpenter, she's a good!

What I propose for these examples is that we are indeed dealing with an extraction of an attributive DegP from within a DP. I propose the following structure for these (where extraction of the DegP proceeds through the specifier of the highest projection in the nominal extended projection):

(18) I don't know [$_{DegP}$ how detailed]$_i$ ~~he wants [t_i' [a t_i list]]~~.

In other words, deletion at PF does indeed repair the otherwise ungrammatical extraction of attributive adjectival phrases.[5] This claim is based not solely on the above sluicing data, however: it is supported by independent facts from VP-ellipsis, comparative deletion, stripping, and gapping in several

---

[4] Though see Sag (1976a: 334) for some problematic examples, taken from Harris (1965, 1968) and Quirk *et al.* (1972: 590).

[5] The grammaticality of the examples in (16c,d), with plurals and mass nouns, shows that the restriction noted for the examples in (9c,d) on pied-piping of these that is found in non-elliptical DegP questions must likewise have its explanation at PF, since the sluiced versions have the same status as their singular, pied-piping, counterparts. Presumably the restriction is located in the kinds of features that are realizable in Kennedy and Merchant's F^0 head (2000a); cf. the restrictions noted by Bennis *et al.* (1998) for a similar domain of data.

languages, as discussed in Kennedy and Merchant (2000*a*). In that work, we develop an approach to the LBC based on properties of the lexicons of individual languages. We propose that a LBC effect arises when a language lacks a particular functional head in the nominal extended projection that can support a [+wh] feature specification. Our proposal is based on facts like those in (19).

(19)   a   Abby wrote a more interesting novel than Ben {wrote, did, Ø}.
        b   *Abby wrote a more interesting novel than Ben wrote [a __ novel].

The examples in (19a) contrast with that in (19b) in having some kind of constituent missing. Take the nearest relative to sluicing, the VP-ellipsis case. Under a deletion approach to VP-ellipsis, the *than*-clause in the example in (19a) will have the structure in (20).

(20)   . . . than [$_{DegP}$ *Op*]$_2$ Ben did [~~write [*t*$_2$ʹ [a *t*$_2$ novel]]~~].

In this example, the degree operator has extracted from the DP *a novel*. In spite of this, the elided version is grammatical, unlike its non-elided counterpart in (19b). In Kennedy and Merchant (2000*a*), we show that the status of examples like (19b) correlates with the status of left-branch wh-extraction in questions in English, Greek, Bulgarian, Polish, and Czech. We link this to a difference in the functional vocabulary of the respective languages. The hypothesis is that in Polish and Czech, where examples like (19b) as well as attributive questions of the form *How lengthy did she write a novel?* are well formed, the lexicon possesses an element that can realize the [+wh] feature on the highest nominal projection, through whose specifier the extraction proceeds. English, Bulgarian, and Greek,[6] on the other hand, which rule out examples like (19b) as well as LBC-violating question formation, lack this element (though English does possess a [−wh] form of the head in question, realized as *of* in variants like *I can't believe he made that long of a film* and *How long of a film did you see?*). In these languages, then, the only way to eliminate the unpronounceable feature combination on this head is either to pied-pipe the entire nominal (leading to the

---

[6] Although I do not have the relevant data from Bulgarian, the same seems to hold for Greek, at least, which allows sluices of the form in (i).

(i)   Proselavan enan psilo   andra,   alla dhen ksero   poso psilo.
       they.hired a.ACC tall.ACC man.ACC but not   I.know how   tall.ACC

       'They hired a tall man, but I don't know how tall.'

Unfortunately, the well-formedness of this example is not particularly revealing, since Greek, unlike English, licenses NP ellipsis after attributive adjectives:

usual *How lengthy a novel did she write?*) or to apply an ellipsis operation to delete a constituent containing the offending structure.

Applying this to the sluicing case above, we have the structure in (21):

(21)   I don't know [$_{DegP}$ how detailed]$_i$ ~~he wants~~ [$_{FP}$ ~~t_i' F^0$_{[+wh]}$~~ ~~[a t_i list]~~].

Extraction of the [+wh] DegP through the highest specifier of the extended projection of the DP (here labelled FP) requires a [+wh] feature on the head F^0, via spec-head agreement. The usual way to check such a feature is to pied-pipe FP, checking the feature in SpecCP, and this option is certainly available in general (see (47) below). What is interesting here, though, is that ellipsis, implemented as deletion at PF, provides a second option for producing a grammatical output. The deletion of the IP containing the unrealizable F^0[+wh], like checking the feature in SpecCP, saves this structure from a PF-crash.

The grammaticality of sluices like (16), then, is accounted for under this analysis. Since the unrealizable [+wh] head remains inside the deletion site (here, the IP), the LBC, construed as a lexical gap in English, will not be triggered.

5.1.1.2 *Dutch (and Some German)*

A similar state of affairs seems to hold in Dutch, with one interesting complication that I return to below. Dutch, like English, does not allow attributive adjectival questions to strand their host DPs (see Corver 1990: ch.10 for extensive discussion):

(22)   *Hoe lang(e)   hebben zij [__ een man] aangesteld?
       how tall(AGR) have   they a   man hired
       ('How tall a man did they hire?')

The possibilities for pied-piping with attributive adjectives are somewhat different from those found in English, though. Standard Dutch in fact lacks any pied-piping strategy, yielding the following paradigm (thanks especially to H. Hendriks for discussion).

(ii)   Enas   eksipnos   andras   ine protimeros apo   enan   psilo.
       a.NOM   smart.NOM   man.NOM   is better   than   a.ACC   tall.ACC

       'A smart man is better than a tall one.'

See Giannakidou and Merchant (1996) and Giannakidou and Stavrou (1999) for discussion of NP-ellipsis in Greek. So *poso psilo* in (i) could simply have the structure [$_{DP}$ poso psilo [$_{NP}$ ~~andra~~]].

(23) a *Hoe lang(e) een man hebben zij   aangesteld?
         how tall(AGR) a   man have   they hired

      b *Hoe lang(e) man hebben zij   aangesteld?
         how tall(AGR) man have   they hired

      c *Hoe een lang(e) man hebben zij   aangesteld?
         how a   tall(AGR) man have   they hired

      d *Hoe'n lang man hebben zij   aangesteld?
         how a tall man have   they hired

      e *Hoe'n lange   man hebben zij   aangesteld?
         how a tall-AGR man have   they hired

         ('How tall a man did they hire?')

      f Een HOE lange   man hebben zij   aangesteld? [echoic]
         a   how   tall-AGR man have   they hired
         'A HOW tall man did they hire?'

In some southern dialects, however, (23e) is grammatical (the data presented here are from the Brabant dialect; thanks to N. Corver, I. Mulders, and R. van Rooy for discussion):

(24)   Hoe'n lange man hebben zij aangesteld?   [Brabants]

This strategy is found in standard Dutch with *zo* 'so', though not with *hoe* 'how', and compares with similar constructions found in German and English (cf. Corver 1990: 319 for the middle Dutch equivalent); (25a,b) both translate as (25c).

(25) a Zo'n lange   man heb ik nooit eerder gezien!
         so a tall-AGR man have I never before seen
                                                  [standard Dutch]

      b So einen großen Mann hab ich nie   zuvor gesehen!
         so a   tall   man have I never before seen
                                                  [German]

      c I've never seen such a tall man before.
      d I've never seen so tall a man before.

Southern Dutch shares with standard Dutch the pattern of acceptability for sluicing attributive adjectives shown in (26a–c) and (26e) (one of the five standard Dutch speakers I consulted rejected even (26a): I have nothing to say about his judgment here). They differ with respect to the possibility of pied-piping in (26d), as above.

(26)　Zij　hebben　een　lange　　man　aangesteld,　maar　ik　weet　niet
　　　　they　have　　a　　tall-AGR　man　hired　　　　　but　I　know　not

　　a　hoe　lang.
　　　　how　tall

　　b　*hoe　lange.
　　　　how　tall-AGR

　　c　*hoe　lang　man.
　　　　how　tall　man

　　d　hoe'n　lange　　(man)　[*in standard Dutch; cf. (23e)]
　　　　how a　tall-AGR　man

　　　　'They hired a tall man, but I don't know how tall (a man).'

　　e　A:　Zij　hebben　een　twee　meter　lange　　man　aangesteld.
　　　　　　they　have　　a　　two　　meter　tall-AGR　man　hired

　　　　　　'They hired a two meter tall man.'

　　　　B:　Een　HOE　lange　　(man)?　[echoic]
　　　　　　a　　how　　tall-AGR　man

　　　　　　'A HOW tall man?'

The grammaticality of (26d,e) is expected, given the well-formedness of the corresponding movement structures in (24) and (23f), with concomitant nominal ellipsis, as discussed in Kester (1996). The surprising fact in (26) is the grammaticality of the bare form of the adjective in (26a), given the ungrammaticality of any of the apparent possible sources for it ((23a,b) or (22)); this contrasts with the equally surprising ungrammaticality of the inflected form of the adjective in (26b): the inflected form of the adjective is required in attributive position with the non-neuter nouns in this environment (*een lang*(e) man* a tall-AGR man).

The bare form of the adjective that shows up in (26a) is, in a sense, unexpected. An adjective modifying a masculine or feminine noun in this attributive use would normally appear in the agreeing form *lange* (the neuter form is *lang* in this environment, and hence is uninformative for our purposes). The bare form *lang* that appears in (26a) is the form of the adjective that appears in predicative uses in Dutch, where no inflection is found, whether questioned or not:

(27)　a　De　man　is　lang(*e).
　　　　　the　man　is　tall(AGR)

　　　　　'The man is tall.'

　　b　*Hoe　lange　　is　de　man?
　　　　　how　tall-AGR　is　the　man

　　　　　('How tall is the man?')

That is, (26a) might seem to be related not to any of the attributive adjectival questions in (23) or (22), but rather to the predicate question in (28):

(28)   Hoe lang is de man (die zij   hebben aangesteld)?
        how tall is the man who they have   hired

        'How tall is the man who they hired?'

Despite this resemblance, I believe that pursuing the similarity between the adjectival sluice in (26a) and the adjectival predicate question in (28) is fruitless.[7] To be able to reduce (26a) to (28), we would have to weaken considerably the propositions that we allow to count as satisfying the focus condition (for example, we'd have to ignore the contribution of the definite determiner), and it is not clear that such a weakening could be accomplished without pulling the focus condition's teeth, and making it unable to render any predictions at all. There is thus little reason, besides the superficial lack of inflection, for pursuing this route.

So where does this leave us? It seems to point to the conclusion that the inflection on attributive adjectives in Dutch is itself the result of feature realization principles operative at PF. Since I would maintain that the derivation of a Dutch sluice like (26a) is parallel to its English counterpart, involving a left-branch extraction from within the DP, the reason that the otherwise attested inflectional *-e* does not appear indicates that the agreement feature on DegP, like other strong features (see Kester 1996), can be deleted at PF. This deletion voids the necessity for realization, even though the host of the realization itself (the adjective) survives the deletion. The remaining question is why the inflection must be absent. One possible answer to this question is to invoke principles of economy of representation: the fewer features one can get away with at PF, the better. Another possibility is that the inflectional schwa is itself structurally pre-

---

[7] Greek supports this decision. Greek requires agreement on adjectives even in predicative position, as in (i) (as above, I gloss only the relevant agreement, that for case; the adjective also declines for number and gender, irrelevant here).

(i)   Poso psilos   ine o   andras?
        how tall.NOM is the.NOM man.NOM

        'How tall is the man?'

If 'attributive adjectival' sluices were actually some form of predicative adjective, we would expect, contrary to fact, that the case on the Greek sluiced adjective would be nominative as in (ii), not the accusative we saw in note 6 above.

(ii)   *Proselavan enan psilo   andra,   alla dhen ksero   poso psilos.
        they.hired a.ACC tall.ACC man.ACC but not I.know how tall.NOM

        ('They hired a tall man, but I don't know how tall.')

sent within the DP (perhaps the head of an adjectival agreement projection in the DP, as proposed by Cinque 1993 and defended for Dutch by Kester 1996): under such a scenario, the moved DegP will simply have stranded its inflection inside the deleted DP. In any case, it is not crucial here how one might implement this intuition; it is crucial only to show that the lack of inflection does not necessarily force us into assuming that the DegP in attributive adjectival sluices does not actually originate in an attributive position. Instead, this lack may open an interesting window into the nature of the inflection itself.

I conclude with some brief remarks on the equivalent German data I have collected. Standard German patterns with standard Dutch in disallowing any sort of inversion of the DegP and the article within the DP; pied-piping is possible only under the echoic reading. (Thanks to S. Winkler for discussion of these examples.)

(29) a *Wie groß(en) einen Center haben sie eingestellt?
          how tall(AGR) a   center have they hired
          ('How tall a center did they hire?')

      b Einen WIE großen Center haben sie eingestellt? [echoic]
         a-AGR how tall-AGR center have they hired
         'They hired a HOW tall center?'

Although judgments are not entirely stable on the relevant sluicing examples (some speakers do not find (30) particularly bad), it does seem that sluicing is fairly degraded, with or without inflection.

(30) ??Sie haben einen großen Center eingestellt, aber ich weiß
        they have a-AGR tall-AGR center hired   but I   know
        nicht, wie groß(en).
        not   how tall(-AGR)
        ('They hired a tall center, but I don't know how tall.)
        (cf. ... aber ich weiß nicht, einen WIE großen. [echoic]
               but I know not   a-AGR how   tall-AGR)

If this judgment stands up to further testing, we are left with the question of why this should be so. One possibility is that German lacks the relevant functional projection (Kennedy and Merchant's FP) entirely, or that some property independent of DegP movement *per se* is ruling out the relevant structures (one option that comes to mind is that certain functional specifiers are unavailable, for whatever reason, as intermediate landing sites for extraction: compare the degradation found even in long wh-movement through intermediate SpecCPs).

Although more cross-linguistic data are needed, I will take the English and Dutch facts as indicating that left-branch violations can in principle be repaired by PF-deletion operations, subject to further language-particular restrictions in some cases.

5.1.1.3 *Attributive Adjectival Sluices and the Focus Conditions*

Still, this does not mean that all kinds of attributive adjectival sluicing will be possible. Strikingly, the kinds of sluicing we have been examining are impossible when there is no overt adjectival correlate in the antecedent clause, as the following data show (cf. (16) above).

(31) a *He wants a list, but I don't know how detailed.
      b *She bought a car, but I don't know how {expensive/fast/big}.
      c *She writes reports, and wait till you see how thorough!
      d *He bought {toys/jewelry}, but he wouldn't say how expensive.
      e *Your brother is a doctor, but it's not clear how smart.
      f *She is a carpenter, but it's not clear how good.

These seem as bad as their overt left-branch extracted counterparts in (6) above. But, given my argumentation so far, in particular the fact that I have argued that the LBC is a PF-phenomenon, the fact that overt extraction is bad can bear no relation to the ill-formedness of the examples in (31). So how do the examples in (31) differ from their well-formed counterparts in (16)? The answer does not lie in the syntax internal to the ellipsis site: in both cases, we are dealing with a licit left-branch extraction. The difference, clearly, is in the potential antecedents made available to resolve the ellipsis.

The contrast between (31) and (16) might seem to support the 'merger' approach proposed by Chung *et al.* (1995). Presumably merger would be able to rescue the impossible left-branch 'extraction', yielding the derivation in (32), where (32b) is the result of IP-copy and merger of the DegPs. (Although this requires a redefinition of merger to allow it to apply to predicates over degrees, assuming that adjectives are not Heimian indefinites, let us suppose that this modification would be innocuous.)

(32) a He wants a detailed list, but I don't know how detailed [$_{IP}$ *e*].
                                                                    S-structure
      b ... [how detailed]^x [$_{IP}$ he wants a [detailed]^x list]   LF

But this approach makes a strong prediction. Since merger is insensitive to islands (here, the LBC), we would expect such 'adjectival merger' to void all islands. This is not the case, as the following examples show.

(33)   a   *She'll be angry if he buys an expensive car, but I don't know how expensive. (vs. It doesn't matter how expensive.[8])
      b   *He got stressed because his boss wants a detailed list, but I don't know how detailed.
      c   *She met a guy who bought an {expensive/fast/big} car, but I don't know how {expensive/fast/big}.
      d   *They want to hire someone who writes thorough reports, and wait till you see how thorough!
      e   *She wants to meet a guy who buys old paintings, but she didn't say how old.

It is not simply that long extraction of DegPs under sluicing is impossible, as (34) shows.

(34)   He said he needed a detailed list, but wait till you hear how detailed!

The contrast between (16) and (33) indicates that the structural solution of merger to the problem of the ill-formedness of the examples in (31) is inadequate. Instead, the desired contrast falls out from the Focus condition. Recall the definitions given in Chapter 1, repeated here:

(35)   GIVENness   (Schwarzschild 1999)
An expression E counts as GIVEN iff E has a salient antecedent A and, modulo ∃-type shifting, A entails F-clo(E).

(36)   **S-Focus condition on IP-ellipsis** (Schwarzschildian version, modified slightly)
An IP α can be deleted or deaccented only if α is contained in a constituent that is GIVEN.

---

[8] The nature of such concessive sluices, which differ in striking ways from their non-concessive counterparts with respect to the ability to sluice over a range of otherwise inaccessible correlates (cf. *She won't talk to anyone—it doesn't matter who!* etc.), must remain a topic for future research. Clearly, though, they indicate that not only structural considerations play a role: the semantics of the embedding predicate must also be taken into account. See Haspelmath (1997: 140–1) for some discussion.

(37)   **e-GIVENness**
       An expression E counts as e-GIVEN iff E has a salient antecedent A and,
       modulo ∃-type shifting,
       (i)   A entails F-clo(E), and
       (ii) E entails F-clo(A)

(38)   **Focus condition on IP-ellipsis**
       An IP α can be deleted only if α is e-GIVEN.

Let us see how these apply to the pair in (39).

(39)   a   She bought a big car, but I don't know how big.
       b   *She bought a car, but I don't know how big.

First, note that the pronunciation of (39a) is that in (40a), not (40b).

(40)   a   She bought a big car, but I don't know HOW big.
       b   *She bought a big car, but I don't know how BIG.

Let us assume for the moment that this indicates that the structure we are
dealing with is that in (41).

(41)   She bought a big car, but I don't know [HOW$_F$ big] [~~she bought [⧸ a~~
       ~~[⧸ car]]~~]

   There are two interrelated questions to be addressed at this point, just as in
the other cases of sluicing examined in Chapter 1. The first has to do with the
application of the general focus condition based on (35), while the second
concerns the application of the narrower condition in (38). Let us begin with
the former.
   In order for the F-marking in (41) to be licit, there must be an alternative to
the question in the CP of the form *(know) whether she bought a big car* (see the
discussion in Chapter 1); in other words, the common ground must contain an
antecedent A that entails the following proposition, derived by replacing
HOW$_F$ in (41) by a variable over quantifiers over degrees—here represented as
Q—and existentially quantifying:

(42)   ∃ Q [I know [Q (λd.she bought a d-big car)]]

And, since *knowing that she bought a big car* entails *knowing whether she bought
a big car*, the S-Focus condition is satisfied.

The second, more narrow condition is satisfied in the following way. The first sentence in (39a) introduces the proposition in (43a), while the F-closure of the deleted IP, assuming reconstuction of the content of the DegP (see Grosu and Landman 1998), will be that in (43b).

(43) a $IP_A' = \exists d[\text{she bought a d-big car}]$
      b $\text{F-clo}(IP_E) = \exists d[\text{she bought a d-big car}]$

Since, in this case, it is the degree quantifier that is focused, the reverse relations will hold as well, namely $IP_E' = \text{F-clo}(IP_A)$. The Focus condition on ellipsis in (38) is, therefore, satisfied.

In (39b), on the other hand, the antecedent IP does not supply the requisite proposition (since $IP_A' = $ *she bought a car*) and the Focus condition is, therefore, not satisfied.

The conclusion, then, is that the constrasts observed here in (16) and (31)[9] are the result of the Focus conditions, not of special operations on ellipsis, nor—and this is the most important point of this section—of syntactic constraints on extraction.

These considerations also militate against an alternative weighed above, that of reducing apparent attributive adjectival sluices like those in (16) to predicative uses of the DegP, as in (44):

(44) She bought a car, but I don't know how big it is.

First, the intonation of (44) is that given in (45a), not (45b):

(45) a . . . but I don't know how BIG it is.
      b * . . . but I don't know HOW big it is.

Deletion of 'it is' in (44), then, would not yield the desired intonation for the grammatical sluices; compare (40). In fact, deletion of 'it is' would incorrectly

---

[9] The contrast in (40), on the other hand, is a result of a different constraint, Schwarzschild's (1999) AvoidF:

(i) **AvoidF**
     F-mark as little as possible, without violating GIVENness.

The example in (40a) satisfies AvoidF, since knowing that she bought a big car does not entail knowing how big a car she bought. The example in (40b), on the other hand, violates AvoidF (even assuming a secondary, perhaps inaudible focus on *how* to satisfy GIVENness). F-marking on BIG in (40b) is superfluous, since the preceding sentence provides an antecedent that entails (42). No violation of GIVENness would be incurred by not F-marking BIG in (40b), since (42) includes the specification that the degrees quantified over are degrees of size (bigness).

generate examples like (31). The attested intonation for (44), the result of the F-marking in (46), illustrates the effects of the general GIVENness condition of Chapter 1: since *big* is not GIVEN, *big* in (44) must be F-marked (or the DegP containing it, if the default accent will fall on the embedded AP):

(46)   She bought a car, but I don't know how [BIG]$_F$ it is.

A final point with respect to DegP sluices is made by the following examples.

(47)   a   He wants a list, but I don't know how detailed a list.
        b   She bought a car, but I don't know how {expensive/fast/big} a car.
        c   ?Your brother is a doctor, but it's not clear how smart a doctor.
        d   She is a carpenter, but it's not clear how good a carpenter.

In these examples, the DP containing the DegP has been pied-piped, yielding the pattern of grammaticality seen above in (9). The fact that these are better than the examples in (31) shows again that the attributive adjectival sluices above are not the result of any hitherto undiscovered process of NP-ellipsis in SpecCP or the like. These differ exactly in requiring a different kind of antecedent to satisfy the Focus condition. Note that the pronunciation again gives us our clue, differing yet again from those seen in the sluices above:

(48)   a   She bought a car, but I don't know how BIG a car.
        b   *She bought a car, but I don't know HOW big a car.
        c   *She bought a car, but I don't know how big a CAR.

The ungrammaticality of (48b,c) is expected: in (48b), *big* is not GIVEN, in violation of GIVENness focus condition, while in (48c), *car* is GIVEN, in violation of AvoidF (see note 9). The grammaticality of (48a) reflects an F-marking parallel to the F-marking in (46) (modulo the possibility that it is the DegP and not simply the AP that is F-marked):

(49)   She bought a car, but I don't know [how [BIG]$_F$ a car]$_2$ [~~she bought t$_2$~~]

Here, both *she bought* and *a car* are given, while *big* is not. Note that, even though *a car* is given, it cannot be deleted (such a deletion would result in the ungrammatical (31b)). This shows that GIVENness is a necessary but not sufficient condition for ellipsis, as argued in Chapter 1: independent restrictions (here, the lack of NP-ellipsis after DegPs in English) play a role as well.

However, there is some reason to believe that the representation in (49) underrepresents the amount of F-marking in the structure. In fact, it seems that the F-marking must percolate up to the DP (cf. Drubig's 1994 notion of Focus-phrase) when an F-marked attributive DegP is extracted (though not necessarily when just the Deg head is F-marked), yielding (50) (I omit the F-marking presumably necessary on the intervening DegP as well):

(50)   She bought a car, but I don't know [how [BIG]$_F$ a car]$_{F_2}$ [~~she bought t~~$_1$]

This seems necessary in light of the contrast between (40a) and (40b). This percolation, together with the natural assumption that a constituent that is F-marked cannot be deleted at PF, rules out the structure in (51), which would otherwise satisfy the Focus condition:

(51)   *She bought a car, but I don't know [$_{DegP}$ how [BIG]$_F$]$_1$ [$_{IP}$ ~~she bought~~ ~~[t$_1'$ a t$_1$ car]$_F$~~]

Note that this is not to say that F-marking on attributive adjectives percolates in general to the DP: this is wrong. For our purposes it is only necessary that the F-marking on DegP, interpreted as a feature, necessarily be shared with the DP when DegP is extracted (via spec-head agreement, as was discussed for the [wh] feature). Though the systems involved are relatively intricate and not fully understood, it seems that there is nothing inherently incompatible between the present account and what is known about F-marking in DegPs.

There might be, however, another way of explaining the impossibility of (51) that eschews positing F-percolation onto DP. Since BIG is F-marked, we can ignore its reconstruction in what follows (cf. the discussion of the contrast sluices in Chapter 1). Nevertheless, we cannot ignore the extraction of the DegP, since this leaves a DP-internal trace. Therefore, the ∃-closure and F-closure of IP$_E$ will be that in (52), which binds the empty variable over gradable adjective meanings that contrast with *big*.

(52)   IP$_E'$ = F-clo(IP$_E$) = ∃P[she bought a P-car]

But one could argue that IP$_A$ does not supply such an entailment. Schwarzschild (1999) notes that his notion of 'contextual entailment' is purposely vague, since it is an open question just what kinds of propositions can be included in the common ground in such a way as to satisfy GIVENness. In this case, though it is possible to reason from the asserted existence of a car to the existence of a size for that car, this second proposition cannot be included in the common ground to satisfy GIVENness: note the oddity of the sequence #*She ate an apple before she ate a GREEN apple* (cf. *She ate an APPLE before she ate a BANANA*). Unfortunately, a number of other questions arise at this point, most prominently the fact that adding a focused, contrasting DegP in the antecedent does not improve matters (*She bought an OLD car, but I don't know how BIG*), leaving the purely syntactic, structural account of (51) (relying as it does on feature passing under wh-extraction) less problematic in this case.

Given the complexities of the semantics of degree phrases (see Kennedy 1999), and the limited work on the focus in them, it is not surprising that some questions remain open. But it seems clear that the resolution of these particular questions should be compatible with the approach to ellipsis taken here, and fit in with an account of degree questions in sluicing—in particular, with an account that posits LBC-violating extraction under deletion.

5.1.1.4 *Left-Branch Subextractions under Sluicing*

A final set of facts indicates that not all left-branch extractions are alike.[10] Corver (1990: ch. 9) notes that subextractions of certain measure phrases from DegPs are possible when the DegP is in predicative position (roughly, those 'measure phrases' that are full gradable DegPs themselves: see Corver 1990: 237 for discussion). He presents several arguments that the extracted DegP orginates within the predicate, and is not simply a VP-adverbial (they can pied-pipe the predicate, for example, unlike VP-adverbs).

(53) a   How badly was he [__ short of funds]?
      b   How easily are these drugs [__ obtainable]?
      c   How well was she [__ prepared]?
      d   How badly was he [__ burned]?

(54) Hoe zwaar   is hij [__ behaard]?   [Dutch]
      how heavily is he   haired

      (lit.) 'How heavily haired is he?' [i.e. How hairy is he?]

These measure phrases are not extractable from attributive position (Corver 1990: ch. 10):

(55) a   *How badly did you meet [a guy [__ short of funds]]?
      b   *How easily did he take [[__ obtainable] drugs]?
      c   *How well have you examined [a [__ prepared] student]?
      d   *How badly did they treat [a [__ burned] man]?

---

[10] Thanks to N. Corver for discussion of this section, and for the Dutch data.

(56) *Hoe zwaar heeft zij een [[__ behaarde] man] ontmoet? [Dutch]
      how heavily has she a haired man met

(lit. 'How heavily haired a man did she meet?')

As Corver shows, these differences must be related to the different structural properties of DegPs occuring in predicate position (where they are properly governed, allowing extraction) versus subextractions from attributive positions. The system proposed in Kennedy and Merchant (2000a) to deal with extraction *of* attributive DegPs does not extend to extraction *from* attributive DegPs. There is at least no a priori expectation that the mechanisms of deletion will be able to repair the deviancies in (55)–(56).

In fact, extraction under sluicing tracks exactly the possibilities for overt extraction found in (53)–(54) versus (55)–(56). The data in (57) and (58) show, for English and Dutch respectively, that sluicing over these measure phrases orginating in predicate DegPs is possible. Their structure is parallel to their overt counterparts in (53)–(54), and is given in (59). (I collapse examples with overt DegP correlates in the antecedent and those without, without indicating intonation in the remnant wh-phrase; these intontations pattern exactly as we saw above, depending on whether the DegP is given or not.)

(57) a He was (badly) short of funds, but I didn't know how badly.
      b These drugs are (easily) obtainable, but you don't want to hear how easily.
      c She was (well) prepared—guess how well!
      d He was (badly) burned, but I don't know how badly.

(58) Hij is (zwaar) behaard, maar ik weet niet hoe zwaar.   [Dutch]
      he is heavily haired but I know not how heavily

(lit.) 'He is (heavily) haired, but I don't know how heavily.'

(59) He was badly burned, but I don't know HOW$_F$ badly [~~he was~~ $_{[DegP}$ t_2 ~~burned]~~].

Crucially, the sluicing counterparts to (55)–(56) are not improved:

(60) a *She met a guy (badly) short of funds, but I didn't know how badly.
      b *He takes (easily) obtainable drugs, but I don't know how easily.
      c *They examined a (well)-prepared student—guess how well!
      d *They treated a (badly) burned man, but I don't know how badly.

(61)   *Zij heeft een behaarde man ontmoet, maar ik weet niet
        she has   a   haired   man met   but I know not
        hoe zwaar.   [Dutch]
        how heavily
        ('She met a haired man, but I don't know how heavily.')

These contrasts indicate that what is ruling out subextractions like (55)–(56) is not the same mechanism that rules out extractions of attributive DegPs in general. Under the account proposed in Kennedy and Merchant (2000*a*), this means that the DegP itself does not project an FP through whose specifier the measure phrase might extract. This seems to be a quite sustainable conclusion: there is no expectation that the FP posited as part of the extended nominal projection would appear in the adjectival projection as well, nor is there the empirical evidence for it (*How easily of obtainable a drug is it?* is impossible, but compare *How obtainable of a drug is it?*).

Of course, when the measure phrase pied-pipes its attributive host DegP, the resulting sluice is grammatical, since the stranded offending F⁰ is deleted:

(62)   a   He wants a longer list, but I don't know how much *(longer).
        b   . . . [$_{DegP}$ how much longer]$_2$ [he wants [$_{FP}$ t_2 ´F⁰ [a t_2 list]]]

Finally, those measure phrases that resist extraction in English require the preposition *by* (see Corver 1990: 220 for some brief discussion, and Abney 1987):

(63)   a   ??(By) how {much/many cm} was he too tall to be an astronaut?
        b   ??(By) how {much/many pounds} was the packet too heavy to be shipped airmail?

Exactly the same pattern is found under sluicing:

(64)   a   He was too tall to be an astronaut, but I don't know ??(by) how {much/ many cm}.
        b   The packet is too heavy to be shipped airmail, but I don't know ??(by) how {much/many pounds}.

These contrasts are important because they indicate that some constraints on extraction—specifically, those responsible for ruling out left-branch *sub*-extractions—do not operate at PF, and hence are not affected by the deletion we have in sluicing; the contrasts also show that sluicing is not some universal panacea to islands, as Ross and others thought. On the other hand, the fact that regular attributive DegP extraction is possible under sluicing argues in favor of the hypothesis that this left-branch effect should indeed be located at PF.

5.1.1.5 *Summary*

This section has discussed a wide range of novel facts from sluicing of attributive adjectives, and has shown that the fact that sluicing is possible with these is compatible with the deletion approach to ellipsis. Extraction of attributive adjectives is ruled out, in some languages, at PF; deletion repairs the resulting structure in the way indicated above. The further intricacies in the data were seen to follow from the Focus condition on ellipsis introduced in Chapter 1, in conjunction with the more general GIVENness condition of Schwarzschild (1999).

5.1.2 COMP-Trace Effects

The second class of extraction restrictions that I will examine are the COMP-trace effects, of which the *that*-trace effect is the most well-known representative. The distribution of these was first noted by Perlmutter (1971) for eleven languages (though he restricts his attention to the complementizers *that* and *for*, the effects are seen also with wh-complementizers such as *if* and *whether* (as noted in Hudson 1972), as well as with *like*), and have been discussed extensively since (Langendoen 1970; Bresnan 1972; Chomsky and Lasnik 1977; Culicover 1992; Déprez 1994; Browning 1996; Roussou 1998). Some typical examples are given in (65).

(65)   a   Which senator is it probable (*that) will resign?
        b   *Who did Sally ask {if/whether} was going to fail?
        c   What did Bob want (*for) to be over the door?
        d   How many students does it seem (*like) will pass?

Although opinions have been divided, it seems likely that the COMP-trace effect, though not particularly well understood, is essentially a PF-phenomenon, as concluded by Perlmutter (1971), Chomsky and Lasnik (1977), Aoun *et al.* (1987), E. Hoekstra (1992), and Culicover (1992) (this last on the basis of adverb amelioration effects discovered by Bresnan 1977*b*; see also Honegger 1996). This has also been suggested recently in de Chene (1995) on the basis of the amelioration found when the subject trace is in a constituent targeted by right node raising:

(66) a ? That's the meeting which$_i$ I've been thinking that, and Jim's been
      saying that, t_i could well be canceled.   (de Chene 1995: 3 (11a))

   b ? Which gangster did the DA claim that, though he couldn't
      absolutely prove, [__ was responsible for the killing]?

De Chene (1995) also gives evidence that the ECP approach is insufficient from
cases of subject/object asymmetries in extraction from clausal complements to
prepositions, which I will not repeat here. Although he does not propose an
analysis, he does conclude that 'the place to look for a new approach to such
[COMP-trace] effects is . . . on the PF-side of the grammar' (p. 4).

   McCloskey (1997) pursues this idea as well, on the basis of the distribution
of subject resumptive pronouns in Swedish. He notes, following Engdahl
(1984), that a certain class of resumptive pronouns in Swedish is limited to,
essentially, what would be COMP-trace environments; an example is given in
(67). If the COMP-trace effect were an ECP effect, the phonological insertion
of such pronouns should not affect the grammaticality of the examples, with
the extraction itself being impossible. If, on the other hand, the COMP-trace
effect is a problem at PF, the 'spelling-out' of the trace as a pronoun could be
expected to satisfy the constraint.

(67)   Vilket ord$_3$ visste ingen hur {det$_3$/*t_3}
        which word knew no-one how it

        stavas?   (Engdahl 1984: 13 (12))
        is.spelled

        'Which word did no one know how it is spelled?'

   Exactly how this effect should be captured is tangential to the current enterprise, and I can do little more than speculate on the general nature the ultimate
analysis of the COMP-trace effect should take. We could presumably formal-
ize this effect in terms of what kinds of features a given language can realize on
its C^{0}s, as was done in the previous section for F^0 in left-branch effects. This line
of analysis would hopefully be able to incorporate the varieties of government
approaches to the COMP-trace effect while continuing to locate the result at
the syntax–lexicon interface (at lexical insertion, in a late-insertion model).
Thus, although there is evidence that we are dealing with a 'phonological'
effect, this does not mean that we must retreat to surface filters as proposed
originally by Perlmutter (1971) (and taken up in Chomsky and Lasnik 1977).
In any case, a fully worked-out theory of this effect is not crucial to us here—
relevant for us is the prediction that any such analysis makes. If the COMP-
trace effect is 'phonological' in the relevant sense, then we do not expect to
find its effects under sluicing. The following examples demonstrate that this
prediction is correct:

(68)   It's probable that a certain senator will resign, but which [~~it's probable that *t* will resign~~] is still a secret.

(69)   Sally asked if somebody was going to fail Syntax One, but I can't remember who [~~Sally asked if *t* was going to fail Syntax One~~] (Chung *et al.* 1995: (86a))

Chung *et al.* used these facts to argue for an LF-copying approach to sluicing, since they assimilated the COMP-trace effect to an ECP violation. But if the COMP-trace effect is located at PF, not at LF, as the other evidence suggests, then the lack of COMP-trace effects under sluicing no longer contradicts the deletion account, as Perlmutter (1971: 112) points out: 'If . . . [an example like (65)] is ungrammatical because of a surface . . . constraint, subsequent application of Sluicing can produce a grammatical sentence. And it does.'

5.1.3 Derived-Position Islands: Topicalizations and Subjects

The third class of islands I will call 'derived-position' islands, and include in English topicalized constituents and subjects (as well as right-dislocated or extraposed constituents). (Here I will concentrate on non-sentential subjects only, though my analysis extends directly to sentential subjects as well, assuming that they originate inside the VP; we will return to them in §5.3.2, however.) Examples are given in (70): extraction is prohibited from a topicalized XP (a), from the subject of a passive or unaccusative (b), and from the subject of a transitive or unergative (c).

(70)   a   *Which Marx brother did she say that [a biography of __], she refused to read?
       b   *Which Marx brother did she say that [a biography of __] {is going to be published/will appear} this year?
       c   *Which Marx brother did she say that [a biographer of __] {interviewed her/worked for her}?

The corresponding sluices, however, are grammatical:

(71)   a   A: A biography of one of the Marx brothers, she refused to read.
           B: Which one?
       b   A biography of one of the Marx brothers {is going to be published/will appear} this year—guess which!

   c A biographer of one of the Marx brothers {interviewed her/worked for her}, but I don't remember which.

I group these together under the rubric 'derived-position' islands, because I assume that, in all of these cases, we are dealing with a constituent that has moved and whose surface position is derived. The idea that I will pursue is that the extraction we see in the grammatical sluicing examples proceeds not from the derived position, which leads to ungrammaticality as in (70), but from the base position.

Let us begin by considering the case of topicalization. Here we can see that the deviance of (70a) is due to the derived position of the object, not to any overall ban on extraction from objects, since the corresponding extraction from an *in situ* object is fine:

(72)   Which Marx brother did she say that she refused to read [a biography of __]?

This fact, I claim, is the key to understanding the grammaticality of the corresponding sluice. I propose that the structure of the sluice is that in (73a), not that in (73b):

(73)   A: A biography of one of the Marx brothers, she refused to read.
    a   B: Which one ~~[she refused to read a biography of *t*]~~?
    b   B: *Which one ~~[a biography of *t*, she refused to read]~~?

In other words, there is no reason to assume that the extraction that feeds sluicing must proceed from a structure isomorphic to the surface structure of the antecedent clause. So far, I have claimed only that deletion is regulated by the Focus condition, not by any additional particular structural requirement. An antecedent that contains a topicalized object as in (73) will still provide the necessary semantic antecedent to satisfy the Focus condition. The sluice in (73a) requires, by the Focus condition, that $\exists x[x$ *is a Marx brother and she refused to read a biography of x]* be entailed by A's utterance. Since this is the case, the sluice is grammatical.

Parallel reasoning applies to the case of subjects. (An alternative would be to consider the subject island itself a PF-effect, a route I will not pursue here.) Let us begin with a passive subject (the same remarks hold, under the usual assumptions, for unaccusative subjects). The sluice in (71b) can have the structure in (74) (I ignore the question of whether there are additional intermediate positions that the subject may have moved through on the way to SpecIP, illustrating the sluice here with the subject in its base position):

(74)   . . . which$_2$ [$_{IP}$ ~~is going to be published [a biography of t_2]~~]

Note first that, under most recent approaches to subject islands, an extraction from a base position (here, the object position) will be allowed. Extraction from SpecIP is banned because it is not the specifier of a complement to an L-related head (or not L-marked (Chomsky 1986*a*: 31), and so on), not simply because extraction is from a subject *per se* (as in Chomsky 1973 and Pollard and Sag 1994: 195). This is borne out by the well-known contrasts in extraction from pre- and post-verbal subjects in Romance (grammatical from post-verbal subjects, not from pre-verbal ones). A similar point can be made on the basis of the following kinds of English examples. In the (a) examples in (75) and (76), the displaced subject in SpecIP is an island to extraction by virtue of its position; the same logical 'subject' in its base position in the (b) examples is not a barrier to extraction.

(75)   a   *Which candidate were [posters of *t*] all over town?
        b   Which candidate were there [posters of *t*] all over town?

(76)   a   *Which candidate did they say [to get *t* to agree to a debate] was hard?
        b   Which candidate did they say it was hard [to get *t* to agree to a debate]?

Since I am not assuming a strict structural isomorphism between the antecedent clause and the deleted IP in sluicing, a structure like (74) will satisfy the Focus condition, while allowing the attested extraction.

The immediate question is how such a structure could be grammatical in English, given that its overt counterpart is impossible:

(77)   *(Guess) [which Marx brother]$_2$ [$_{IP}$ __ is [$_{VP}$ going to be published [a biography of t_2]]]]

The standard answer to the impossibility of an unfilled SpecIP in English is some version of the extended projection principle (the EPP), essentially a stipulation that SpecIP must be filled (see Chomsky 1981). In recent formulations (Chomsky 1995; Alexiadou and Anagnostopoulou 1998), the EPP has been conceived of as the result of certain featural requirements of I^0: for English, Chomsky claims that I^0 has a 'strong' EPP feature, where 'strong' means that the feature is uninterpretable at the PF-interface and hence must be checked before Spell-Out (this being the mechanism forcing overt movement in the system). This approach to the EPP makes an interesting prediction from the present perspective. If a 'strong' feature does not reach the PF interface as a result of deletion, then the absence of the associated checking movement should not matter. This is exactly the difference between the grammatical (74) and the ungrammatical (77). The latter violates the EPP, since the 'strong' feature on I^0 has not been checked, and has reached the PF-interface intact, causing the derivation to crash. In (74), however, although the 'strong' feature has not been checked, it has been deleted along with the rest of the IP, and therefore does not reach the PF-interface to cause a crash. This account of the grammaticality of subject extractions, being based on a feature implementation of the EPP, is thus parallel to the account offered above for the amelioration of left-branch violations under ellipsis.

The same account applies to subjects of transitive and unergative verbs, if the internal subject hypothesis is correct—if there are positions inside the VP from which A'-movement can extract a subconstituent, we expect to be able to void the subject island in the same way we did for subjects of passives and unaccusatives. The deleted structure in (71c), then, must be as follows:

(78)   A biographer of one of the Marx brothers interviewed her, but I don't remember which$_3$ $[_{IP}$ ── $[_{VP}$ a biographer of t_3 interviewed her$]]$.

Depending on exactly what formulation of the barrierhood of SpecIP one adopts, the grammaticality of extraction as in (78) might bear on whether the subject originates as a specifier of VP or as an adjunct to VP, seeming to favor the former. (This relates also to questions of whether barrierhood should be formulated in terms of θ-government (as in Chomksy 1986a: 14–15) or L-relatedness (as Chomsky 1998 suggests). The choice is not crucial here.)

An obvious question at this point is whether the fact that the subject remains low at Spell-Out, in violation of the EPP, has any further consequences for interpretation. The answer is no, but it is worth seeing why this expectation might arise and why it is not fulfilled. Given commonly held assumptions, IP of (74) should not be able to host further movement. This would follow from the Strict Cycle Condition, which forbids A'-movement out of an IP followed by A-movement inside that IP (or in general, if this condition is reduced along the lines of Chomsky's (1995) Extension Condition, no XP movement can target a position structurally inferior to the highest node in the tree; see Collins 1997 for a recent approach). If the Strict Cycle Condition applies also to post-Spell-Out movement, then we expect to see a scope-freezing effect for subjects in a structure like (74).

This expectation is not borne out. Consider the examples in (79), where indefinite subjects interact with modals and negation.

(79)   a   Five pictures of one of the victims might be distributed to the press, but I can't remember which one₂ [~~IP~~ ~~might be~~ [~~VP~~ ~~distributed [five pictures of t₂] to the press]~~].

       b   Five pictures of one of the victims weren't distributed to the press, but I can't remember which one₂ [~~IP~~ ~~weren't~~ [~~VP~~ ~~distributed [five pictures of t₂] to the press]~~].

If the subject *five pictures of t₂* were frozen in its base position by the Strict Cycle Condition even after Spell-Out, we would predict that (79b), for example, would admit only the ¬∃ reading. In fact, both the ¬∃ and ∃¬ readings are possible here, the latter given in (80) (if anything, the latter is preferred):

(80) $\lambda p[\exists x[victim(x) \wedge p= \ulcorner[\exists_i Y[picture(Y, of \ x) \wedge \neg distributed(Y, to \ the \ press)]]]]]$

For purposes of scope, the Strict Cycle Condition does not apply, since all instances of QR are counter-cyclic under standard assumptions as well. But we might predict that A-movement of the subject after Spell-Out will be impossible, since the 'strong' feature on I^0 that drives this movement has been deleted. But if the Case features on the subject DP still need to be checked, we might have Greed-violating Case-driven A-movement after Spell-Out after all. (Some recent theorizing has even sought to reduce all A-movement to feature movement, with subject DPs possibly base-generated outside the VP; see Pesetsky 1998*b* and Manzini and Roussou 2000, and Hornstein 1999 for a related approach.)

These questions are, however, difficult to test. One possibility is to test whether the subject out of which extraction under sluicing has occurred can come to bind a higher pronoun. If it can, we have evidence that it has undergone A-movement, since A'-movement of this kind triggers a weak crossover violation. Although the facts are subtle, I believe that the evidence does indicate that such binding is possible, and therefore that we have evidence that covert phrasal A-movement has taken place. The relevant data are given in (81).

(81)   a   [Every biography of one of the Marx brothers]₁ seemed to its₁ author to be definitive, but I don't remember (of) which (Marx brother).

       b   [Every soldier from one of the airborne battalions]₂ seemed to his₂ commander to be sick, but I don't know (from) which (battalion).

In these examples, cross-clausal binding is impossible (cf. *Every soldier₂ was sick, but I don't know whether his₂ commander knew*). Since the examples are nonetheless grammatical, we have evidence that covert phrasal A-movement is occurring. The derivation for (81b) is sketched below:

(82) a   Spell-Out
          ... which (battalion)$_3$ [~~IP~~ [~~VP~~ seemed to his$_2$ commander to be [~~IP~~ [every solider from one of t_3]$_2$ sick]]]
      b   A-movement at LF
          ... which (battalion)$_3$ [$_{IP}$ [every soldier from one of t_3]$_2$ seemed to his$_2$ commander [$_{IP}$ t_2' to be t_2 sick]]

In (82b), DP$_2$ has raised by A-movement, coming to bind *his*$_2$. This movement is necessary, assuming that bound variable anaphora requires c-command at LF. This movement cannot be simply A'-movement, since such movement would give us a weak crossover effect that is not attested.

One might expect that a similiar argument for covert phrasal movement in these cases could be constructed by examining the effects of Principle C of the Binding Theory. As (83a) shows, overt A-movement can bleed Principle C. This should be compared with (83b), where the subject remains *in situ*, triggering a Principle C violation.

(83) a   Many reports about Clinton$_2$ seemed to him$_2$ to be on TV during the summit.
      b   *There seemed to him$_2$ to be many reports about Clinton$_2$ on TV during the summit.

In the comparable cases of sluicing, no Principle C effect is seen:

(84) One of Albright$_3$'s reports on one of the Balkan countries seemed to her$_3$ to have been leaked to the press, though I don't know which (of the Balkan countries).

Comparable to (82), I give the derivation of (84) in (85):

(85) a   Spell-Out
          ... which$_1$ [$_{IP}$ [$_{VP}$ seemed to her$_3$ to have been leaked [one of Albright$_3$'s reports on t_1] to the press]]
      b   LF
          ... which$_1$ [$_{IP}$ [one of Albright$_3$'s reports on t_1]$_2$ [$_{VP}$ seemed to her$_3$ t_2' to have been leaked t_2 to the press]]

If this were all that needed to be said, the grammaticality of (84) would provide another argument in favor of phrasal A-movement at LF, since phrasal

A'-movement at LF does not generally repair Principle C violations (though see Sauerland 1998, Fox 2000, and Merchant 2000*a* for a qualification relating to antecedent-contained deletion). Unfortunately, the status of (84) cannot actually tell us much, since it is known independently that Principle C effects are not attested under ellipsis. As we saw in Chapter 1, Fiengo and May (1994) have documented this surprising fact for VP-ellipsis, but it holds for sluicing as well, as shown in Merchant (1999*a*). Consider, for instance, (86):

(86)   They said they wanted to hire Abby$_3$, but she$_3$ didn't know why.

If this sluice were resolved as in (87a), we would expect a Principle C violation. Instead, the material that is deleted is that in (87b), in line with the analysis of the parallel facts for VP-ellipsis presented in Chapter 1.

(87)   a   *she$_3$ didn't know why ~~they wanted to hire Abby~~$_3$.
        b   she$_3$ didn't know why ~~they wanted to hire her~~$_3$.

Since there are no Principle C effects under ellipsis in general, the fact that (84) is grammatical unfortunately can tell us nothing about the LF position of the subject. 'Vehicle change' effects do not alter the argument based on the examples in (81), however, since, even though universals are indeed equivalent to pronouns under ellipsis in some contexts, and assuming that the pronoun could be given the correct interpretation, the occurrence of a pronoun for the whole DP would eliminate the extraction site, since pronouns cannot contain extraction sites.

Note that I am not claiming that sluicing out of subjects always requires an expletive (*there* or *it*) in the deletion site. For the case of *there* in particular, the variability in scope of indefinite subjects argues against a hidden *there*, since *there* forces narrow scope for its associate. And several authors have shown that there is evidence against phrasal A-movement to replace *there*: Williams (1984), den Dikken (1995), and Pesetsky (1998*b*). The relation between *there* and its associate is not one of phrasal movement (perhaps feature movement, irrelevant for binding theory, scope, and quantifier-variable binding). Indeed, the *there*-insertion equivalent to (82) above does not allow the required variable binding, indicating again that the *there*-associate relation is not one of phrasal A-movement at LF:

(88)   There seemed (*to his$_2$ commander) to be [a soldier]$_2$ sick.

But this fact does not militate against the analysis proposed above. In the sluicing cases, there is no *there* there, and hence whatever it is that blocks phrasal movement in cases like (88) is not operative.

This analysis also has implications for Diesing's (1992) Mapping Hypothesis. Diesing (1992) proposes that material in SpecIP at LF is mapped into the restriction of quantificational adverbs, while material inside the VP is mapped into the scope. She adopts a Kamp–Heimian analysis of indefinites as open predicates, and posits that existential closure applies at the VP-level. Furthermore, subjects of stage-level (SL) predicates are base-generated in SpecVP, undergoing raising to SpecIP prior to Spell-Out, and able to reconstruct or not as the case may be, while subjects of individual-level (IL) predicates are base-generated in SpecIP, and cannot be interpreted inside the VP (that is, they cannot be subject to existential closure; SpecVP is occupied by PRO). If Diesing's conjecture about the structural differences between these kinds of predicates is correct, we should find corresponding differences in whether their subjects allow extractions. Subjects of SL predicates should allow extraction under sluicing; subjects of IL predicates, being base-generated in SpecIP, should not. The data in (89), exhibiting both kinds of predicates, do not bear out this predicted contrast, however—all are equally grammatical.

(89)   a   Pictures of one of the astronauts weren't available at press time, but I can't remember which one.   (SL)

   b   Pictures of one of the astronauts weren't visible at press time, but I can't remember which one.   (SL or IL)

   c   Writing samples of one of the astronauts weren't legible, but I can't remember which one.   (IL)

   d   Pictures of one of the astronauts weren't printable, but I can't remember which one.   (IL)

   e   Eggplants from one of the islands are poisonous—you better find out which one before you go!   (IL)

For example, (89e), having the IL predicate *poisonous*, should not allow a derivation of the necessary kind, sketched in (90), since the subject *eggplants* from which extraction proceeds does not occur in SpecVP, by hypothesis.

(90)   *. . . which one$_i$ [$_{IP}$ [eggplants from t_i]^i are [$_{VP}$ PRO^i poisonous]]

These considerations suggest that the correct account of the effects she discovered cannot be the structural one she proposed; see also Fernald (1994, 2000), who reaches this conclusion on independent grounds.

In summary, the deletion account is compatible with topicalization structures because these are equivalent to their unmoved counterparts in the ellipsis site. It is compatible with subjects for the same reason, though the movement of subjects in English to SpecIP is not optional in the general case. If the EPP is implemented as a 'strong' feature, as in Chomsky (1995), the absence of subject island effects is expected, as we saw to be the case with their left-branch cousins.

Two interesting further conclusions followed from the implementation presented here: first, that there must be at least some species of covert *phrasal* A-movement, and, secondly, that Diesing's structural solution to the differences between stage- and individual-level predicates is incompatible with the proposed account of extractions out of subjects under sluicing.

5.1.4 Coordinate Structure Constraint I: The Conjunct Condition

There are two subparts to Ross's (1967) Coordinate Structure Constraint (CSC), as stated in (91) (Ross 1967 (1986: 98–99), number (4.84)).

(91)   In a coordinate structure, no conjunct may be moved, nor may any element contained in a conjunct be moved out of that conjunct.

These two conditions are illustrated by the examples in (92): extraction of a conjunct in (92a), and extraction out of a conjunct in (92b).

(92)   a   *Which senator did they persuade Kennedy and __ to jointly sponsor the legislation?
        b   *What movie did Bob both go to a restaurant and see __ at the Nick that night?

In this section, I will concentrate on the first kind of extraction, which I will refer to as the *conjunct condition*, following Postal's (1992) terminology (the second kind will be taken up in the next section). This distinction was made originally in Grosu (1973), and elaborated in Grosu (1981: 53–60).

Ross (1969) noticed that sluicing provides some amelioration of the conjunct condition. His example (71) is given here in (93).

(93)   Irv and someone were dancing together, but I don't know who.

The status of such examples has been the subject of some debate. Ross marked his original example with ??, while Lakoff (1970) revises this to full acceptability without comment. Baker and Brame (1972) take issue with

Lakoff's revision, noting that 'many speakers find it completely ungrammatical' (p. 61). L. Levin (1982) gives the following example (her (42b)) without comment, indicating complete acceptability:

(94)   Janet and one of the boys were holding hands, but I don't remember which one.

Chung *et al.* (1995) also note this variation, providing the following example, which they note is only slightly odd:

(95)   ?They persuaded Kennedy and some other Senator to jointly sponsor the legislation, but I can't remember which one.   (Chung *et al.* 1995: (83b))

To these we can add examples like (96).

(96)   a   Ben baked the cake and something else, but I don't know what.
        b   Abby was a member of the Students for a Democratic Society and one other organization, but it wasn't clear which.
        c   President Kim Dae Jung and a 'senior American representative'— the White House has not said who—will deliver speeches. (*International Herald Tribune*, 29 Mar. 2000, p. 2)

I will thus take it that sluicing over a conjunct is in principle possible, and must be allowed by the syntax.[11]

Given the present enterprise of reducing sluicing to deletion, the grammaticality of these examples requires that the conjunct condition be a condition whose effects are due to a principle operative at PF, not a principle that bans extraction of a conjunct as a condition on movement rules. The representation of an example like (95) will therefore be as follows:

(97)   . . . but I can't remember which one₁ [~~they persuaded Kennedy and t₁ to jointly sponsor the legislation~~]

---

[11] One point of variability regards the nature of the subjects involved. All the examples in the literature contain predicates that require a plural subject (Ross's 'together', Chung *et al.*'s 'jointly', Levin's 'hold hands'); examples where this is not the case, or indeed where a strictly distributive reading of the predicate is forced, are sometimes worse:

(i)   a   *Mark and another boy each won a prize, but I don't remember who.
       b   *Some shaft and the coupler were broken—guess which!

The conjunct condition, then, must be something along the lines of Grosu's (1981: 56) Null Conjunct Constraint, which states that conjuncts may not be phonetically null. This claim, that the conjunct condition is a condition operative at PF, has interesting support from sentences that seem to be deviant because of the presence of a null conjunct, but are not usually derived by movement under current analyses. (Munn 1993 also denies that the conjunct condition is a constraint on extraction.) These data fall into four classes: null VPs, Right Node Raising structures, null pronouns and null topics, and illicit across-the-board extractions.

The first of these is VP-ellipsis. As Grosu (1973, 1981: 53) notes, a null VP cannot be coordinated with an overt one. His example is given in (98):

(98)   *I couldn't lift this weight, but I know a boy who could [__ and lift a crowbar, too].

In judging this example, one must be careful not to add a pause before *and*; such a pause renders the example grammatical but irrelevant. In such a case, we have instead a parallel to *Bob can sing—and dance, too!* (cf. *You should do it, and quickly (too)!*; see Progovac 1999 for discussion of these 'adjunct *and*' clauses). We can construct examples where such a factor does not play a role, however, by adding a 'left-bracket' element like *both* or *either*, or by reversing the order of the conjuncts. Such examples are unambigously impossible.

(99)   Bob can juggle, and
    a   *Abby both can [__ and sing], too.
    b   *Abby can [sing and __], too.
    c   *Abby can either [__ or sing].
    d   *Abby can either [sing or __].

Although it has sometimes been suggested that VP-ellipsis could be reducible to VP-topicalization in English (Johnson 1997; Postal 1998: 180), parallel arguments can be constructed for sluicing and NP-ellipsis, where a topicalization analysis is much less likely. The relevant data are given in (100) and (101).

At the least, the unacceptability of these examples argues against a conjunction reduction analysis for conjoined subjects (see the discussion below of conjoined VPs). But appealing to the lack of distributivity by itself cannot account for the full range of data, since examples like (96) are well formed. In (96c), in particular, the intended reading *is* distributive: the dignitaries are to give separate speeches, not a joint one.

(100) a *Abby invited someone, but I don't know who$_2$ [__ and Ben kissed t_2].

     b *Abby invited someone, but I don't know who$_2$ [Ben kissed t_2 and __].

(101) a *I have five cats, but he has six [__ and dogs]!

     b *I have five cats, but he has six [dogs and __]!

The second argument comes from the apparent sensitivity of Right Node Raising (RNR) to the conjunct condition, as noted by Ross (1967). The following example is from McCawley (1988):

(102) *Tom is writing an article on Aristotle and, and Elaine has just published a monograph on Mesmer and, Freud.

If RNR is in fact a prosodic deletion phenonemon, as argued convincingly by Wilder (1995) and Swingle (1995), then the ungrammaticality of (102) must also follow from constraints on deletion, not movement. (See in particular Swingle 1995: 58 n. 34, who shows how her theory of RNR as deletion handles this kind of example.)

Another kind of support comes from various null proforms. In Greek, for example, null subjects are possible, but these cannot be coordinated with non-null DPs (similar data hold, to my knowledge, in various Romance and Slavic languages[12]). Compare the grammatical overt pronominal forms in the subject coordinations with their ungrammatical null counterparts. The order of the conjuncts is irrelevant (thanks to A. Giannakidou for judgments).

(103) a {Aftos/*pro} kai o Pavlos ine adherfia.
        he   *pro and the Paul are siblings*

        'He and Paul are siblings.'

     b {Esi /*pro} kai o Pavlos iste adherfia.
        you.sg pro and the Paul are siblings

        'You and Paul are siblings.'

---

[12] A potential counterexample comes from Irish, as analyzed in McCloskey and Hale (1984) and McCloskey (1986) (and Old Irish, as in McCloskey 1991*b*). In this language, it is possible to have configurations like (i), where a null left conjunct can trigger agreement:

(i)   V$_{[\alpha F]}$ [DP pro$_{[\alpha F]}$ Conj DP] . . .

One possibility, suggested to me by Jim McCloskey, is that the agreement material is the left conjunct, and has prosodically cliticized onto V—this pattern is sensitive to adjacency in a way that suggests this is plausible, though space prevents a detailed discussion here.

c {Ego/*pro} kai o Pavlos imaste adherfia.
   I   pro and the Paul are   siblings
   'I and Paul are siblings.'

(104) a O Pavlos kai {aftos/*pro} ine adherfia.
         the Paul and he   pro are siblings
         'Paul and he are siblings.'

      b O Pavlos kai {esi /*pro} iste adherfia.
         the Paul and you.sg pro are siblings
         'Paul and you are siblings.'

      c O Pavlos kai {ego/*pro} imaste adherfia.
         the Paul and I   pro are   siblings
         'Paul and I are siblings.'

A parallel argument comes from various 'topic-drop' constructions in German and East Asian languages (see Huang 1984). These are typically analyzed as involving a null operator in the left periphery of the clause; in German, this is SpecCP. This operator, although it fulfils the V2 requirement of German, cannot be coordinated with overt material:

(105) A: Hat er dir   seine Infos   gegeben—zum Beispiel,
         has he you.DAT his   vitals.ACC given   for   example

         seinen Namen?
         his   name.ACC
         'Did he give you his personal information—for example, his name?'

      B: a (*und sein Alter) wollte er nicht sagen.
            and his age   wanted he not   say
            'That (and his age), he didn't want to say.'

         b (*Sein Alter und) wollte er nicht sagen.
            his   age   and wanted he not   say
            '(His age and) that, he didn't want to say.'

Another kind of argument comes from constructions where extraction would be expected to be licit in an across-the-board (ATB) manner, but the result of which would leave one or both conjuncts null. As noted by Grosu, whole conjuncts cannot be removed across the board, as in (106a), nor may ATB movement affect a subpart of a conjunct and a whole conjunct, as in (106b,c), taken from Gazdar *et al.* (1985: 178); (see also Gazdar *et al.* 1982 and Sag and Fodor 1994).

(106)   a   *Which books did Bob read [__ and __]?
         b   *I wonder who you saw [__ and [a picture of __]].
         c   *I wonder who you saw [[a picture of __] and __].

More complicated examples are provided by constructions where the conjunction has an 'intensifying' import (Grosu 1981: 55). These examples, from
Grosu (1981: 55), are given in (107) and (108).[13]

(107)   *Here is the picture of Mary which John is looking for __ and {only /
         nothing but} __.

(108)   a   John is growing eagerer and eagerer (to meet Mary) every minute.
         b   *Eagerer though John seemed to be growing __ and __, Mary was
             still reluctant to introduce herself to him.
             (cf. Eagerer and eagerer though John seemed to be growing . . .)

Since ATB extraction is in principle possible, and the conditions on ATB
extraction seem to be met in these examples, an independent constraint is
needed to rule out examples like (106)–(108). The Null Conjunct Constraint
does just that.

Finally, in a somewhat more speculative vein, if the conjunct condition is a
PF-phenomenon, we may expect to find resumptive pronouns ameliorating
the effects of conjunct extraction. While this is in general true in several languages that have robust resumptive pronoun strategies like Irish, this effect
seems also to be attested in English, as in (109).

(109)   a   That's the guy$_2$ that they were going to kill [you and him$_2$]
             together.
         b   Which wine$_3$ would you never serve it$_3$ and sushi together?
             (Pesetsky 1998*a*: 366 n. 28)

But it is difficult to tell whether these structures actually indicate that a trace of
movement can be 'spelled out' as a pronoun inside an island, as a way of repair-
ing the island effect (as proposed, for example, by Pesetsky 1998*a*), or whether
these examples are simply making use of the general strategy for interpreting
resumptive pronouns linked to an operator base-generated in its A′-position
(see Merchant 1999*c* for discussion). Instead, we must find an environment

---

[13] Example (107) may in fact be ruled out on independent grounds by Kuno and Takami's
(1997) *Ban on Out-of-Scope Extraction* or Tancredi's (1990) *Principle of Lexical Association*, which
can be read as requiring operators like *only* in English to associate to overt lexical material in their
c-command domain.

where we know that the normal resumptive interpretation strategy is impossible, and then see if a resumptive pronoun can occur in such an environment as a conjunct nonetheless. Such an environment is discussed by Sells (1984): resumptive pronouns cannot be linked to relative-clause operators when the relative clause forms part of the restriction of a universal,[14] as in (110):[15]

(110)　　*Every guy that you got upset when Betsy started dating him turned out fine in the end.

The crucial test, then, is to determine whether a resumptive pronoun can occur as a conjunct in such a relative clause. Such a resumptive pronoun could only be the result of a PF-spell out process turning a trace of movement into a pronoun, since the regular strategy of base-generated operator and resumptive pronoun is unavailable (for reasons discussed by Sells 1984). Relevant data are given in (111):

(111)　　a　?(?)Every guy that you thought {[[he and Betsy]/that [Betsy and him]} would make a good couple turned out to be a psycho in the end.

　　　　b　?(?)She interviewed every guy that you saw Betsy and him together.

Unfortunately, judgments on these are difficult: they seem better than (110), but not as good as (109a). Pending clearer data, then, the results of this test remain inconclusive.

We have thus seen at least four different areas where null conjuncts are pro-

---

[14] This generalization is the subject of some debate; Prince (1990) has shown that the constraints on actual use of resumptives in relative clauses are not quite so clear cut.

[15] Note that these contrasts, illustrated in (i), make an interesting prediction with respect to antecedent-contained deletion (ACD) structures as well.

(i)　　a　?I read the (same) book that Charlie made the claim that you had read it.
　　　　b　*I read every book that Charlie made the claim that you had read it.

Since resumptives can ameliorate subjacency effects as in (ia), then, to the extent that they can co-occur with the determiners that license ACD (*the* allows ACD to some extent: *I gave him₂ the book Charlie₂ wanted me to*), we should find a comparable amelioration of the subjacency effects discovered by Haïk (1987). The data in (ii) show this to be true.

(ii)　　a　?I read the (same) book that Charlie made the claim that you had.
　　　　b　*I read every book that Charlie made the claim that you had.

These data indicate that the trace of QR (even DPs headed by *the* must raise, as the lack of a principle C effect in the italicized example in the previous paragraph also shows) can be equivalent to a resumptive pronoun, as expected under the semantic reanalysis of 'vehicle change' effects presented in Chapter 1.

hibited, none of which is plausibly analyzed as involving extraction. This lends support to the hypothesis that the Null Conjunct Constraint, whatever the best account of its effects may be, applies to PF representations,[16] regardless of whether the null conjunct was the result of movement or not. If the Null Conjunct Constraint operates at PF, we expect that sluicing should ameliorate the defect of structures arising from single conjunct extractions, as is the case.

5.1.5 Summary

In the above sections, we have examined the ability of sluicing seemingly to extract constituents out of a variety of islands: left branches, COMP-trace environments, derived positions (topicalizations and subjects), and conjuncts. In each case, I argued that the extraction itself was licit, contrary to naive expectation based on comparison with the overt counterpart, but that the deviance was rendered ineffectual by deletion at PF. In each case, I showed that there was independent reason for believing that the locus of these island effects is in the phonological component. This was cashed out in various ways, some more explicit than others, as our current understanding of the phenomena permits. But no particular implementation of these claims is crucial to the main hypothesis supported by the sluicing data: that certain island effects are not necessarily structural in the usual sense, but rather should be located at PF.

5.2 E-TYPE ANAPHORA UNDER SLUICING

Before continuing with the next class of islands, a bit of background is needed. In this section, which builds on Merchant (1999*a*), I show that certain traces of movement in an antecedent IP are equivalent to E-type pronouns in the deleted IP. This will set the stage for an understanding of several of the facts we will consider in the next section.

---

[16] One remaining issue that I will not solve here is the fact, noted by Rodman (1976) and others since (see Ruys 1992 for discussion), that conjuncts cannot scope independently. If the conjunct condition is only a PF condition, the constraints on scoping in coordinations must follow not from constraints on QR, but on semantic restrictions on the interpretation of such structures (see Winter 1998).

Related to this is the status of wh-*in-situ* in conjuncts. Although Fiengo, Huang, Lasnik, and Reinhart (1988: 81) report that (i) is only slightly deviant (the question mark is their judgment),

(i)   ?Who saw John and who?

5.2.1 The Problem: A′-Traces under Sluicing

The problem, given any approach to the resolution of IP-ellipsis, arises quite simply: IPs that contain A′-traces license deletion of IPs that apparently do not—that is, trace-containing IPs can provide the necessary antecedent IP to resolve a sluice. Constructed examples are given in (112), and some attested ones are in (113)–(115).

(112)   a   The report details what IBM did and why.
        b   Who did the suspect call and when?
        c   We know which families bought houses on this block, but we don't know which (houses), yet.
        d   It was clear which families had mowed their lawns, but we can only guess with which brands of lawnmower.
        e   The judge had records of which divers had been searching the wreck, but not of how long.
        f   The hospital spokeswoman told us which patients had died, but she wouldn't say when.
        g   The Guinness Book records how long some alligators can hold their breaths, but not which (ones).
        h   Though Abby eventually told us who she saw that night, she never revealed where.

(113)   a   That's a gazebo. But I don't know who built it or why.   (overheard conversation, Santa Cruz, 15 Sept. 1996)
        b   A ride-along with an officer shows who gets ticketed, and why. (*San Jose Mercury News*, 9 Aug. 1996)
        c   A chronology was the first step in piecing together what had happened—which had to precede figuring out why.   (Robinson 1994: 222)
        d   They didn't have any clear idea of what they were going to try to do, or why.   (Robinson 1994: 535)
        e   What's proposed and why.   (*San Jose Mercury News*, headline, 28 Nov. 1996)

similar examples are judged by Bresnan (1975), Pesetsky (1982: 618), and Postal (1992: 33) as unacceptable (see also Ginzburg 1992: 171, who notes that 'for many speakers, [such an example] can be used only to reprise [as an echo question—JM]'); I tend to side with the latters' judgment as well. These facts are only problematic if wh-*in-situ* must move at LF: if so, and if the conjunct condition applies at this level as well, the latter authors' judgments can be accounted for. From the current perspective, these facts must follow from the semantic mechanisms, and not from a constraint on movement.

(114)   a   [The Smart Toilet] is a paperless device that not only accommo-
            dates calls of nature, but also 'knows' who's using it and how.
            (*San Jose Mercury News*, 6 Aug. 1996)

        b   What interveners are able to 'get out of the way', and how?
            (Szabolcsi and Zwarts 1993: 14)

        c   Investigators want to know who is supplying the drugs—and
            how—since Kevorkian's medical license was suspended in 1991.
            (*San Jose Mercury News*, 17 Aug. 1996)

(115)   a   [The police asked] who'd seen him last and where.   (Tartt 1994:
            294)

        b   But R. C. Lahoti, a High Court judge appointed to lead the inves-
            tigation of the accident, must decide who will decode the recorders
            and where.   (*San Jose Mercury News*, 30 Nov. 1996)

        c   He only wanted to know whom they had met, and where.
            (Robinson, 1996: 515)

Even multiple wh-phrases may be in the antecedent IP:

(116)   a   We need to know who saw what, and when.

        b   This is Washington, where everyone keeps track of who crossed
            whom and when.   (*New York Times Magazine*, 23 July 2000)

        c   [He] makes no empirical claims concerning what domain will be
            opaque for what relations, [or] why.   (Szabolcsi and Zwarts 1993:
            240 n. 4)

        d   You know exactly who will laugh at which particular kind of joke,
            and for how long.   (slightly altered ex. from de Bernières 1995: 33)

        e   He wasn't even certain who within his own family was entitled to
            what, or why.   (Kress 1993: 109)

        f   Entitlement, after all, was the entire issue. Who got what, and
            how, and why.   (Kress 1993: 108)

Traces of QRed constituents in the antecedent IP can also give rise to the same
effect.

(117)   a   The suspect phoned everyone on this list, but we don't know
            when.

        b   Most gangs will be at the rumble, though it's not clear why.

        c   Every boy scout helped, though most didn't know why.

        d   (Only a) few boats looked for survivors, though it's not clear
            why.

e At least five guerrillas survived the raids, but no one could figure out how.

f The duke hid exactly six of the jewels, and even Holmes didn't know where.

If structural isomorphism required exact identity between the antecedent IP and the deleted one, we would have the representative LFs in (118), where the struck-through material has been deleted at PF; exactly the same problem would arise for a copying approach. These LFs have the glaring defect that the wh-trace in the second conjunct is unbound. Under normal circumstances we would expect an unbound trace to give rise to spectacular ungrammaticality—but these examples show that it does not.

(118) a ... [$_{CP}$ what$_1$ [$_{IP}$ IBM did t_1]] and [$_{CP}$ why [$_{IP}$ ~~IBM did t_1~~]]

b [$_{CP}$ who$_2$ did [$_{IP}$ the suspect call t_2]] and [$_{CP}$ when [$_{IP}$ ~~the suspect call t_2~~]]

The key to explaining the acceptability of these examples is the fact that they have interpretations parallel to the sentences in (119), which contain overt pronouns anaphoric to preceding non-c-commanding wh-phrases, but no ellipsis.

(119) a The report details what$_1$ IBM did and why IBM did it$_1$.

b Who$_2$ did the suspect call and when did the suspect call him$_2$?

c Most gangs$_3$ will be at the rumble, though it's not clear why they$_3$'ll be there.

d Every boy scout$_4$ helped, though most$_5$ didn't know why they$_{4/5}$ helped.

While no analysis has ever been proposed for sentences like those in (112)–(117), ones like those in (119a,b) were discussed in Bolinger's seminal paper (1978) and more recently in Comorovski (1996). Comorovski mentions them only in passing, since her main interests lie elsewhere, and attributes the possibility of an anaphoric link of the observed kind to the existential presuppositions of wh-questions. Whether or not this is the correct approach to the feasibility of such anaphoric links in the first place, this observation obviously does not solve the problem raised by the elliptical sentences in (112)–(117).

Note especially that none of these examples is plausibly the result of some novel, mysterious application of across-the-board (ATB) movement of the first wh-phrase out of both conjuncts. Such an ATB account would obviously run into numerous problems (phrase-structural, to begin with, as well as island violations); in addition, there are many examples that are not coordinate structures of the kind necessary for ATB extraction (see Merchant 1999*a* for additional examples).

5.2.2 The Solution: 'Vehicle Change' and E-Type Pronouns

The solution I will propose is now familiar in general form: I will assimilate the deleted IPs to their non-elided counterparts above. I propose simply that the LFs of deleted IPs like those in (118) are in fact fully parallel in the relevant respects to the LFs of sentences like (119)—specifically, that wh-traces (and traces of QR) license the deletion of pronouns in these circumstances.

As mentioned in Chapter 1, Fiengo and May (1994) propose and defend a mechanism for capturing exactly this kind of syntactic sleight of hand: 'vehicle change' (see also van den Wyngaerd and Zwart 1991, Brody 1995, Kennedy 1997, and Giannakidou and Merchant 1998). 'Vehicle change' in essence defines certain equivalence classes under ellipsis; this is given in its general form in (120). For our purposes, the relevant instantiation of 'vehicle change' would be the one given schematically in (121), which states that non-pronominals may be treated as pronominals under ellipsis. Specifically, a variable like a wh-trace can be treated as a pronominal—its 'pronominal correlate', in Fiengo and May's term, as in (122).

(120)   *Vehicle change* (Fiengo and May 1994: 218 ff.)
        Nominals can be treated as non-distinct with respect to their pronominal status under ellipsis.

(121)   [−pronominal] $=_e$ [+pronominal]
        (where $=_e$ means 'forms an equivalence class under ellipsis with')

(122)   [−a, −p] (variable or name) $=_e$ [−a, +p] (*pronominal correlate* = ^{P}e)

Fiengo and May take pains to argue that 'vehicle change' is syntactic, and has syntactic effects, and is not simply relevant at some more abstract level of semantic equivalence (as in property-anaphora treatments of ellipsis). They show that the pronominal correlates of names and wh-traces under VP-ellipsis do not trigger Principle C violations, do trigger Principle B, and do not respect islands, all of which they assume are syntactic phenomena. Though their discussion is limited exclusively to VP-ellipsis, the first and third of these properties can be observed under sluicing as well. Of course, if structural isomorphism is rejected, we have no reason not to posit regular pronouns in the ellipsis site, as I do here. The same conclusions hold.

5.2.2.1 *'Vehicle Change' under Sluicing*

Let us begin with the Binding Theory effect—namely, the disappearance of Principle C effects. Example (123) presents a standard case of a Principle C violation with a name. If the trace of a moved wh-phrase is copied under a co-indexed c-commanding pronoun, as in (124a), however, no deviance arises, contrary to naive expectation, since featurally names and wh-traces are indistinct. For Fiengo and May, 'vehicle change', however, converts the trace into its pronominal correlate, as in the LF given in (124b), in which the variable t_4 is realized as its pronominal correlate $^Pe_4$; $^Pe_4$, being [+pronominal], is no longer subject to Principle C. In terms of the theory defended here, this means that the deleted IP simply contains a pronoun, as in (124c).

(123)   *The detectives wanted to know whether they₃ knew why Sue hated the Thompsons₃.

(124)   a   The detectives wanted to know who₄ [Sue hated t_4] and whether they₄ knew why.

   b   . . . they₄ knew why [**Sue hated** $^Pe_4$]

   c   . . . they₄ knew why [~~Sue hated them~~₄]

Principle B is not testable, since in sluicing an entire IP is elided, so no example with a clause-mate c-commanding pronoun can be constructed.

   Secondly, we find that the normal binding relation between a wh-phrase and its bound trace, which is constrained by islands, is relaxed under this type of sluicing as well. In other words, the pronominal correlate of a reconstructed trace can find its antecedent outside an island. This is indeed trivially true under sluicing, since sluicing involves wh-islands to begin with, but even embedding the CP immediately dominating the sluiced IP inside another island does not affect the status of these examples. Again, normal binding could not be expected to hold in the first place, since the wh-phrase does not c-command the pronominal correlate.

   The following example is structured as follows. The (a) example is a control, showing the ungrammaticality of extraction from the island (here, a subject; see Merchant 1999*a* for this kind of sluice inside twenty-four other kinds of islands as well). The (b) example shows that a wh-link into a non-elided IP is impossible. The (c) example gives a version with no ellipsis, but with a pronoun linked to the wh-antecedent. This link from a pronominal element is what makes the sluiced version in the (d) example grammatical, as its LF in (e) shows.

(125)   a   *Which crime$_4$ did the FBI admit that ⟨solving t_4⟩ will prove difficult?

         b   *The FBI knows which truck$_4$ was rented, but ⟨figuring out from where t_4 was rented⟩ has proven difficult.

         c   The FBI knows which truck$_4$ was rented, but ⟨figuring out from where it$_4$ was rented⟩ has proven difficult.

         d   The FBI knows which truck$_4$ was rented, but ⟨figuring out from where⟩ has proven difficult.

         e   . . . figuring out from where [it$_4$ was rented] has proven difficult.

Thus all available evidence indicates that we are dealing with a pronoun in the ellipsis site. These effects, in conjunction with their structural isomorphism condition, are Fiengo and May's motivation for proposing the operation of 'vehicle change'. But the same effects follow directly if the ellipsis site contains a regular pronoun at all levels of representation, as seen in Chapter 1. In what follows, then, I will simply represent the element in question as a pronoun, though continuing at times to use the useful term 'vehicle change' to refer to the fact that A′-traces license the deletion of pronouns under certain circumstances, and 'pronominal correlate' as the pronoun deleted under these conditions.

5.2.2.2 *Interpreting the Result of 'Vehicle Change'*

An account of the anaphoric link between the pronominal correlate and its antecedent must distinguish them from regular bound wh-traces or bound pronouns. These are essentially a subspecies of donkey pronouns: anaphoric on a preceding quantificational expression, yet not bound by it.[17]

Let us take as our working example (126a) and its associated LF, parallel to its unelided counterpart in (127) (I ignore the trace of *when*, irrelevant here):

(126)   a   Which suspect did Abby call, and when?

         b   [$_{CP}$ which suspect$_2$ did [$_{IP}$ Abby call t_2]] and [$_{CP}$ when [$_{IP}$ Abby call him$_2$]]

(127)   Which suspect did Abby call, and when did she call him?

---

[17] The interested reader is referred to Merchant (1999*a*), where further evidence is presented that the assimilation of these pronouns to E-type pronouns is correct, based on the distribution of quantificational variability effects in these constructions.

The immediate question to be addressed is the same question with respect to this kind of data that we asked in Chapter 1: does the fact that the IP can be deleted follow from the Focus condition? As we have done before, we assume for simplicity that traces of wh-movement, like pronouns, translate as variables. Assume for the moment that pronouns and variables are translated by the same rule (recall Chapter 1, definition (4)), both yielding $g(2)$ in this case. Given this, the Focus condition is satisfied, since, in this case, the IP_A and IP_E yield the following:

(128)   a $IP_E' = $ F-clo$(IP_E) = $ Abby called $g(2)$
         b $IP_A' = $ F-clo$(IP_A) = $ Abby called $g(2)$

This result should follow regardless of one's approach to donkey anaphora, since the Focus condition is defined on entailments, not structures: the set quantified over by the wh-phrase (its trace) should be the set picked out by the donkey pronoun in the deleted IP, however this is implemented. Since equivalent deaccenting is possible in the cases in (119), I conclude that the Focus conditions are insensitive to the differences between 'regular' pronouns and donkey pronouns (if indeed 'regular' pronouns themselves cannot just be analyzed as a limited case of E-type pronouns).

One might have hoped that the behavior of donkey anaphora under ellipsis might shed light on the proper analysis of donkey anaphora itself, helping us decide among the several alternatives that have been proposed in the literature (see Heim 1990, Groenendijk and Stokhof 1991, Lappin and Francez 1994, and Chierchia 1995). Unfortunately for such an investigation, it seems that, to the extent that the approaches successfully handle the core data, they will extend without modification to the data presented here.

The above facts do raise one interesting question for E-type approaches such as that of Evans (1980) and Heim (1990), in which a definite description is filled in for the pronoun, which seem the most promising available. Semantically, as long as this description picks out the correct individual(s) (as it is designed to do), the Focus condition will be satisfied, of course. If this 'replacement' is to be done syntactically, though, we are faced with the question—given the data just presented—why such a definite description behaves like a pronoun with respect to the Binding Theory. Presumably, this question falls under the larger question of how such descriptions can be pronounced as pronouns in the first place, if indeed they are syntactically complex descriptions.

For this reason, I will set aside the complex questions regarding the translation and analysis of donkey anaphora, adopting an E-type approach; I will continue to translate even donkey pronouns as (simple) variables for perspicacity in what follows—the reader, however, should keep this convenient fiction in mind.

5.2.3 Summary

The investigation of the behavior of A'-traces in antecedents to deleted IPs has provided evidence for a number of conclusions. First, I argued that these traces are equivalent to pronouns, satisfying the Focus condition of Chapter 1. The fact that what is deleted is a pronoun explains the absence of effects associated with standard variables—namely, that Principle C effects and island-sensitivity are not attested. I suggested further an interpretation of these pronominal correlates as E-type pronouns anaphoric on wh-phrases, parallel to E-type pronouns anaphoric on other non-c-commanding quantifiers investigated in the literature on donkey anaphora, and parallel in particular to the pronouns occurring in similar cases of IP-deaccenting.

5.3 PROPOSITIONAL ISLANDS

With this much as background, I turn now to the second class of islands, called class C at the outset of this chapter, which are distinguished by having one feature in common: in all cases, the island in question contains a constituent that is propositional. I will, therefore, call islands in this class 'propositional islands', without intending this descriptive term to signify anything about the nature of the islandhood involved. The core idea in analyzing these cases will be that the extraction proceeds only locally, from out of the embedded propositional domain, and that the interpretative effect of the island (that is, the fact that the interpretation is restricted in such a way as to have made us think that there was extraction from out of an island to begin with) can be derived through the independently needed mechanisms of E-type anaphora and modal subordination. My goal here is not to explore the accounts of these latter phenomena in any depth, but rather to concentrate on the syntactic aspects of the extraction, in particular the fact that we can avoid island-violating extractions by employing these mechanisms.

I begin with a consideration of relative-clause islands of various types, and then move on to adjunct clauses and certain Coordinate Structure Constraint violations.

5.3.1 Relative Clauses

This section discusses two kinds of relative clauses, traditionally known as indicative and subjunctive. For indicative relatives, I show that, given the results of the previous section, the trace of the relative operator can license the deletion of a pronoun in an IP, and that this fact derives the desired interpretation. Some complications arise in the case of subjunctive relatives, but these are handled by modal subordination. The analysis presented here is representative for the analyses in the coming sections, which have essentially the same character.

5.3.1.1 *Indicative Relatives*

Recall that sluicing out of relative clauses appears to be possible:

(129) a They hired someone who speaks a Balkan language—guess which!
       b They hired someone who speaks a lot of languages—guess how many!

These contrast with regular extraction, as in (130).

(130) a *Guess which (Balkan language) they hired someone who speaks!
       b *Guess how many (languages) they hired someone who speaks!

One might take the contrast between (129) and (130) to indicate, as in the cases in § 5.1, that relative clauses are PF-islands. This conclusion is unlikely to be correct, however—unlike the improvement noted above in comparatives for left-branch extractions, for example, the equivalent extractions out of relative clauses inside *than*-clauses remain ill formed (cf. Introduction, example (5), and Chapter 4 note 5):

(131) a *Abby hired someone who speaks a rarer Balkan language than
          Op_1 Ben did ~~hire someone who speaks [t_1 'a t_1 Balkan language]~~.
       b *Abby hired someone who speaks more Balkan languages than
          Op_1 Ben did ~~hire someone who speaks [t_1 Balkan languages]~~.

What I propose instead is that the parallel between (129) and (130) is only apparent, and that the sluices in (129) do not in fact contain an island. Instead, I propose that they have a structure like the following:

(132) a Guess which$_1$ [~~she speaks t_1~~]!
       b Guess how many$_2$ [~~he speaks t_2~~]!

These are thus parallel to their overt counterparts in (133).

(133)   a   They hired someone who speaks a Balkan language—guess which
            she speaks!
        b   They hired someone who speaks a lot of languages—guess how
            many he speaks!

The interpretation of the sluicing examples will be identical to that of their
non-elided counterparts. The meaning of the antecedent clause is given in
(134a), and that of the sluiced CP in (134b). (I begin to use world variables here
for reasons that will become clear in the following section; here @ = the actual
world [more commonly represented as W_0], following the notation of von
Stechow 1996.)

(134)   a $\lambda w.\exists y[\textbf{balkan-language}_@(y) \wedge \exists x[\textbf{speak}_w(x, y) \wedge \textbf{hire}_w(\textbf{they}, x)]]$
        b $?y[\textbf{balkan-language}_@(y) \wedge \textbf{speak}_w(x, y)] =$
            $\lambda p.\exists y[\textbf{balkan-language}_@(y) \wedge p = \lambda w[\textbf{speak}_w(x, y)]]$

Let us see how the structures leading to these interpretations will satisfy the
Focus condition. Recall the relevant definition:

(135)   **e-GIVENness**
        An expression E counts as e-GIVEN iff E has a salient antecedent A and,
        modulo ∃-type shifting,
        (i)   A entails F-clo(E), and
        (ii)   E entails F-clo(A)

The general focus condition requires that $[[[\text{WHICH}_F \text{ (Balkan language)}]_1$
she$_6$ speaks $t_1]]^g$, regardless of whether the IP internal to the CP is elided or not,
satisfy GIVENness; as demonstrated in detail in Romero (1998), a sentence such
as *(I know whether) she speaks a Balkan language*, inferrable from the first conjunct of (129), provides an appropriate antecedent to license the F-marking
seen in both (129) and its non-elliptical counterpart in (133). What remains to
be shown is that the IP internal to this CP, when elided, satisfies the stronger
condition based on e-GIVENness as well. Let us therefore consider the deleted
IP in (132a).

First, let us assume for convenience, and apparently correctly, that F-
marking does not remain on traces of moved F-marked constituents. Secondly,
to be fully explicit, we have to assume that the NP ellipsis in [$_{DP}$ WHICH
[$_{NP}$ ~~Balkan language~~]], which we have been ignoring throughout, contributes
its meaning in some way to the deleted IP. The most straightforward way is
to assume the copy theory of movement, yielding something like (136) for the
deleted IP (see Sauerland 1998 for detailed discussion of the contribution of
traces):

(136)   [$_{IP}$ she$_6$ speaks [x Balkan language]]

Further, we let $[\![\text{she}_6^{E\text{-}type}]\!]^g = g(6) \in D_E$. The result of replacing the F-marked material and of existentially closing the unbound variable then is the following:

(137) $IP_E' = \text{F-clo}(IP_E) = \exists x.g(6)$ speaks x and x is a Balkan language

The embedded IP of the antecedent clause, given in (138), can serve as an antecedent to this, provided as above that the value assigned to *she*$_6^{E\text{-}type}$ is the same as the value assigned to t_6.

(138) $[\![[_{IP} t_6 \text{ speaks a Balkan language}]]\!]^g = \lambda w.\exists y[\textbf{balkan-language}_@(y) \wedge \textbf{speak}_w(g(6),y)]$

This gives the following for IP$_A$:

(139) $IP_A' = \text{F-clo}(IP_A) = \exists x.g(6)$ speaks x and x is a Balkan language

So IP$_A$ and IP$_E$, stand in the required relations, as desired.

This equivalence between a trace in the antecedent and a pronoun in the ellipsis site is the same as that discussed in the previous section for the traces of wh-XPs in questions and under QR. It should come as no surprise that the traces of wh-movement in relative clauses give rise to the same effects. Again, unless we are committed to a particular kind of structural identity condition on the deleted IP, no explicit appeal to a syntactic mechanism of 'vehicle change' is necessary. The pronoun in the ellipsis site will qualify as deletable under the Focus condition only if its index is the same as that of the trace in the antecedent. The interpretation of this pronoun, as in the previous section, will be that of an E-type pronoun, since it is not bound by the relative operator. This predicts that, if an E-type pronoun is impossible in a given context, the sluice will fail, just as the overt versions fail. That this prediction is correct is shown by the deviance of the following examples.

(140)   a   They hired {*no/??few} people who spoke a lot of languages— guess how many!
         b   *They didn't hire anyone who speaks a Balkan language, but I don't remember which.

These correspond exactly to the degree of deviance associated with their overt counterparts:

(141)   a   They hired {*no/??few} people who spoke a lot of languages—
             guess how many they$^{E\text{-}type}$ spoke!
         b   *They didn't hire anyone who speaks a Balkan language, but I
             don't remember which she$^{E\text{-}type}$ speaks.

The antecedent DPs in these cases, headed by *no, few*, and the negative polarity *any*, respectively, do not in general license E-type anaphora, as is well
known. Under some circumstances, however, E-type anaphora is licensed with
few, at least (though not with *no*), as in the following attested example (as in
Evans's (1980) original examples (5) and (7)).

(142)   The May day was still quite chilly and few people were out. I looked
         at them$^{E\text{-}type}$ idly across the intervening MacArthur Lock...
         (Paretsky 1984: 150)

   To the extent that such anaphora is possible, then, we expect sluices relying
on this kind of anaphora to be correspondingly improved. This seems to dove-
tail with the reactions of informants, who sometimes hestitate on judging the
relevant examples (those in (140) with *few*), no doubt indicating that they are
attempting to construct the relevant context to allow the anaphora, usually
with poor results.[18]
   These contrasts are replicated with traces of QR in antecedent IPs as well.
When the QRed DP licenses cross-sentential anaphora, sluicing exhibits the
ambiguity shown in (143)–(146).

(143)   Everyone helped, but I don't know why.
         a   = ... why everyone helped
         b   = ... why they$^{E\text{-}type}$ helped

(144)   Five scouts helped, but I don't know why.
         a   = ... ?why five scouts helped
         b   = ... why they$^{E\text{-}type}$ helped

(145)   At least three flags will be flown; when will be announced later today.
         a   = ... ?when at least three flags will be flown
         b   = ... when they$^{E\text{-}type}$ will be flown

(146)   Exactly five officers were fired, but I don't know why
         a   = ... why exactly five were fired
         b   = ... why they$^{E\text{-}type}$ were fired

---

[18] In some cases, comp-set anaphora is possible (see Moxey and Sandford 1993), a possibility
I put aside here.

In each case, there is a systematic ambiguity in what is deleted. The sluice can be interpreted as either (a) or (b), which represent the structures of the deleted material. The (a) examples are expected, since they are exactly equivalent to the antecedent IP, by the following logic. Take for example (146a). For the sluice to have this reading, the deleted IP is as in (147).

(147)   [$_{IP}$ ~~exactly five were fired~~]

Clearly, since this is identical to the antecedent, its deletion is licensed by the Focus condition. Here, IP_A and IP_E are as in (148).

(148)   a $IP_E' = \exists_5!x.x$ were fired
         b $IP_A' = \exists_5!x.x$ were fired

The availability of the (b) readings is again the result of the fact that the Focus condition can evaluate a pronoun as equivalent to a trace. So, for (146b), we have:

(149) $IP_E = $ [$_{IP}$ ~~they~~$_2$$^{E\text{-}type}$ ~~were fired~~] $= g(2)$ were fired

The lower IP segment of the antecedent IP after QR of *exactly five officers* supplies IP_A:

(150)   a   [$_{IP}$ ~~[exactly five officers]~~$_2$ ~~[$_{IP}$ t_2 were fired]~~]
         b $IP_A = $ [$_{IP}$ ~~t_2 were fired~~]

This equivalence will go through only provided that the anaphora can be resolved in the first place (that is, just scoping a correlate to provide a structurally useful antecedent IP segment is not enough). If the antecedent DP is downward entailing, such anaphoric links will be difficult or impossible, as the following data show.

(151)   No one helped, but I don't know why.
         a   = . . . why no one helped
         b   ≠ . . . *why they$^{E\text{-}type}$ helped

(152)   Few scouts helped, but I don't know why.
         a   = . . . why few scouts helped
         b   ≠ . . . *why they$^{E\text{-}type}$ helped

(153)   Fewer than six states voted for Mondale—the big question is why.
         a   = fewer than six (i.e., so few) voted for him
         b   = ? they$^{E\text{-}type}$ voted for him (i.e., why those six voted for him at all)

These could satisfy the Focus condition as above, if it were the case that only structural conditions had a role to play. But the conditions on the availability of such anaphora are not structural, but rather semantic/pragmatic. The fact that these sluices are unambiguous, in contrast to those in (143)–(146) has nothing to do with the mechanisms that resolve ellipsis or sluicing in particular—they follow from general constraints on the availability of E-type anaphora.

The conclusion that quantified antecedents can license deletion of pronouns is supported as well by the following data (showing as well that Safir's 1999 claim that the traces of QR are immune to 'vehicle change' cannot be sustained).

(154)   a   I met with every suspect$_1$, though most$_2$ claimed I hadn't.
         b   Everyone$_1$ helped, though most$_2$ weren't sure why.

These examples are ambiguous in a way similar to the examples in (143)–(146), with the interesting difference that here, when the trace of QR in the antecedent is equivalent to a pronoun, this pronoun is bound by the local, c-commanding quantifier (let us call this an example of 'rebinding'), as in (155). (Note that Binding Theory tests show that we have a pronoun, not a syntactic variable, in the ellipsis site: Principle C is voided, but Principle B is not.)

(155)   a   . . . most$_2$ claimed I hadn't [~~met with them$_2$~~].
         b   . . . most$_2$ weren't sure why [~~they$_2$ helped~~].

This is not simply telescoping, and is impossible if the rebinding quantifier has a different restriction:

(156)   I met with every suspect$_1$, though most cops$_2$ claimed I hadn't.
         a   = [met with {every suspect/them$_1$}]
         b   ≠ [met with them$_2$]

These may be taken to provide support for the copy theory of A′-movement, if the restriction *in situ* is something like [*x suspect*], interpreted as a definite description (see Sauerland 1998, Fox 2000). This conclusion only goes through, of course, if pronouns are themselves minimal spell-outs of such definite descriptions (as in the traditional analysis of E-type pronouns), since the same interpretive restrictions are found with overt pronouns in the equivalent deaccented counterparts:

(157)   I met with every suspect$_1$, though most cops$_2$ claimed I hadn't *met with them*$_{\{1/*2\}}$.

Interestingly, these anaphoric possibilities track set/subset relations (assume: *lifer'* $\subset$ *inmate'*). Compare the interpretations available for (158) and (159) to those possible for (160) and (161) (parallel, again, to their overt deaccented counterparts, as the reader may verify).

(158)   I met with every inmate$_1$, though {many/most} lifers$_2$ said I hadn't.
    a   = [met with them$_1$]
    b   = [met with them$_2$]

(159)   I met with every lifer$_2$, though {many/most} inmates$_1$ said I hadn't.
    a   = [met with them$_2$]
    b $\neq$ [met with them$_1$]

(160)   I met with most inmates$_1$, though many lifers$_2$ didn't want me to.
    a   = [meet with {most/the} inmates]
    b   = [meet with them$_2$]

(161)   I met with most lifers$_2$, though many inmates$_1$ didn't want me to.
    a   = [meet with {most/the} lifers]
    a $\neq$ [meet with them$_1$]

When the second quantifier is a subset of the first, rebinding is possible (as in (158b), (160b)); otherwise, rebinding is not possible.

Whether these data should in fact be accounted for using the copy theory of movement depends in part on what the correct analysis is of the structure of anaphoric pronouns—essentially whether they have internal structure, and, if so, exactly what shape this structure takes. One possible difficulty in reducing these data to a purely structural account over a more general semantic-pragmatic account is the fact that the same anaphoric possibilities show up with 'situational' *it*, as the data in (162) and (163) show.

(162)   I met with every inmate$_1$, though {many/most} lifers$_2$ didn't like/denied it.
    a   *it*= [that I met with every inmate]
    b   *it*= [that I met with them$_2$]

(163)   I met with every lifer₂, though {many/most} inmates₁ didn't like/
            denied it.
        a   *it* = [that I met with every lifer]
        b   *it* ≠ [that I met with them₁]

It is generally assumed that this *it* is not derived by deletion (see especially Bresnan 1971 for arguments). If this is true, then the inferential similarities should be derived by general mechanisms of cross-sentential anaphora, and not from structural conditions encoded by a copy theory. The obvious other conclusion is that even this *it* is derived by a mechanism of 'minimal spell-out', encoding complex structure see (see Akmajian 1970, Grinder and Postal 1971, Hankamer and Sag 1976, and McCawley 1998: ch.11 for discussion).[19]

In sum, there is substantial evidence that the availability of certain interpretations for elided structures falls out from independently needed devices for anaphoric resolution, E-type or otherwise.

5.3.1.2 *Subjunctive Relatives and Modal Subordination*

Up to this point, we have been concerned with relative clauses occurring in DPs that could be taken to have referents in the real world. In several languages with robust indicative/subjunctive mood distinctions, such as Greek, French, and Catalan, the predicates inside such relative clauses appear in the indicative, indicating that the DP in which they occur must outscope any intensional operators (that is, the descriptive content must be evaluated with respect to the world of the speaker). The solution to the apparent island nature of the relative clauses examined above relied on this fact, using E-type anaphora to resolve the posited pronoun in the deleted IP. Such a strategy cannot extend directly to subjunctive relative clauses, however. (See Quine 1960, Farkas 1985, Giannakidou 1997, 1998, and Quer 1998 for discussion of the scopal properties of these clauses.) This is because DPs that are modified by relative clauses whose predicates are in the subjunctive must take scope under an intensional operator— therefore, no referent in the speaker's world is guaranteed.

A naive view might lead us to think that this fact would imply that sluicing over correlates in subjunctive relatives would not be possible. This is in fact false, as the following data from Greek and English demonstrate. In Greek,[20] the

---

[19] By Lakoff's (1968) test—if such pronouns occur in Bach–Peters sentences, they must be non-derived pronouns—this *it* is non-derived: '**The guy who denied *it*** was arrested for *wire-tapping his employee's offices.*'

[20] Thanks to A. Giannakidou for judgments and discussion of the Greek examples in this section.

embedded verbs are preceded by the subjunctive particle *na*; in English, which lacks a morphological subjunctive in these cases, we find the simple present form.

(164)   Theli na vri ena imerologio pu na exi grapsi enas
        wants SUBJ find a   diary   that SUBJ has written a

        stratigos   tou Nixon, alla dhen thimame   pjos.
        general of.the Nixon but not I.remember which

        'She wants to find a diary that a general of Nixon's may have written, but I don't remember which (general).'

(165)   Psaxnun kapjon pu na   milai mia valkaniki glossa, alla
        they.seek someone that SUBJ speaks a   Balkan   language but

        dhe ksero   pja.
        not I.know which

        'They're looking for someone who (would) speak(s) a Balkan language, but I don't know which.'

(166)   They want to hire someone who speaks a Balkan language, but I don't know which.

The Greek examples allow only for the *de dicto* reading of the indefinite DP object of the intensional predicate, while the English is ambiguous (though for present purposes we will be concerned only with the narrow scope reading). Thus the antecedent clause of (165) has only the reading given in (167b) (modulo the scope of the embedded indefinite *a Balkan language*, which must have wide scope to license the sluice in the first place) and does not permit the reading in (167a); I will restrict attention to the English case of this reading as well—for the remainder of this section, we can ignore the wide-scope reading.

(167)   a $\neq \exists y[\textbf{Balkan-language}_@(y) \wedge \exists x[\textbf{person}_@(x) \wedge \textbf{speak}_@(x,y) \wedge \textbf{want}_@(\textbf{they}, \lambda w[\textbf{hire}_w(\textbf{they},x)])]]$
        b $= \exists y[\textbf{Balkan-language}_@(y) \wedge \textbf{want}_@(\textbf{they}, \lambda w[\exists x[\textbf{person}_w(x) \wedge \textbf{speak}_w(x,y) \wedge \textbf{hire}_w(\textbf{they},x)]])]$

Since in these cases, there is no individual whose existence is entailed, it makes no sense to think of the pronoun in the sluiced IP as referring to that individual. The key to this puzzle is given by the behavior of pronominals in intensional contexts, however. As investigated especially in Roberts (1989, 1996), it is possible for anaphora to succeed across sentence boundaries in some cases just in case the sentence in which the pronoun occurs contains one of an appropriate class of modal markers. Some of her examples are given in (168).

(168) a You should buy a lottery ticket$_1$. It$_1$ might be worth a million dollars.
       b He wants to marry a Norwegian$_2$. She$_2$ should like the cold.
       c If you (should) see a finch$_3$, stop moving. It$_3$ might get scared off.

This property of modal contexts applies equally in questions (see Groenendijk 1998 and van Rooy 1998 as well):

(169) a A patient might come in complaining of pressure in the head. What questions should you ask him?
       b Where can I find an Italian newspaper, and how much will it cost?

Roberts dubs this possibility 'modal subordination', and shows convincingly that it is primarily a pragmatic phenomenon. The exact account of modal subordination is not crucial here, only that it is possible—it is this possibility that permits a pronoun in the sluice to be used. The sluices in (165) and (166) are equivalent to the following overt continuations.

(170) a . . . pja *(na) milai.
             which SUBJ *speaks*
       b . . . which she {should speak/*speaks}.

In these cases, some kind of modal element is necessary. In Greek, this is supplied simply by the use of the subjunctive, which is obligatory in this case. In English, presumably because of the lack of robust subjunctive morphology, a full modal must be used. This is the same as the fact that some kind of modal must be used to trigger modal subordination in the standard cases in (168), as well as in questions (the anaphora is successful only on the undesired widescope use of the indefinite in the first sentence in English):

(171) a You should buy a lottery ticket. #It is worth a million dollars.
       b #Where can I find an Italian newspaper, and how much does it cost?

The same contrast obtains in Greek, where the data leave no room for ambiguity, unlike the English, since the presence of a subjunctive relative will require narrow scope of the indefinite with respect to the intensional operator in the first sentence.

(172)   Theli   na   pandrefti mia norvigidha pu   na   exei
         he.wants SUBJ *marries   a   Norwegian   who* SUBJ *has*

         polla lefta.
         much money

         a   Prepi   na   tis   aresi   to   krio.
              it.is.necessary SUBJ *her   pleases   the   cold*

         b   #Tis aresi   to   krio.
              her pleases   the   cold

         'He wants to marry a Norwegian who has a lot of money. She {should like/#likes} the cold.'

Returning to the sluices in (165) and (166), then, the ability of pronouns in intensional contexts to pick up antecedents in previous embedded contexts will account for the observed data. The sluices, then, simply are the IP-deleted versions of (170) above:

(173)   a   . . . pja₂ ~~pro₆ na milai t₂~~.
              which   SUBJ speaks

         b   . . . which ~~she₆ should speak t₂~~.

These will have roughly the semantics given in (174):[21]

(174) $?y[\textbf{balkan-language}_@(y) \wedge \square \textbf{ speak}_w(g(6),y)] =$
         $\lambda p \exists y[\textbf{balkan-language}_@(y) \wedge p(@) \wedge p = \lambda w' \forall w[w'Rw \rightarrow$
         $\textbf{speak}_w(g(6),y)]]$

This deletion will satisfy the Focus condition just in case there is an antecedent that can yield the formula in (175).

(175) $\exists y[\textbf{balkan-language}_@(y) \wedge \square\textbf{speak}_w(g(6), y)]$

---

[21] Here I use the standard definitions given in Hughes and Cresswell (1996). Let a model be an ordered triple M = ⟨W, R, V⟩, where R is an accessibility relation over W, W a non-empty set of worlds, and V is a valuation function over propositional variables such that V(p,w) = 1 iff V assigns the value 1 to p in w, and V(p,w) = 0 iff V assigns the value 0 to p in w. Then we define the necessity operator $\square$ as in (i):

   (i) $V(\square\phi, w) = 1$ if $\forall w' [wRw' \rightarrow V(\phi, w') = 1]$, otherwise $V(\square\phi, w) = 0$

Modal subordination is just restricting R by the modal base f (i.e., by excluding those worlds w_i from the range of R which are not in $\cap f(w)$).

We can assume that the subjunctive in the relative clause provides the □ operator,[22] unseen morphologically in English. It is the presence of the subjunctive—translated as some kind of modal operator—in the deleted IP that licenses the modally subordinated anaphora.

This derives the desired interpretation of the sluices in (164)–(166), but does so without having to claim that the island is itself present or reconstructed in the missing IP in the sluice. Instead, the appropriate restriction to the 'want-worlds' that is part of the meaning of these sluices is a by-product of modal subordination.

Just as we saw that the E-type anaphora involved in the sluices with indicative relatives is sensitive to discourse functions (see the discussion of (140) and (141)), the modally subordinated anaphora needed in the case of the subjunctive relatives is also ruled out when the antecedent cannot license cross-sentential anaphora, regardless of whether there is deletion or not. I illustrate this fact with the clearest cases—emphatic negative polarity items in Greek with subjunctive relatives (see Giannakidou 1998: ch. 4, and 2000 for the scopal properties of Greek emphatic NPIs). Such DPs do not license cross-sentential anaphora even with a modal element.

(176)   *Dhen ithelan   na proslavoun KANENAN pu na milai
         not   *wanted.they SUBJ hire*   *anyone   that SUBJ speaks*
        mia valkaniki glossa, alla dhen ksero pja.
         a   Balkan   language but not I.know which
        ('*They didn't want to hire anyone who speaks a Balkan language, but
        I don't know which.' (cf. 140b))

(177)   *Dhen ithelan   na proslavoun KANENAN pu na milai
         not   *wanted.they SUBJ hire*   *anyone   that SUBJ speaks*
        mia valkaniki glossa, alla dhen ksero pja na milai.
         a   Balkan   language but not I.know which SUBJ speaks
        ('*They didn't want to hire anyone who speaks a Balkan language, but
        I don't know which s/he (would) speak(s).' (cf. (141b)))

---

[22] Simplifying somewhat, this would mean that the sentence with the subjunctive relative would have a translation like that in (i):

   (i) $\exists y[\text{balkan-language}_@(y) \land \textbf{want}_@(\textbf{they}, \lambda w[\exists x[\textbf{person}_w(x) \land \forall w'[wRw' \rightarrow \textbf{speak}_{w'}(x,y)] \land \textbf{hire}_w(\textbf{they},x)]])]$

See especially Quer (1998) for a more refined view. For my purposes, it is not crucial exactly what the semantics of □ is, just that it is the same for the subjunctive both in the subjunctive relative clause and in the modal subordination-triggering question.

In sum, then, it is possible to sluice over a correlate in a relative clause just in case the independent constraints regulating the distribution of (E-type) anaphora are met: again, we see that nothing particular to sluicing need be said. This is a very attractive feature of the present approach over those that posit various operations found only under ellipsis or permit exceptions to structural isomorphism.

5.3.2 Adjuncts and Sentential Subjects

The above analysis extends directly to adjuncts, since these also can introduce modal bases restricting the evaluation of subsequent modal operators. The prototypical case is the protasis of a conditional, but the same holds of concessive, reason, and temporal adjuncts as well (in fact, in their veridical uses, these latter are even simpler, parallel to the case of the indicative relatives above).

(178)   If Ben talks to someone, Abby will be mad, but I don't remember who.

It is standard to analyze the *if*-clause as restricting a (possibly covert) adverb of quantification (see Kratzer 1981, de Swart 1991, and von Fintel 1994). The same holds for other adjuncts (see discussion and references in Kratzer 1998 and Giannakidou and Zwarts, forthcoming). This formalization is given in (179), parallel to the cases examined above.

(179) $\exists x[\textbf{person}_@(x) \wedge \forall w[\textbf{talk-to}_w(\textbf{ben}, x) \rightarrow \textbf{mad}_w(\textbf{abby})]]$

The sluice in (178) will have the structure in (180a), having the translation in (180b):

(180)   a   ... who [~~he talks to~~ ___]
          b $?x[\textbf{person}_@(x) \wedge \Box\textbf{talk-to}_w(\textbf{ben}, x)]$

Here again, modal subordination must restrict the domain of $\Box$ to those worlds that satisfy the consequent of the conditional in the antecedent. This effect can be paraphrased as something like 'who he would have to talk to [to make Abby mad]' or, less naturally, 'who he might talk to in the Abby-mad worlds'. Interestingly, although I have eliminated the island *per se* from the base structure of the sluice, it remains a fact that there seems to be no particularly natural way to express the meaning of the missing material overtly. This contrasts with the case of the relative clauses above, where, especially in languages with overt mood marking, the relevant non-elliptical version is possible. Whether this should be a matter for concern or not is not entirely clear to me at this point. Perhaps this is simply another case where, speaking pre-theoretically, language prefers an 'economical' solution; the parallel that suggests itself is with E-type pronouns, where filling in some overt, explicit description is unwieldy at best. Since this fact has not prevented many analysts from assuming that such a description is in fact constructed, I will not let the strangeness of any overt version of (180) concern me further here. Perhaps the awkwardness should be related to the fact that the 'subjunctive' in English, which we might assume is the form of the verb that the overt antecedent in the protasis takes based on the parallel forms in languages with overt morphological marking (not to be confused with the form of the verb that occurs in the complement to predicates like *require* etc., which are also often termed subjunctive), cannot occur without an overt binder for its world variable. This contrast, whatever properties of the defective subjunctive morphology in English that it follows from, can be seen in the fact that non-modals cannot support modal subordination in contexts parallel to those in (169) above:

(181)   *Where can I find an Italian newspaper$_4$, and how much does it$_4$ cost?

For sentential subjects, we have several options. In the case of veridical sentential subjects, there is no reason to suppose that we have extraction out of the subject CP at all, since there is no interpretive difference:

(182)   [$_{CP}$ That Maxwell killed the judge] was proven, but it's still not clear with what.

Since the subject CP is true in the actual world (that is, V($[\![CP]\!]$, @) = 1), there is no reason on grounds of interpretation to claim that the sluice has the structure in (183a) over that in (183b).

(183)   a   . . . with what$_2$ [[~~Maxwell killed the judge t_2~~] ~~was proven~~].
         b   . . . with what$_2$ [~~Maxwell killed the judge t_2~~].

In fact, it has often been noted that fronted sentential subjects tend to be factive (Kiparsky and Kiparksy 1970: 167), but, as pointed out especially in Svenonius (1994: 77), they need not be. When they are not, we will need to have recourse either to the kind of discourse subordination effect discussed above, or we can claim that the extraction proceeds from the base position of the CP, as was argued for non-sentential subjects in §5.1.3. I am not aware of any evidence that would help us decide between these alternatives at this point, so I will leave the choice between them in abeyance.

5.3.3 Coordinate Structure Constraint II: Extraction out of a Conjunct

Similar considerations come into play in the analysis of extraction out of conjuncts, in particular out of VP conjuncts, which I will restrict my attention to here as the most problematic and interesting of the potential cases (extraction out of just one CP conjunct or the like will be readily amenable to the treatment sketched above for sentential subjects, if only a single CP is in the deletion site). At issue are cases like the following.

(184)   a   Bob ate dinner and saw a movie that night, but he didn't say which.
        b   Bob ate dinner and saw a couple of movies that night, but he didn't say how many.
        c   Bob saw a movie and ate an expensive dinner that night, but he didn't say how expensive.

I will assume that the structure of such examples involves VP coordination, and not some kind of operation of conjunction reduction applying to conjoined IPs (given the well-formedness of *No-one$_2$ ate dinner and saw a movie that night*, which cannot be derived from the impossible **No-one$_2$ ate dinner and he$_2$ saw a movie that night*, see Winter 1998 for recent discussion and references). I will further assume that coordinated VPs are indeed islands, a sometimes debated assumption defended forcefully in Postal (1998: ch. 3).

With these assumptions, the deleted IPs cannot be those in (185), since these should have the same status as their overt counterparts in (186).

(185)   a   . . . which$_1$ ~~[he ate dinner and saw t_1 that night]~~.
        b   . . . how many$_2$ ~~[he ate dinner and saw t_2 that night]~~.
        c   . . . how expensive$_3$ ~~[he saw a movie and ate [t_3' a t_3 dinner] that night]~~.

(186)   a   ??Which movie$_1$ did Bob eat dinner and see t_1 that night?
        b   *How many movies$_2$ did Bob eat dinner and see t_2 that night?
        c   *How expensive a dinner$_3$ did Bob see a movie and eat t_3 that night?

Chung *et al.*'s solution (1995) to this problem is to allow binding into a conjunct, via merger. For them, an example like (184a) would have the structure in (187) at LF (modulo vehicle change, presumably):

(187)   . . . which^x [he ate dinner and saw [a movie]^x that night].

Since merger, unlike sprouting, is by hypothesis insensitive to islands, the sluice in (184a) is well formed. Unfortunately for this account, examples like the following are also well formed.

(188)   a   I packed up all the dishes and dumped them without telling her where.
         b   He sold his farm and moved away, but no one knows where to.
         c   Abby quit and got a new job—guess what as!
         d   Ben was sitting in the back and playing the trumpet, but I couldn't tell how loudly.

Under the Chung *et al.* (1995) system, the resolution of these sluices would have to involve sprouting, which is posited to be sensitive to islands.

   An alternative would be to claim that the ban on extraction out of conjuncts is a PF-effect, as argued above for the ban on extraction of conjuncts.[23] But this would leave the following contrasts mysterious—when the subject is headed by the determiner *no*, sluices of all kinds are impossible, whether with overt correlates or not.

(189)   a   *No farmer sold his farm and moved to a certain town—I don't remember which.
         b   *No one quit and got a new job—guess what as!
         c   *Nobody was sitting in the back and playing one of the horns, but I couldn't tell {which/how loudly}.
         d   *Not one critic ate dinner and saw a couple of movies that night, but I don't know how many.

   If extraction out of the conjunct were itself possible, these examples should have the same status as an example like the following:

(190)   Which town did no farmer move to?

And indeed, as seen above in (151)–(153), it is possible in some instances to sluice over IPs containing downward-entailing DPs:

---

[23] It is somewhat difficult to construct examples relevant for testing this claim directly, especially since it is not clear what exactly would be going wrong at PF to cause the ungrammaticality. The example in (i), to the extent that it tests this, shows that simply embedding the illicit extraction site in an ellipsis site does not remedy the island violation. (The examples in (ii) give various controls.)

(191)   No one moved to a certain town—guess which!

The fact that the sluices in (189) fail provides the key to the puzzle. I propose that the deleted IP contains an E-type pronoun licensed by the VP-internal subject. Thus, instead of (192a) as the deleted IP for the sluice in (184a), I propose that the IP that is deleted is in fact that given in (192b).

(192)   a   . . . *which [~~he₆ ate dinner and saw *t* that night~~].
        b   . . . which [~~he₆ saw *t* that night~~].

This IP can be deleted just in case there is an antecedent that entails (193), where $g(6)$ is an E-type pronoun, as above.

(193) $\exists x[\textbf{movie}(x) \wedge \textbf{saw}(g(6), x, \textbf{that-night})]$

And we can indeed infer (193) from the first sentence of (184a), *Bob₆ ate dinner and saw a movie that night*. In the cases in (189), however, no such inference goes through, since no E-type interpretation will be available. Again, the sluices have the same status as their overt counterparts with pronouns:

(194)   a   Bob ate dinner and saw a movie that night, but he didn't say which he saw.
        b   *No farmer sold his farm and moved to a certain town—I don't remember which he moved to.

The availability of sluicing, then, will track the availability of E-type anaphora in these contexts. This also correctly predicts that there will be no difference between 'merger' and 'sprouting' cases:

(195)   Ben was sitting in the back and playing the trumpet, but I couldn't tell how loudly (he was playing it).

These examples also point to the difficulty in imposing a strict structural isomorphism requirement on the sluiced material. Here, such a requirement would have to be relaxed enough to allow a VP to license deletion of

(i)   *Abby ate a more expensive dinner than Ben saw a movie and then {ate/did}.
(ii)   a   Abby ate a more expensive dinner than Ben did.
        b   Abby ate dinner; Ben saw a movie first and then did.

an entire IP. No such difficulty arises for the present account, however, since the semantic condition can be satisfied independently of how much structure is projected in the phrase that provides the antecedent.

5.4 SELECTIVE ('WEAK') ISLANDS

The behavior of sluicing out of selective islands is illuminating in that it demonstrates again that sluicing does not confer some kind of absolute immunity to islandhood—in fact, as we will see, sluicing over implicit correlates in selective islands sometimes gives rise to a deviance that cannot be explained in any syntactic way at all. This fact lends support to the range of analyses in the literature (Kroch 1989; Comorovski 1989; Szabolcsi and Zwarts 1993; Kuno and Takami 1997; Honcoop 1998) that claim that selective islandhood is a semantic or pragmatic phenomenon, not a syntactic one at all (contra Rizzi 1990, 1994; Manzini 1998).

The question of sluicing and selective islands has been investigated in Albert (1993), Sauerland (1996), Romero (1998), and Merchant (2000c). Here the discussion will be limited to reviewing the conclusions reached in those works, and showing that the relevant data are compatible with a deletion account of the syntax of sluicing.

Albert (1993) was the first to notice that sluicing over implicit correlates (either implicit arguments or adjuncts) shows a systematic sensitivity to selective islands.[24] Some of his data, for implicit arguments, are reproduced in (196); (197) is from Merchant (2000c):

(196) a   *Nigel nevers hunts, but I don't remember what.
       b   *No one drank, but I can't say which kind of wine.
       c   *The new chef refused to bake, but we don't recall what.
       d   *No one talked, but it's not clear to whom.
       e   *Mitch refused to go to the party, but we can't remember who with.
       f   *Reggie avoids reading novels, but I don't know what about.
       g   *It's hard for Megan to dance, but I don't know who with.
       h   *Mario denied Sally got in a fight, but it's unclear who with.
       i   *Judy rarely borrows a car, but I can't recall whose.

---

[24] I omit from consideration here sluices with *why*. Such sluices have a number of interesting properties that would lead us afield here, such as their variants including negation (*She didn't leave, but I don't know why not.*). See Horn (1978: 164–5) and Merchant (2000d) for discussion.

(197) a *No nurse was on duty, but we don't know when.
 b *A nurse is rarely on duty—guess when!

Extraction of certain kinds of wh-expressions from the environments in (196) and (197) are deviant, as is well known (see the above works for examples). What is surprising about the data in (196)–(197) is that the wh-phrases that are the remnants of the sluicing in those examples do not in fact show this deviance under overt extraction:

(198) a What does Nigel never hunt?
 b Which kind of wine did no one drink?
 c What does Reggie avoid reading novels about?

(199) a When was no nurse on duty?
 b When is a nurse rarely on duty?

The contrast between the licit extractions in (198)–(199) and the impossible sluices in (196)–(197) is problematic for Chung *et al.*'s (1995) account of island sensitivities as being a property of their 'sprouting' operation: in these cases, the chain connecting the operator and the 'sprouted' trace should be well formed, since the extraction is possible, yet the sluices remain deviant.

It is also not the case that sluicing overt implicit correlates is deviant in all cases (we have seen numerous examples to the contrary before), nor even when, say, an adverb of quantification occurs. Consider the contrast in (200), from Albert (1993: 1 (1)).

(200) a Sonny always eats around noon, but I don't know what.
 b *Sonny rarely eats around noon, but I don't know what.

To these we can add the parallel contrast in the following examples:

(201) a Ralph bought an old boat, but I don't know how old.
 b *No one bought an old boat, but I don't know how old.

(202) Jake {always/*rarely} takes his eggs salty—wait till you hear how salty!

The key to understanding these contrasts comes from the scopal properties of the implicit correlates: implicit arguments and adjuncts always take narrowest scope in their domain, as noted by Mittwoch (1982) and others (see Romero 1998: 38–9 for further references and discussion). This being the case, these contrasts can be explained by the requirement for scopal parallelism between the implicit quantifier in the antecedent clause and the quantifier associated with the wh-phrase in the sluicing clause. In the first clause in (197a), for example, the implicitly bound temporal variable has narrow scope with respect to *no nurse*, as in (203a), and does not have the reading expressed in (203b). It is this second reading that would have to be available for the sluice in (197a) to be well formed.

(203)   a $\neg\exists x[\mathbf{nurse}(x) \wedge \exists t[\mathbf{on\text{-}duty}(x, \text{at } t)]]$
         b $\exists t \neg\exists x[\mathbf{nurse}(x) \wedge \mathbf{on\text{-}duty}(x, \text{at } t)]$

This follows from the Focus condition, as Romero (1998) shows in detail. As she notes, when the intervenor is not downward monotonic, sluicing is possible (as in (200a), (201a) and (202)), because such elements are equivalent to E-type elements in the deleted IP (as seen above).

It is thus not necessarily the type of the sluiced wh-phrase that matters, so much as the possibility for the correlate, overt or implicit, to take the necessary clause-level (that is, outside the modal) scope. This accounts for the following gradability in judgments, where the remnant wh-phrase remains constant (an amount phrase, typically highly sensitive to extraction islands); the grammaticality of the resulting sluice depends on the ability of the amount phrase in the antecedent to take clausal scope, reflecting differences in how robustly certain kinds of antecedents license anaphora in modally subordinated contexts.

(204)   a   He wants to marry someone who speaks {a certain number of/??several/*Ø} languages, but I don't know how many.
         b   She needs to interview someone who has been in {a predetermined number of/??several/??some/*Ø} S. American countries—I don't know how many.
         c   We'll get reprimanded if {some special number of/*more than one/*some/*many/*Ø} customers complain, but I forgot how many.
         d   He wants to marry someone with {a certain amount of/*Ø} money, but he didn't say how much.

In summary, the contrasts discussed in this section illustrate that the conditions on acceptability in sluicing can relate directly to scopal parallelism requirements, and cannot be derived solely from structural conditions. This conclusion is perfectly compatible with the deletion approach advocated here, although since these conditions are ultimately not syntactic in nature, it is not particularly revealing as a probe on the syntactic nature of ellipsis.

5.5 SUMMARY

This chapter has shown that the data presented in Chapter 3 relating to islands and form-identity effects can be successfully handled by a deletion-based theory of ellipsis as applied to sluicing. While the form-identity effects follow directly from this approach, the apparent island insensitivity requires in some part a rethinking of our notions of syntactic islandhood (selective islands, at least, not being syntactic in any case). On the one hand, I argued that a large class of islands are in effect irrelevant to the investigation of islandhood under sluicing—those that properly contain a propositional domain—since there is no reason to assume that the deleted material contains an analog to the overt island. On the other hand, this left a residue of interesting effects that had to be reanalyzed as essentially products of ill-formedness at PF, and I presented independent evidence in each case that this was a plausible and coherent alternative.

The picture that emerges, then, is that we need a more pluralistic view of islandhood than is often assumed, and that various components of the grammar may give rise to extraction deviations. It is only by looking at extraction from out of an ellipsis site that we can begin to determine what parts of the grammar are responsible for what kinds of constraints on extraction. Our view of some of these matters has in effect been occluded by the overt, audible syntax—there is, it seems, much to be learned from undertaking the difficult task of investigating the inaudible structures underlying ellipsis, the syntax of silence.

Conclusion

The present work has been built on an examination of two of the best-studied and most intriguing areas in syntax and semantics: ellipsis and wh-movement. Although these two areas have garnered immense interest by themselves, their intersection—sluicing—has remained largely neglected. I believe this neglect is unfortunate, and that, especially by investigating sluicing, which is cross-linguistically much more widespread than the kinds of ellipsis more commonly studied, new light can be shed on a number of long-standing puzzles and questions in both areas.

This assertion is more than simply an article of faith: in examining a much wider range of data than is usually brought to bear on these questions, a number of surprising and theoretically challenging generalizations were uncovered, generalizations that could not, or only with difficulty, have emerged from studying other kinds of ellipsis. These include the form-identity generalizations of Chapter 3 and the sluicing-COMP generalization of Chapter 2. And, perhaps most interestingly, it was shown in Chapter 5 that our conception of islandhood must be refined in fundamental ways, leading to a pluralistic view of islands, with extraction deviancies distributed over different components of the grammar.

An important point to keep in mind is that I have *not* proposed a replacement for the general focus conditions discussed widely in the literature, which apply equally to structures that contain and do not contain ellipsis sites. These *containment* conditions remain in force, and I have had nothing new to say about them. The point that I have been pursuing is that such containment conditions must be supplemented by an *identity* condition, a condition that applies at the level of the ellipsis itself, and regulates only the ellipsis site, insensitive in general to material outside the ellipsis site. It is this identity condition, usually considered to be of a syntactic nature, that I have been at pains to show can and should be formulated in terms very similar, though not identical, to the containment conditions. This is the basis of the identity condition based on e-GIVENness, related to the containment condition based on GIVENness.

A significant advantage of defining and localizing this identity condition on ellipsis sites themselves is that, by doing so, we can for the first time begin to build a theory that links what are traditionally known as the 'licensing' and 'identification' requirements on ellipsis sites. It was proposed in Chapter 2 that these requirements can both be imposed by the E feature, which is given a local feature-matching requirement (encoding 'licensing') as well as a well-defined semantics (the 'identification' by e-GIVENness).

I have endeavored throughout also to show that it is not only possible, but in fact necessary, to combine a theory of ellipsis based on semantic identity with ellipsis sites that have complete internal syntactic structure, unpronounced. A theory such as the one proposed here can put aside the false dichotomy that runs through much of the discussion of ellipsis: semantic approaches to ellipsis resolution are often seen as requiring the absence of syntactic structure in the ellipsis site, while evidence that there is syntax in ellipsis has often been used to claim that ellipsis resolution is based on identity of syntactic structures. But we have seen here that these different strands of evidence are in fact not in competition at all: it is perfectly coherent, and indeed desirable, to countenance syntactically active and complete structures that are unpronounced by virtue of a semantic relationship with an antecedent. Such an approach captures the best of both worlds, while providing insight into problems that have plagued the narrower approaches, problems that have sometimes been named (such as the problem of 'vehicle change') but have never received a satisfactory solution. Though in several respects the present proposal must be seen as only the first step, I am optimistic that such an approach is correct in its essential theoretical orientation and I am hopeful that it will prove flexible enough to meet the challenges presented by other elliptical constructions as successfully as it has sluicing.

References

Abney, Steven (1987). 'The English Noun Phrase in its Sentential Aspect', Ph.D. thesis, MIT.

Ackema, Peter, and Neeleman, Ad (1998). 'Optimal Questions'. *Natural Language and Linguistic Theory*, 16: 443–90.

Adger, David, and Quer, Josep (1997). 'Subjunctives, Unselected Embedded Questions, and Clausal Polarity Items', in K. Kusumoto (ed.), *Proceedings of the 27th Meeting of the North Eastern Linguistic Society*. Amherst, MA: Graduate Student Linguistic Society, 1–15.

Aissen, Judith (1992). 'Topic and Focus in Mayan'. *Language*, 68: 43–80.

Akmajian, Adrian (1970). 'The Role of Focus in the Interpretation of Anaphoric Expressions', in S. Anderson and P. Kiparsky (eds.), *A Festschrift for Morris Halle*. New York: Holt, Rinehart and Winston, 215–26.

Albert, Chris (1993). 'Sluicing and Weak Islands', MS, University of California, Santa Cruz.

Alexiadou, Artemis, and Anagnostopoulou, Elena (1998). 'Parametrizing AGR: Word Order, V-Movement, and EPP-Checking'. *Natural Language and Linguistic Theory*, 16: 491–539.

Anagnostopoulou, Elena (1994). 'Clitic Dependencies in Greek', Ph.D. thesis, Salzburg University.

——van Riemsdijk, Henk, and Zwarts, Frans (1997) (eds.), *Materials on Left Dislocation*. Amsterdam: John Benjamins.

Anderson, Stephen (1996). 'How to Put your Clitics in their Place'. *Linguistic Review*, 13: 165–91.

——(2000). 'Towards an Optimal Account of Second Position Phenomena', in J. Dekkers, F. van der Leeuw, and J. van de Weijer (eds.), *Optimality Theory: Phonology, Syntax, and Acquisition*. Oxford: Oxford University Press, 302–33.

Aoun, Joseph (1985). *A Grammar of Anaphora*. Cambridge, MA: MIT Press.

——and Benmamoun, Elabbas (1998). 'Minimality, Reconstruction, and PF Movement'. *Linguistic Inquiry*, 29: 569–97.

——Hornstein, Norbert, Lightfoot, David, and Weinberg, Amy (1987). 'Two Types of Locality', *Linguistic Inquiry*, 18: 537–77.

Asher, Nicholas, Hardt, Daniel, and Busquets, Joan (1997). 'Discourse Parallelism, Scope, and Ellipsis', in A. Lawson (ed.), *Proceedings of the 7th conference on Semantics and Linguistic Theory*. Ithaca, NY: Cornell University, 19–36.

Baker, C. L., and Brame, Michael (1972). '"Global Rules": A Rejoinder'. *Language*, 48: 51–75.

Baltin, Mark, and Postal, Paul (1996). 'More on Reanalysis Hypotheses'. *Linguistic Inquiry*, 27: 127–45.

Bayer, Josef (1984). 'COMP in Bavarian'. *Linguistic Review*, 3: 209–74.

——(1996). *Directionality and Logical Form: On the Scope of Focussing Particles and Wh-in-Situ*. Dordrecht: Kluwer.

Bechhofer, Robin (1976*a*). 'Reduced Wh-Questions', in J. Hankamer and J. Aissen (eds.), *Harvard Studies in Syntax and Semantics 2*. Harvard University, Cambridge, MA, 31–67.

——(1976*b*). 'Reduction in Conjoined Wh-Questions', in J. Hankamer and J. Aissen (eds.), *Harvard Studies in Syntax and Semantics 2*. Harvard University, Cambridge, MA, 68–120.

——(1977). 'A Double Analysis of Reduced Wh-Questions', in J. Kegl *et al.* (eds.), *Proceedings of the 7th Meeting of the North Eastern Linguistic Society*. Amherst, MA: Graduate Student Linguistic Society, 19–31.

Beck, Sigrid (1996). 'Quantified Structures as Barriers for LF Movement'. *Natural Language Semantics*, 4: 1–56.

Beghelli, Filippo, and Stowell, Tim (1997). 'Distributivity and Negation: The Syntax of *Each* and *Every*', in A. Szabolcsi (ed.), *Ways of Scope Taking*. Dordrecht: Kluwer, 71–107.

Bennis, Hans (1986). *Gaps and Dummies*. Dordrecht: Foris.

——(1995). 'The Meaning of Structure: The *wat voor* Construction Revisited', in M. den Dikken and K. Hengeveld (eds.), *Linguistics in the Netherlands 1995*. Amsterdam: J. Benjamins, 25–36.

—— Corver, Norbert, and den Dikken, Marcel (1998). 'Predication in Nominal Phrases'. *Journal of Comparative Germanic Linguistics*, 1: 85–117.

den Besten, Hans (1978). 'On the Presence and Absence of Wh-Elements in Dutch Comparatives'. *Linguistic Inquiry*, 9: 641–71.

——(1989). 'Studies in West Germanic Syntax'. Ph.D. thesis, Tilburg University.

Bissell, Teal (1999). 'Antecedent-Contained Deletion and Null Pronominal Variables'. MA thesis, University of California, Santa Cruz.

Bolinger, Dwight (1972). *Degree Words*. The Hague: Mouton.

——(1978). 'Asking More than One Thing at a Time', in H. Hiz (ed.), *Questions*. Dordrecht: Reidel, 107–50.

Borer, Hagit (1981). 'Parametric Variation in Clitic Constructions'. Ph.D. thesis, MIT.

Bošković, Željko (1995). 'Participle Movement and Second Position Cliticization in Serbo-Croatian'. *Lingua*, 96: 245–66.

Bouton, Lawrence (1970). 'Antecedent-Contained Proforms', in *Papers from the 6th Regional Meeting of the Chicago Linguistic Society*. Chicago: Chicago Linguistic Society, 154–67.

Bresnan, Joan (1971). 'A Note on the Notion "Identity of sense anaphora"'. *Linguistic Inquiry*, 2: 589–97.

——(1972). 'Theory of Complementation in English Syntax'. Ph.D. thesis, MIT.

——(1975). 'Comparative Deletion and Constraints on Transformations'. *Linguistic Analysis*, 1: 25–74.

——(1977*a*). 'Transformations and Categories in Syntax', in R. E. Butts and J. Hintikka (eds.), *Basic Problems in Methodology and Linguistics*. Dordrecht: Reidel, 261–82.

——(1977*b*). 'Variables in the Theory of Transformations', in P. Culicover, T. Wasow, and A. Akmajian (eds.), *Formal Syntax*. New York: Academic Press, 157–96.

Brody, Michael (1995). *Lexico-Logical Form: A Radically Minimalist Theory*. Cambridge, MA: MIT Press.

Browne, Wayles (1972). 'Conjoined Question Words and a Limitation on English Surface Structures'. *Linguistic Inquiry*, 3: 222–6.

——(1974). 'On the Problem of Enclitic Placement in Serbo-Croatian', in R. D. Brecht and C. V. Chvany (eds.), *Slavic Transformational Syntax*. Ann Arbor: Michigan Slavic Materials, 36–52.

Browning, M. A. (1987). 'Null Operator Constructions'. Ph.D. thesis, MIT.

——(1996). 'CP Recursion and *that-t* Effects'. *Linguistic Inquiry*, 27: 237–55.

Büring, Daniel (1995). 'On the Base Position of Embedded Clauses in German'. *Linguistische Berichte*, 159: 370–80.

——(1997). *On the Meaning of Topic and Focus: The 59th Street Bridge Accent*. London: Routledge.

——(forthcoming). 'Let's Phrase It! Focus, Word Order, and Prosodic Phrasing in German Double Object Constructions'. in G. Müller and W. Sternefeld (eds.), *Competition in Syntax*. Amsterdam: John Benjamins.

——and Hartmann, Katharina (1999). 'V3 or not V3?' MS, University of California, Santa Cruz and University of Frankfurt.

Chao, Wynn (1987). 'On Ellipsis'. Ph.D. thesis, University of Massachusetts, Amherst.

——and Sells, Peter (1983). 'On the Interpretation of Resumptive Pronouns', in P. Sells and C. Jones (eds.), *Proceedings of the 13th Meeting of the North Eastern Linguistic Society*. Amherst, MA: Graduate Student Linguistic Society, 47–61.

de Chene, Brent (1995). 'Complementizer-Trace Effects and the ECP'. *Geneva Generative Papers*, 3: 1–4.

Chierchia, Gennaro (1995). *Dynamics of Meaning*. Chicago: University of Chicago Press.

Chomsky, Noam (1972). 'Some Empirical Issues in the Theory of Transformational Grammar', in S. Peters (ed.), *The Goals of Linguistic Theory*. Englewood Cliffs, NJ: Prentice-Hall, 63–130.

——(1973). 'Conditions on Transformations', in S. Anderson and P. Kiparsky (eds.), *A Festschrift for Morris Halle*. New York: Holt, Rinehart, and Winston, 232–86.

——(1981). *Lectures on Government and Binding*. Dordrecht: Foris.

——(1986*a*). *Barriers*. Cambridge, MA: MIT Press.

—— (1986*b*). *Knowledge of Language*. New York: Praeger.

—— (1995). *The Minimalist Program*. Cambridge, MA: MIT Press.

—— (1998). 'Minimalist Inquiries: The Framework'. MS, MIT.

—— and Lasnik, Howard (1977). 'Filters and Control'. *Linguistic Inquiry*, 8: 425–504.

—— —— (1993). 'Principles and Parameters Theory', in J. Jacobs, A. von Stechow, W. Sternefeld, and T. Vennemann (eds.), *Syntax: An International Handbook of Contemporary Research*. Berlin: De Gruyter, 506–70.

Chung, Sandra, Ladusaw, William, and McCloskey, James (1995). 'Sluicing and Logical Form'. *Natural Language Semantics*, 3: 239–82.

Cinque, Guglielmo (1990). *Types of A′ Dependencies*. Cambridge, MA: MIT Press.

—— (1993). 'On the Position of Modifiers in the Romance NP'. MS, University of Venice.

—— (1999). *Adverbs and Functional Heads: A Cross-Linguistic Perspective*. Oxford: Oxford University Press.

Collins, Chris (1997). *Local Economy*. Cambridge, MA: MIT Press.

Comorovski, Ileana (1989). 'Discourse-Linking and the *wh*-Island Constraint', in J. Carter and R.-M. Déchaine (eds.), *Proceedings of the 19th Meeting of the North Eastern Linguistic Society*. Amherst, MA: Graduate Student Linguistic Society, 78–96.

—— (1996). *Interrogative Phrases and the Syntax–Semantics Interface*. Dordrecht: Kluwer.

Corver, Norbert (1990). 'The Syntax of Left Branch Constructions'. Ph.D. thesis, Tilburg University.

Culicover, Peter (1992). 'The Adverb Effect: Evidence against ECP Accounts of the *that-t* Effect', in A. Schafer (ed.), *Proceedings of the 23rd Meeting of the North Eastern Linguistic Society*. Amherst, MA: Graduate Student Linguistic Society, 97–111.

—— and McNally, Louise (1998) (eds.), *The Limits of Syntax* (Syntax and Semantics 29). San Diego: Academic Press.

Dalrymple, Mary, Shieber, Stuart, and Pereira, Fernando (1991). 'Ellipsis and Higher-Order Unification'. *Linguistics and Philosophy*, 14: 399–452.

Deacon, Terrence (1997). *The Symbolic Species: The Co-Evolution of Language and the Brain*. New York: Norton.

Delin, Judy (1992). 'Properties of *it*-Cleft Presuppositions'. *Journal of Semantics*, 9: 289–306.

Demirdache, Hamida (1991). 'Resumptive Chains in Restrictive Relatives, Appositives, and Dislocation Structures'. Ph.D. thesis, MIT.

Déprez, Viviane (1994). 'A Minimal Account of the *that-t* Effect', in G. Cinque, J. Koster, J.-Y. Pollock, L. Rizzi, and R. Zanuttini (eds.), *Paths towards Universal Grammar: Studies in Honor of Richard S. Kayne*. Washington: Georgetown University Press, 121–35.

Diesing, Molly (1992). *Indefinites*. Cambridge, MA: MIT Press.

den Dikken, Marcel (1995). 'Binding, Expletives, and Levels'. *Linguistic Inquiry*, 26: 347–54.

den Dikken, Marcel, Meinunger, André, and Wilder, Chris (1998). 'Pseudoclefts and Ellipsis', in A. Alexiadou, N. Fuhrhop, P. Law, and U. Kleinhenz (eds.), *ZAS Working Papers in Linguistics 10*. Berlin: Zentrum für Allgemeine Sprachwissenschaft, 21–71.

Dobrovie-Sorin, Carmen (1993). *The Syntax of Romanian*. The Hague: Mouton.

Doron, Edit (1982). 'The Syntax and Semantics of Resumptive Pronouns'. *Texas Linguistics Forum 19*. Austin: University of Texas, 1–48.

—— (1990). 'V-Movement and VP-Ellipsis'. MS, Hebrew University of Jerusalem.

—— (1999). 'V-Movement and VP-Ellipsis', in S. Lappin and E. Benmamoun (eds.), *Fragments: Studies in Ellipsis and Gapping*. Oxford: Oxford University Press, 124–40.

Dowty, David (1991). 'Thematic Proto-Roles and Argument Selection'. *Language*, 67: 547–619.

Drubig, Bernhard (1994). 'Island Constraints and the Syntactic Nature of Focus and Association with Focus'. *Arbeitspapiere des Sonderforschungsbereichs*, 340/51.

Dryer, Matthew (1997). Handout from Typology Class, Linguistic Society of America Institute, Cornell University, Ithaca, NY.

Engdahl, Elisabet (1984). 'Parasitic Gaps, Resumptive Pronouns, and Subject Extractions'. MS, University of Wisconsin, Madison.

Erteschik-Shir, Nomi (1977). *On the Nature of Island Constraints*. Bloomington: IN: Indiana University Linguistics Club.

—— (1992). 'Resumptive Pronouns in Islands', in H. Goodluck and M. Rochemont (eds.), *Island Constraints: Theory, Acquisition, and Processing*. Dordrecht: Kluwer, 89–108.

Evans, Gareth (1980). 'Pronouns'. *Linguistic Inquiry*, 11: 337–62.

Fanselow, Gisbert (1990). 'Scrambling as NP-Movement', in G. Grewendorf and W. Sternefeld (eds.), *Scrambling and Barriers*. Amsterdam: John Benjamins, 113–40.

Farkas, Donka (1981). 'Quantifier Scope and Syntactic Islands', in R. Hendrick, C. Masek, and M. F. Miller (eds.), *Papers from the 17th Regional Meeting of the Chicago Linguistic Society*. Chicago: Chicago Linguistic Society, 59–66.

—— (1985). *Intensional Descriptions and the Romance Subjunctive Mood*. New York: Garland.

Fernald, Theodore (1994). 'On the Nonuniformity of the Individual- and Stage-Level Effects'. Ph.D. thesis, University of California, Santa Cruz.

—— (2000). *Predicates and Temporal Arguments*. Oxford: Oxford University Press.

Fiengo, Robert, and May, Robert (1994). *Indices and Identity*. Cambridge, MA: MIT Press.

—— Huang, C.-T. James, Lasnik, Howard, and Reinhart, Tanya (1988). 'The Syntax of wh-in-situ', in H. Borer (ed.), *Proceedings of the 7th West Coast Conference on Formal Linguistics*. Stanford, CA: Center for the Study of Language and Information, 81–98.

Fillmore, Charles (1965). *Indirect Object Constructions in English and the Ordering of Transformations*. The Hague: Mouton.

—— (1986). 'Pragmatically Contolled Zero Anaphora', in V. Nikiforidou, M. Van-Clay, M. Niepokuj, and D. Feder (eds.), *Proceedings of the 12th Meeting of the Berkeley Linguistic Society*. Berkeley, CA: Berkeley Linguistic Society, 95–107.

Finer, Daniel (1997). 'Contrasting A′-Dependencies in Selayarese'. *Natural Language and Linguistic Theory*, 15: 677–728.

von Fintel, Kai (1994). 'Restrictions on Quantifier Domains'. Ph.D. thesis, University of Massachusetts, Amherst.

Fox, Danny (1999). 'Reconstruction, Binding Theory, and the Interpretation of Chains'. *Linguistic Inquiry*, 30: 157–96.

——(2000). *Economy and Semantic Interpretation*. Cambridge, MA: MIT Press.

Fukaya, Teruhiko (1998). 'On So-called "Sluicing" in Japanese'. MS, University of Southern California.

Gazdar, Gerald, Pullum, Geoffrey, Sag, Ivan, and Wasow, Thomas (1982). 'Coordination and Transformational Grammar'. *Linguistic Inquiry*, 13: 663–76.

——Klein, Ewan, Pullum, Geoffrey, and Sag, Ivan (1985). *Generalized Phrase Structure Grammar*. Cambridge, MA: Harvard University Press.

Giannakidou, Anastasia (1997). 'The Landscape of Polarity Items'. Ph.D. thesis, University of Groningen.

——(1998). *Polarity Sensitivity as (Non)veridical Dependency*. Amsterdam: John Benjamins.

——(2000). 'Negative . . . Concord?', *Natural Language and Linguistic Theory*, 18: 457–523.

——and Merchant, Jason (1996). 'On the Interpretation of Null Indefinite Objects in Greek', in J. Veloudis and M. Karali (eds.), *Studies in Greek Linguistics 17*, Thessaloniki: University of Thessaloniki, 141–55.

————(1998). 'Reverse Sluicing in English and Greek'. *Linguistic Review*, 15: 233–56.

——and Stavrou, Melita (1999). 'Nominalization and Ellipsis in the Greek DP'. *Linguistic Review*, 16: 295–333.

——and Zwarts, Frans (forthcoming), 'Temporal/Aspectual Operators and (Non)veridicality', in A. Giorgi, J. Higginbotham, and F. Pianesi (eds.), *Tense and Mood Selection*. Oxford: Oxford University Press.

Ginzburg, Jonathan (1992). 'Questions, Queries and Facts: A Semantics and Pragmatics for Interrogatives'. Ph.D. thesis, Stanford University.

——(in preparation). 'Questions and the Semantics of Dialogue'. MS, Hebrew University of Jerusalem.

Goodluck, Helen, and Rochemont, Michael (1992) (eds.), *Island Constraints: Theory, Acquisition, and Processing*. Dordrecht: Kluwer.

Grewendorf, Günther, and Poletto, Cecilia (1991). 'Die Cleft-Konstruktion im Deutschen, Englischen, und Italienischen', in G. Fanselow and S. Felix (eds.), *Strukturen und Merkmale syntaktischer Kategorien*. Tübingen: Gunter Narr, 174–216.

Grinder, John, and Postal, Paul (1971). 'Missing Antecedents'. *Linguistic Inquiry*, 2: 269–312.

Groenendijk, Jeroen (1998). 'On Modal Subordination in Questions'. MS, Institute for Logic, Language, and Computation, University of Amsterdam.

——and Stokhof, Martin (1991). 'Dynamic Predicate Logic'. *Linguistics and Philosophy*, 14: 39–100.

Groenendijk, Jeroen and Stokhof, Martin (1997). 'Questions', in J. van Benthem and A. ter Meulen (eds.), *Handbook of Logic and Language*. Amsterdam: Elsevier, 1055–1124.

Grohmann, Kleanthes (1998). 'Syntactic Inquiries into Discourse Restrictions on Multiple Interrogatives'. *Groninger Arbeiten zur germanistischen Linguistik*, 42:1–60.

—— (2000). 'Prolific Peripheries: A Radical View from the Left'. Ph.D. thesis, University of Maryland, College Park.

Grosu, Alexander (1973). 'On the Nonunitary Nature of the Coordinate Structure Constraint'. *Linguistic Inquiry*, 4: 88–92.

—— (1974). 'On the Nature of the Left Branch Condition'. *Linguistic Inquiry*, 5: 308–19.

—— (1981). *Approaches to Island Phenomena*. Amsterdam: North-Holland.

—— (1994). *Three Studies in Locality and Case*. London: Routledge.

—— and Landman, Fred (1998). 'Strange Relatives of the Third Kind'. *Natural Language Semantics*, 6: 125–70.

Gunlogson, Christine (in preparation). 'Rising Declaratives'. Ph.D. thesis, University of California, Santa Cruz.

Gussenhoven, Carlos (1983). *On the Grammar and Semantics of Sentence Accents*. Dordrecht: Foris.

Haïk, Isabelle (1987). 'Bound VPs that Need to Be'. *Linguistics and Philosophy*, 10: 503–30.

Hankamer, Jorge (1979). *Deletion in Coordinate Structures*. New York: Garland.

—— and Sag, Ivan (1976). 'Deep and Surface Anaphora'. *Linguistic Inquiry*, 7: 391–428.

Hardt, Daniel (1992). 'VP Ellipsis and Semantic Identity', in S. Berman and A. Hestvik (eds.), *Proceedings of the Stuttgarter Ellipsis Workshop. Arbeitspapiere des Sonderforschungsbereichs*, 340/29.

—— (1993). 'Verb Phrase Ellipsis: Form, Meaning, and Processing'. Ph.D. thesis, University of Pennsylvania.

—— (1999). 'Dynamic Interpretation of Verb Phrase Ellipsis'. *Linguistics and Philosophy*, 22: 185–219.

Harris, Zelig (1965). 'Transformational Theory'. *Language*, 41: 363–401.

—— (1968). *Mathematical Structures of Language*. New York: Interscience Publishers.

Haspelmath, Martin (1997). *Indefinite Pronouns*. Oxford: Oxford University Press.

Heim, Irene (1982). 'The Semantics of Definite and Indefinite NPs'. Ph.D. thesis, University of Massachusetts, Amherst.

—— (1990). 'E-Type Pronouns and Donkey Anaphora'. *Linguistics and Philosophy*, 13: 137–77.

—— and Krazter, Angelika (1998). *Semantics in Generative Grammar*. London: Blackwell.

Hendriks, Petra, and de Hoop, Helen (forthcoming). 'Optimality Theory Semantics'. *Linguistics and Philosophy*.

Higgins, F. Roger (1973). 'The Pseudo-Cleft Construction in English'. Ph.D. thesis, MIT.

Hirschberg, Julia, and Ward, Gregory (1991). 'Accent and Bound Anaphora'. *Cognitive Linguistics*, 2: 101–21.

Hirschbühler, Paul (1978). 'The Syntax and Semantics of WH-constructions', Ph.D. thesis, University of Massachusetts, Amherst.

——(1981). 'The Ambiguity of Iterated Multiple Questions', *Linguistic Inquiry*, 12: 135–46.

Hoekstra, Eric (1992). 'On the Parametrisation of Functional Projections in CP', in A. Schafer (ed.), *Proceedings of the 23rd Meeting of the North Eastern Linguistic Society*. Amherst, MA: Graduate Student Linguistic Society, 191–204.

Hoekstra, Jarich (1993). 'The Split CP Hypothesis and the Frisian Complementizer System'. MS, Fryske Akademy, Ljouwert.

——(1995). 'Preposition Stranding and Resumptivity in West Germanic', in H. Haider, S. Olsen, and S. Vikner (eds.), *Studies in Comparative Germanic Syntax*. Dordrecht: Kluwer, 95–118.

——and Marácz, László (1989). 'The Position of Inflection in West Germanic'. *Working Papers in Scandinavian Syntax*, 44: 75–88.

Höhle, Tilman (1983). 'Akzent in Fragewörtern'. MS, Universität Tübingen.

Hoji, Hajime (forthcoming). 'Surface and Deep Anaphora, Sloppy Identity, and Experiments in Syntax', in A. Barss and T. Langendoen (eds.), *Explaining Linguistics*. London: Blackwell.

——and Fukaya, Teruhiko (1999). 'Stripping and Sluicing in Japanese and Some Implications', in S. Bird, A. Carnie, J. Haugen, and P. Norquest (eds.), *Proceedings of the 18th West Coast Conference on Formal Linguistics*. Somerville, MA: Cascadilla Press, 145–58.

Holmberg, Anders, and Platzack, Christer (1995). *The Role of Inflection in Scandinavian Syntax*. Oxford: Oxford University Press.

Honcoop, Martin (1998). 'Dynamic Excursions on Weak Islands'. Ph.D. thesis, Leiden University.

Honegger, Mark (1996). 'A Phonological Account of the "Adverb Effect" and *That-t* Violations', in *Proceedings of the 1996 Meeting of the Formal Linguistics Society of Mid-America*.

Horn, Laurence (1978). 'Remarks on Neg-Raising', in Peter Cole (ed.), *Pragmatics* (Syntax and Semantics 9). New York: Academic Press, 129–220.

Hornstein, Norbert (1995). *Logical Form: From GB to Minimalism*. Oxford: Blackwell.

——(1999). 'Movement and Control'. *Linguistic Inquiry*, 30: 69–96.

——and Weinberg, Amy (1981). 'Case Theory and Preposition Stranding'. *Linguistic Inquiry*, 12: 55–91.

Huang, C.-T. James (1982). 'Logical Relations in Chinese and the Theory of Grammar'. Ph.D. thesis, MIT.

——(1984). 'On the Determination and Reference of Empty Pronouns'. *Linguistic Inquiry*, 15: 531–74.

Hudson, R. A. (1972). 'Why it is that that *that* that Follows the Subject is Impossible'. *Linguistic Inquiry*, 3: 116–18.

Hughes, G. E., and Cresswell, M. J. (1996). *A New Introduction to Modal Logic*. London: Routledge.

Inoue, Kazuko (1976). *Kenkei bunpoo to nihongo*. Tokyo: Taishukan.

Inoue, Kazuko (1978). *Nihongo-no bunpoo kisoku.* Tokyo: Taishukan.

Jacobson, Pauline (1992). 'Antecedent-Contained Deletion in a Variable Free Semantics', in C. Barker and D. Dowty (eds.), *Proceedings from the 2nd Conference on Semantics and Linguistic Theory.* Columbus, OH: Ohio State University, 193–214.

Johnson, Kyle (1997). 'What VP Ellipsis Can Do, and What it Can't, but Not Why'. MS, University of Massachusetts, Amherst.

Johnston, Michael (1994). 'The Semantics of Adverbial Adjuncts'. Ph.D. thesis, University of California, Santa Cruz.

Joseph, Brian (1980). 'Recovery of Information in Relative Clauses: Evidence from Greek and Hebrew'. *Journal of Linguistics,* 16: 237–44.

Kamp, Hans (1981). 'A Theory of Truth and Discourse Representation', in J. Groenendijk, M. Stokhof, and T. Janssen (eds.), *Formal Methods in the Study of Language.* Amsterdam: Mathematisch Centrum, 277–322.

Karttunen, Lauri, and Peters, Stanley (1979). 'Conventional Implicature', in C.-K. Oh and D. Dineen (eds.), *Presupposition* (Syntax and Semantics 11). New York: Academic Press, 1–56.

Kayne, Richard (1981). 'On Certain Differences between French and English'. *Linguistic Inquiry,* 12: 349–71.

——(1994). *The Antisymmetry of Syntax.* Cambridge, MA: MIT Press.

Keenan, Ed. (1971). 'Names, Quantifiers, and the Sloppy Identity Problem', *Papers in Linguistics,* 4: 211–32.

Kehler, Andrew (1993). 'The Effect of Establishing Coherence in Ellipsis and Anaphora Resolution', in *Proceedings of the 31st Annual Meeting of the Association for Computational Linguistics,* Columbus, OH, 62–9.

——(2000). *Coherence, Reference, and the Theory of Grammar.* Stanford, CA: Center for the Study of Language and Information.

Kennedy, Christopher (1997). 'VP-Deletion and "Nonparasitic" Gaps'. *Linguistic Inquiry,* 28: 697–707.

——(1999). *Projecting the Adjective: The Syntax and Semantics of Gradability and Comparison.* New York: Garland.

——(2000). 'Comparative Deletion and Optimality in Syntax'. MS, Northwestern University.

——and Merchant, Jason (1997). 'Attributive Comparatives and Bound Ellipsis'. Linguistics Research Center Report LRC-97-3, University of California, Santa Cruz.

————(1999). 'Attributive Comparatives and the Syntax of Ellipsis', in F. Corblin, C. Dobrovie-Sorin, and J.-M. Marandin (eds.), *Empirical Issues in Formal Syntax and Semantics 2: Selected Papers from the Colloque de Syntaxe et Sémantique de Paris.* The Hague: Thesus, 233–53.

————(2000*a*). 'Attributive Comparative Deletion'. *Natural Language and Linguistic Theory,* 18: 89–146.

————(2000*b*). 'The Case of the "Missing CP" and the Secret Case'. MS, Northwestern University and University of Groningen.

Kester, Ellen-Petra (1996). 'The Nature of Adjectival Inflection'. Ph.D. thesis, University of Utrecht.

Kiss, Katalin (1998). 'Identificational Focus versus Information Focus'. *Language*, 74: 245–73.

Kiparksy, Paul, and Kiparsky, Carol (1970). 'Fact', in M. Bierwisch and K. E. Heidolph (eds.), *Progress in Linguistics*. The Hague: Mouton, 143–73.

Kizu, Mika (1997). 'A Note on Sluicing in Wh-in-Situ Languages'. MS, McGill University.

Klein, Maarten (1977). 'Appositionele constructies in het Nederlands', Ph.D. thesis, Nijmegen University.

Klein, Wolfgang (1993). 'Ellipse', in J. Jacobs, A. von Stechow, W. Sternefeld, and T. Vennemann (eds.), *Syntax: An International Handbook of Contemporary Research*. Berlin: De Gruyter, 763–99.

Kluender, Robert (1998). 'On the Distinction between Strong and Weak Islands: A Processing Perspective', in P. Culicover and L. McNally (eds.), *The Limits of Syntax* (Syntax and semantics 29). San Diego: Academic Press, 241–79.

Koopman, Hilda, and Sportiche, Dominique (1982). 'Variables and the Bijection Principle'. *Linguistic Review*, 2: 139–60.

Kratzer, Angelika (1981). 'On the Notional Category of Modality', in H. Eikmeyer and H. Rieser (eds.), *Words, Worlds, and Contexts*. Berlin: De Gruyter, 38–74.

——(1998). 'Scope or Pseudoscope? Are there Wide-Scope Indefinites?', in S. Rothstein (ed.), *Events and Grammar*. Dordrecht: Kluwer, 163–96.

Kroch, Anthony (1989). 'Amount Quantification, Referentiality, and Long *wh*-Movement'. MS, University of Pennsylvania.

Kuno, Susumu, and Takami, Ken-ichi (1997). 'Remarks on Negative Islands'. *Linguistic Inquiry*, 28: 553–76.

Kuroda, S.-Y. (1968). Review of C. Fillmore, *Indirect Object Constructions in English and the Ordering of Transformations*. *Language*, 44: 374–78.

Kuwabara, K. (1996). 'Multiple Wh-Phrases in Elliptical Clauses and Some Aspects of Clefts with Multiple Foci', in *Formal Approaches to Japanese Linguistics 2* (MIT Working Papers in Linguistics 29). Cambridge, MA, 97–116.

Ladusaw, William, and Dowty, David (1988). 'Toward a Nongrammatical Account of Thematic Roles', in W. Wilkins (ed.), *Thematic Relations* (Syntax and Semantics 21). San Diego: Academic Press, 62–74.

Lakoff, George (1968). 'Pronouns and Reference'. Bloomington, IN: Indiana University Linguistics Club. Appears in McCawley (1976), 273–335.

——(1970). 'Global Rules'. *Language*, 46: 627–39.

——(1972). 'The Arbitrary Basis of Transformational Grammar'. *Language*, 48: 76–87.

Langendoen, D. Terence (1970). *Essentials of English Grammar*. New York: Holt, Rinehart, and Winston.

Lappin, Shalom (1996). 'The Interpretation of Ellipsis', in S. Lappin (ed.), *The Handbook of Contemporary Semantic Theory*. Oxford: Oxford University Press, 145–75.

Lappin, Shalom and Francez, Nissim (1994). 'E-Type Pronouns, I-Sums, and Donkey Anaphora'. *Linguistics and Philosophy*, 17: 391–428.

Lasnik, Howard (1999). 'On Feature Strength: Three Minimalist Approaches to Overt Movement'. *Linguistic Inquiry*, 30: 197–217.

——and Saito, Marmoru (1984). 'On the Nature of Proper Government'. *Linguistic Inquiry*, 15: 235–89.

Legendre, Géraldine (1999). 'Morphological and Prosodic Alignment at Work: The Case of South-Slavic Clitics', in K. Shahin, S. Blake, and E.-S. Kim (eds.), *Proceedings of the 17th West Coast Conference on Formal Linguistics*. Stanford, CA: Center for the Study of Language and Information, 436–50.

——(2000), 'Morphological and Prosodic Alignment of Bulgarian Clitics', in J. Dekkers, F. van der Leeuw, and J. van de Weijer (eds.), *Optimality Theory: Phonology, Syntax, and Acquisition*. Oxford: Oxford University Press.

Levin, Beth, and Rappaport, Malka (1988). 'What to Do with θ-Roles', in W. Wilkins (ed.), *Thematic Relations* (Syntax and Semantics 21). San Diego: Academic Press.

Levin, Lori (1982). 'Sluicing: A Lexical Interpretation Procedure', in J. Bresnan (ed.), *The Mental Representation of Grammatical Relations*. Cambridge, MA: MIT Press, 590–654.

Lewis, G. L. (1967). *Turkish Grammar*. Oxford: Oxford University Press.

Lightfoot, David (2000). 'Ellipses as Clitics', in K. Schwabe and N. Zhang (eds.), *Ellipsis in Conjunction*. Tübingen: Niemeyer, 79–94.

Lobeck, Anne (1991). 'The Phrase Structure of Ellipsis', in S. Rothstein (ed.), *Perspectives on Phrase Structure* (Syntax and Semantics). San Diego: Academic Press, 81–103.

——(1995). *Ellipsis: Functional Heads, Licensing, and Identification*. Oxford: Oxford University Press.

——(1999). 'VP Ellipsis and the Minimalist Program: Some Speculations and Proposals', in S. Lappin and E. Benmamoun (eds.), *Fragments: Studies in Ellipsis and Gapping*. Oxford: Oxford University Press, 98–123.

López, Luis (2000). 'Ellipsis and Discourse-Linking'. *Lingua*, 110: 183–213.

Maling, Joan, and Sprouse, Rex (1995). 'Structural Case, Specifier-Head Relations, and the Case of Predicate NPs', in H. Haider, S. Olsen, and S. Vikner (eds.), *Studies in Comparative Germanic Syntax*. Dordrecht: Kluwer, 167–86.

McCawley, James (1976) (ed.), *Notes from the Linguistic Underground* (Syntax and Semantics 7). New York: Academic Press.

——(1988). *The Syntactic Phenomena of English*. Chicago, IL: Chicago University Press.

——(1998). *The Syntactic Phenomena of English*. 2nd edn. Chicago, IL: Chicago University Press.

McCloskey, James (1979). *Transformational Syntax and Model Theoretic Semantics: A Case Study in Modern Irish*. Dordrecht: Reidel.

——(1986). 'Inflection and Conjunction in Modern Irish'. *Natural Language and Linguistic Theory*, 4: 245–81.

—— (1990). 'Resumptive Pronouns, A′-Binding, and Levels of Representation in Irish', in R. Hendrick (ed.), *The Syntax of the Modern Celtic Languages* (Syntax and Semantics 23). San Diego: Academic Press, 199–248.

—— (1991*a*). 'Clause Structure, Ellipsis and Proper Government in Irish'. *Lingua*, 85: 259–302.

—— (1991*b*). 'A Note on Agreement and Coordination in Old Irish', in S. Chung and J. Hankamer (eds.), *A Festschrift for William Shipley*. Santa Cruz, CA: Syntax Research Center, 105–14.

—— (1991*c*). '*There, It*, and Agreement'. *Linguistic Inquiry*, 22: 563–7.

—— (1996). 'On the Scope of Verb Raising in Irish'. *Natural Language and Linguistic Theory*, 14: 47–104.

—— (1997). 'Resumptive Pronouns'. Handout from talk presented at meeting of the Netherlands Institute for Advanced Study, Wassenaar.

—— (2000). 'Quantifier Float and *Wh*-Movement in an Irish English'. *Linguistic Inquiry*, 31: 57–84.

——and Hale, Ken (1984). 'On the Syntax of Person-Number Inflection in Modern Irish'. *Natural Language and Linguistic Theory*, 1: 487–533.

McDaniel, Dana (1989). 'Partial and Multiple Wh-Movement'. *Natural Language and Linguistic Theory*, 7: 565–604.

——McKee, Cecile, and Bernstein, Judy (1998). 'How Children's Relatives Solve a Problem for Minimalism'. *Language*, 74: 308–34.

Manzini, Rita (1998). 'A Minimalist Theory of Weak Islands', in P. Culicover and L. McNally (eds.), *The Limits of Syntax* (Syntax and Semantics 29). San Diego: Academic Press, 185–210.

——and Roussou, Anna (2000). 'A Minimalist Theory of A-Movement and Control'. *Lingua*, 110: 409–47.

Marvin, Tatjana (1997). 'Wh-Movement in the Generative Theory with Special Reference to Slovene'. Diploma thesis, University of Ljubljana.

May, Robert (1991). 'Syntax, Semantics, and Logical Form', in A. Kasher (ed.), *The Chomskyan Turn*. Oxford: Blackwell, 334–59.

Merchant, Jason (1998). '"Pseudosluicing": Elliptical Clefts in Japanese and English', in A. Alexiadou, N. Fuhrhop, P. Law, and U. Kleinhenz (eds.), *ZAS Working Papers in Linguistics 10*. Berlin: Zentrum für Allgemeine Sprachwissenschaft, 88–112.

—— (1999*a*). 'E-Type A′-Traces under Sluicing', in K. Shahin, S. Blake, and E.-S. Kim (eds.), *Proceedings of the 17th West Coast Conference on Formal Linguistics*. Stanford, CA: Center for the Study of Language and Information, 478–92.

—— (1999*b*). 'Resumptive Operators, Case, and Sluicing'. Paper presented at the 75th annual meeting of the Linguistic Society of America, Los Angeles, CA.

—— (1999*c*). 'On the Form of Resumptive-Binding Operators'. MS, University of California, Santa Cruz.

—— (2000*a*). 'Economy, the Copy Theory, and Antecedent-Contained Deletion'. *Linguistic Inquiry*, 31: 566–75.

—— (2000*b*). 'Antecedent-Contained Deletion in Negative Polarity Items'. *Syntax*, 3: 144–50.

Merchant, Jason (2000c). 'LF Movement and Islands in Greek Sluicing'. *Journal of Greek Linguistics*, 1: 39–62.

——(2000d). 'Why No(t)?' MS, University of Groningen.

——(forthcoming). 'Swiping in Germanic', in J.-W. Zwart and W. Abraham (eds.), *Studies in Germanic Syntax*. Amsterdam: John Benjamins.

Mikkelsen, Line (forthcoming). 'Expletive Subjects in Subject Relative Clauses', in J.-W. Zwart and W. Abraham (eds.), *Studies in Germanic Syntax*. Amsterdam: John Benjamins.

Milapides, Michael (1990). 'Aspects of Ellipsis in English and Greek'. Ph.D. thesis, University of Thessaloniki.

Miller, Philip (1991). 'Clitics and Constituents in Phrase Structure Grammar'. Ph.D. thesis, Utrecht University.

Mittwoch, Anita (1982). 'On the Difference between "Eating" and "Eating Something": Activities vs. Accomplishments'. *Linguistic Inquiry*, 13: 113–21.

Moxey, L. M., and Sandford, A. J. (1993). *Communicating Quantities*. Hillsdale NJ: Erlbaum, Hove.

Müller, Gereon (1995). *A-Bar Syntax*. Berlin: Mouton de Gruyter.

——and Sternefeld, Wolgang (1993). 'Improper Movement and Unambiguous Binding'. *Linguistic Inquiry*, 24: 461–507.

Munn, Alan (1993). 'Topics in the Syntax and Semantics of Coordinate Structures'. Ph.D. thesis, University of Maryland, College Park.

Niño, María-Eugenia (1997). 'The Multiple Expression of Inflectional Information and Grammatical Architecture', in F. Corblin *et al.* (eds.), *Empirical Issues in Formal Syntax and Semantics: Selected Papers from the Colloque de Syntaxe et Sémantique de Paris 1995*. Bern: Peter Lang, 127–47.

Nishigauchi, Taisuke (1986). 'Quantification in Syntax'. Ph.D. thesis, University of Massachusetts, Amherst.

——(1998). ' "Multiple sluicing" in Japanese and the Functional Nature of *Wh*-Phrases'. *Journal of East Asian Linguistics*, 7: 121–52.

Nishiyama, Kunio, Whitman, John, and Yi, Eun-Young (1996). 'Syntactic Movement of Overt Wh-Phrases in Japanese and Korean'. *Japanese/Korean Linguistics 5*. Stanford, CA: Center for the Study of Language and Information, 337–51.

Oppenrieder, Wilhelm (1991). 'Preposition Stranding im Deutschen? Da will ich nichts von hören!', in G. Fanselow and S. Felix (eds.), *Strukturen und Merkmale syntaktischer Kategorien*. Tübingen: Gunter Narr, 159–73.

Partee, Barbara, and Bach, Emmon (1981). 'Quantification, Pronouns, and VP Anaphora', in J. Groenendijk, M. Stokhof, and T. Janssen (eds.), *Formal Methods in the Study of Language*. Amsterdam: Mathematisch Centrum, 445–81.

Perlmutter, David (1971). *Deep and Surface Structure Constraints in Syntax*. New York: Holt, Rinehart, and Winston.

Pesetsky, David (1982). 'Paths and Categories'. Ph.D. thesis, MIT.

——(1987). 'Wh-in-situ: Movement and Unselective Binding', in E. Reuland and A. ter Meulen (eds.), *The Representation of (In)definiteness*. Cambridge, MA: MIT Press, 98–129.

—— (1998*a*). 'Some Optimality Principles of Sentence Pronunciation', in P. Barbosa, D. Fox, P. Hagstrom, M. McGinnis, and D. Pesetsky (eds.), *Is the Best Good Enough?* Cambridge, MA: MIT Press, 337–83.

—— (1998*b*). 'Phrasal Movement and its Kin'. MS, MIT.

Pollard, Carl, and Sag, Ivan (1994). *Head-Driven Phrase Structure Grammar*. Chicago: University of Chicago Press.

Pollmann, T. (1975). 'Een regel die subject en copula deleert?' *Spektator*, 5: 282–92.

Postal, Paul (1992). 'The Status of the Coordinate Structure Constraint'. MS, IBM.

—— (1996). 'Islands'. Paper presented at Western Conference on Linguistics 96, University of California, Santa Cruz. Revised version to appear in M. Baltin and C. Collins (eds.), *The Handbook of Syntactic Theory*. Oxford: Blackwell.

—— (1998). *Three Investigations of Extraction*. Cambridge, MA: MIT Press.

Potts, Christopher (1999). 'Vehicle Change and Anti-Pronominal Contexts'. MS, New York University.

Potsdam, Eric (1998). *Syntactic Issues in the English Imperative*. New York: Garland.

Prince, Ellen (1978). 'A Comparison of WH-clefts and IT-clefts in Discourse', *Language*, 54: 883–906.

—— (1990). 'Syntax and Discourse: A Look at Resumptive Pronouns', in *Proceedings of the 16th Meeting of the Berkeley Linguistic Society*. Berkeley, CA: Berkeley Linguistics Society, 482–97.

Progovac, Ljiljana (1999). 'Events and Economy of Coordination'. *Syntax*, 2: 141–59.

Prüst, Hub (1993). 'Gapping and VP Anaphora'. Ph.D. thesis, University of Amsterdam.

—— and Scha, Remko (1990*a*). 'VP Ellipsis Induces Clausal Parallelism', in R. Bok-Bennema and P. Coopmans (eds.), *Linguistics in the Netherlands 1990*. Dordrecht: Foris, 123–32.

—— —— (1990*b*). 'A Discourse Perspective on Verb Phrase Anaphora', in M. Stokhof and L. Torenvliet (eds.), *Proceedings of the 7th Amsterdam Colloquium*. Institute for Logic, Language, and Information, University of Amsterdam, 451–74.

—— van den Berg, Martin, and Scha, Remko (1994). 'Discourse Grammar and Verb Phrase Anaphora'. *Linguistics and Philosophy*, 17: 261–327.

Pullum, Geoffrey (1991). *The Great Eskimo Vocabulary Hoax and Other Irreverent Essays on the Study of Language*. Chicago: University of Chicago Press.

—— and Zwicky, Arnold (1997). 'Licensing of Prosodic Features by Syntactic Rules: The Key to Auxiliary Reduction'. Paper presented at the annual meeting of the Linguistic Society of America, Chicago.

Puskás, Genoveva (1999). *Word Order in Hungarian: The Syntax of A'-positions*. Amsterdam: John Benjamins.

Quer, Josep (1998). 'Mood at the Interface'. Ph.D. thesis, Utrecht University.

Quine, W. V. O. (1960). *Word and Object*. Cambridge, MA: MIT Press.

Quirk, R., Greenbaum, S., Leech, G., and Svartvik, J. (1972). *A Grammar of Contemporary English*. London: Seminar Press.

Reinhart, Tanya (1995). 'Interface Strategies'. OTS working papers 95–002, Utrecht University.

Reinhart, Tanya (1997). 'Quantifier Scope: How Labor is Divided between QR and Choice Functions'. *Linguistics and Philosophy*, 20: 335–97.

Reis, Marga (1985). 'Satzeinleitende Strukturen im Deutschen: Über COMP, Haupt- und Nebensätze, *w*-Bewegung und die Doppelkopfanalyse', in W. Abraham (ed.), *Erklärende Syntax des Deutschen*. Tübingen: Gunter Narr, 271–311.

van Riemsdijk, Henk (1978). *A Case Study in Syntactic Markedness: The Binding Nature of Prepositional Phrases*. Dordrecht: Foris.

——(1983). 'The Case of German Adjectives', in F. Heny and B. Richards (eds.), *Linguistic Categories: Auxiliaries and Related Puzzles I*. Dordrecht: Reidel, 223–52.

——(1997). 'Left Dislocation', in E. Anagnostopoulou *et al.* (1997), 1–12.

Rizzi, Luigi (1990). *Relativized Minimality*. Cambridge, MA: MIT Press.

——(1994). 'Argument/Adjunct (A)symmetries', in G. Cinque, J. Koster, J.-Y. Pollock, L. Rizzi, and R. Zanuttini (eds.), *Paths towards Universal Grammar: Studies in Honor of Richard S. Kayne*. Washington: Georgetown University Press, 367–76.

——(1995). 'The Fine Structure of the Left Periphery'. MS, University of Geneva.

Roberts, Craige (1989). 'Modal Subordination and Pronominal Anaphora in Discourse'. *Linguistics and Philosophy*, 12: 683–721.

——(1996). 'Anaphora in Intensional Contexts', in S. Lappin (ed.), *The Handbook of Contemporary Semantic Theory*. Oxford: Blackwell, 215–46.

Rodman, Robert (1976). 'Scope Phenomena, "Movement Transformations", and Relative Clauses', in B. Partee (ed.), *Montague Grammar*. New York: Academic Press, 165–76.

Romero, Maribel (1997*a*). 'Recoverability Conditions for Sluicing', in F. Corblin *et al.* (eds.), *Empirical Issues in Formal Syntax and Semantics: Selected Papers from the Colloque de Syntaxe et Sémantique de Paris 1995*. Bern: Peter Lang, 193–216.

——(1997*b*). 'The Correlation between Scope Reconstuction and Connectivity Effects', in E. Curtis, J. Lyle, and G. Webster (eds.), *Proceedings of the 16th West Coast Conference in Formal Linguistics*. Stanford, CA: Center for the Study of Language and Information, 351–66.

——(1998). 'Focus and Reconstruction Effects in Wh-Phrases'. Ph.D. thesis, University of Massachusetts, Amherst.

Rooth, Mats (1985). 'Association with Focus'. Ph.D. thesis, University of Massachusetts, Amherst.

——(1992*a*). 'Ellipsis Redundancy and Reduction Redundancy', in S. Berman and A. Hestvik (eds.), *Proceedings of the Stuttgarter Ellipsis Workshop*. Arbeitspapiere des Sonderforschungsbereichs 340, No. 29.

——(1992*b*). 'A Theory of Focus Interpretation'. *Natural Language Semantics*, 1: 75–116.

——(1996). 'Focus', in S. Lappin (ed.), *The Handbook of Contemporary Semantic Theory*. Oxford: Blackwell, 271–97.

van Rooy, Rob (1998). 'Modal Subordination in a Dynamic Semantics'. MS, Institute for Logic, Language, and Computation, University of Amsterdam.

Rosen, Carol (1976). 'Guess What About?', in A. Ford, J. Reighard, and R. Singh (eds.), *Papers from the 6th Meeting of the North Eastern Linguistic Society.* Montreal: Montreal Working Papers in Linguistics, 205–11.

Ross, John R. (1967). 'Constraints on Variables in Syntax'. Ph.D. thesis, MIT.

—— (1969). 'Guess Who?', in R. Binnick, A. Davison, G. Green, and J. Morgan (eds.), *Papers from the 5th Regional Meeting of the Chicago Linguistic Society.* Chicago: Chicago Linguistic Society, 252–86.

—— (1986). *Infinite Syntax!* Norwood, NJ: Ablex.

Roussou, Anna (1998). 'Features and Subject Dependencies: *that-t* Phenomena Revisited'. MS, University of Wales, Bangor.

Rudin, Catherine (1985). *Aspects of Bulgarian Syntax: Complementizers and Wh-Constructions.* Columbus, OH: Slavica Publishers.

Rullmann, Hotze (1995). 'Maximality in the Semantics of WH-Constructions'. Ph.D. thesis, University of Massachusetts, Amherst.

Ruys, Eddy (1992). 'The Scope of Indefinites'. Ph.D. thesis, Utrecht University.

Safir, Ken (1999). 'Vehicle Change and Reconstruction in A′-Chains'. *Linguistic Inquiry*, 30: 587–620.

Sag, Ivan (1976*a*). 'Deletion and Logical Form'. Ph.D. thesis, MIT.

—— (1976*b*). 'A Note on Verb Phrase Deletion'. *Linguistic Inquiry*, 7: 664–71.

—— and Fodor, Janet D. (1994). 'Extraction without Traces', in *Proceedings of the 13th West Coast Conference on Formal Linguistics.* Stanford, CA: Center for the Study of Language and Information, 365–84.

Sauerland, Uli (1996). 'Guess How?', in J. Costa, J. Goedemans, and R. van Vijver (eds.), *Proceedings of the 4th Conference of the Student Organization of Linguistics in Europe.* Leiden: Student Organization of Linguistics in Europe, 297–309.

—— (1998). 'The Meaning of Chains'. Ph.D. thesis, MIT.

Schwabe, Kerstin (2000). 'Coordinate Ellipsis and Information Structure', in K. Schwabe and N. Zhang (eds.), *Ellipsis in Conjunction.* Tübingen: Niemeyer, 247–69.

Schwarzschild, Roger (1999). 'Givenness, AvoidF, and Other Constraints on the Placement of Accent'. *Natural Language Semantics*, 7: 141–77.

Sells, Peter (1984). 'Syntax and Semantics of Resumptive Pronouns'. Ph.D. thesis, University of Massachusetts, Amherst.

Shieber, Stuart, Pereira, Fernando, and Dalrymple, Mary (1996). 'Interactions of Scope and Ellipsis'. *Linguistics and Philosophy*, 19: 527–52.

Shimoyama, Junko (1995). 'On "Sluicing" in Japanese', MS, University of Massachusetts, Amherst.

Shlonksy, Ur (1988). 'Complementizer-Cliticization in Hebrew and the Empty Category Principle'. *Natural Language and Linguistic Theory*, 6: 191–205.

von Stechow, Arnim (1996). 'Against LF Pied-Piping'. *Natural Language Semantics*, 4: 57–110.

Suñer, Margarita (1998). 'Resumptive Restrictive Relatives: A Crosslinguistic Perspective'. *Language*, 74: 335–64.

Svenonius, Peter (1994). 'Dependent Nexus: Subordinate Predication Structures in English and the Scandinavian Languages'. Ph.D. thesis, University of California, Santa Cruz.

de Swart, Henriëtte (1991). 'Adverbs of Quantification: A Generalized Quantifier Approach'. Ph.D. thesis, University of Groningen.

Swingle, Kari (1995). 'On the Prosody and Syntax of Right Node Raising'. Qualifying paper, University of California, Santa Cruz.

Szabolcsi, Anna, and Zwarts, Frans (1993). 'Weak Islands and Algebraic Semantics for Scope Taking'. *Natural Language Semantics*, 1: 235–84.

Takahashi, Daiko (1994). 'Sluicing in Japanese'. *Journal of East Asian Linguistics*, 3: 265–300.

Takami, Ken-ichi (1992). *Preposition Stranding: From Syntactic to Functional Analyses*. Berlin: Mouton de Gruyter.

Tancredi, Chris (1990). 'Not Only *Even*, but Even *Only*'. MS, MIT.

—— (1992). 'Deletion, Deaccenting, and Presupposition'. Ph.D. thesis, MIT.

Taraldsen, Knut Tarald (1986). '*Som* and the Binding Theory', in L. Hellan and K. Koch Christensen (eds.), *Topics in Scandinavian Syntax*. Dordrecht: Reidel, 149–84.

Tomioka, Satoshi (1995). '[Focus]$_F$ Restricts Scope: Quantifiers in VP Ellipsis', in M. Simons and T. Galloway (eds.), *Proceedings of the 5th conference on Semantics and Linguistic Theory*, Ithaca, NY: Cornell University, 328–45.

—— (1996). 'On the Mismatch between Variable Binding and Sloppy Identity', in J. Camacho, L. Choueiri, and M. Watanabe (eds.), *Proceedings of the 14th West Coast Conference on Formal Linguistics*. Stanford, CA: Center for the Study of Language and Information, 541–56.

—— (1997). 'Focusing Effects and NP Interpretation in VP Ellipsis'. Ph.D. thesis, University of Massachusetts, Amherst.

—— (1999). 'A Sloppy Identity Puzzle'. *Natural Language Semantics*, 7: 217–41.

Trissler, Susanne (1993). 'P-Stranding im Deutschen', in F.-J. d'Avis *et al.* (eds.), *Extraktion im Deutschen I*, 247–91. *Arbeitspapiere des Sonderforschungsbereichs*, 340/34.

Vat, Jan (1981). 'Left Dislocation, Connectedness, and Reconstruction'. *Groninger Arbeiten zur germanistischen Linguistik*, 20. Reprinted in Anagnostopoulou *et al.* (1997), 67–92.

Vikner, Sten (1991). 'Relative *der* and other C^0 Elements in Danish'. *Lingua*, 84: 109–36.

—— (1995). *Verb Movement and Expletive Subjects in the Germanic Languages*. Oxford: Oxford University Press.

Wahba, Wafaa Abdel-Faheem Batran (1984). 'Wh-Constructions in Egyptian Arabic'. Ph.D. thesis, University of Illinois, Urbana-Champaign.

Webelhuth, Gert (1992). *Principles and Parameters of Syntactic Saturation*. Oxford: Oxford University Press.

Wilder, Chris (1995). 'Some Properties of Ellipsis in Coordination'. *Geneva Generative Papers*, 2: 23–61.

Williams, Edwin (1977). 'Discourse and Logical Form'. *Linguistic Inquiry*, 8: 103–39.

—— (1984). '*There*-Insertion'. *Linguistic Inquiry*, 15: 131–53.

—— (1986). 'A Reassignment of the Functions of LF'. *Linguistic Inquiry*, 17: 265–99.

Wiltschko, Martina (1993). 'ProPPs im Deutschen'. MA thesis, Universität Wien.

Winkler, Susanne (1997). 'Ellipsis and Information Structure in English and German: The Phonological Reduction Hypothesis'. *Arbeitspapiere des Sonderforschungsbereichs*, 340/121.

Winter, Yoad (1997). 'Choice Functions and the Scopal Semantics of Indefinites'. *Linguistics and Philosophy*, 20: 399–467.

—— (1998). 'Flexible Boolean Semantics'. Ph.D. thesis, Utrecht University.

vanden Wyngaerd, Guido, and Zwart, Jan-Wouter (1991). 'Reconstruction and Vehicle Change', in F. Drijkoningen and A. van Kemenade (eds.), *Linguistics in the Netherlands 1991*. Amsterdam: John Benjamins, 151–60.

—— —— (1999). 'Antecedent-Contained Deletion as Deletion', in R. van Bezooijen and R. Kager (eds.), *Linguistics in the Netherlands 1999*. Amsterdam: John Benjamins, 203–16.

Zwart, Jan-Wouter (1993). 'Dutch Syntax: A Minimalist Approach'. Ph.D. thesis, University of Groningen.

SOURCES OF ATTESTED EXAMPLES

de Bernières, Louis (1994). *Captain Corelli's Mandolin*. New York: Vintage International.

Brin, David (1991). *Earth*. New York: Tor Books.

Dexter, Peter (1988). *Paris Trout*. New York: Penguin.

Kress, Nancy (1993). *Beggars in Spain*. New York: Avon.

O'Brien, Tim (1994). *In the Lake of the Woods*. New York: Penguin.

Paretsky, Sarah (1984). *Deadlock*. New York: Ballantine.

Robinson, Kim Stanley (1994). *Green Mars*. New York: Bantam.

—— (1993). *Red Mars*. New York: Bantam.

Tartt, Donna (1994). *The Secret History*. Boston: Back Bay.

Voskuil, J. J. (1996) *Meneer Beerta: Het Bureau I*. Amsterdam: Van Oorschot.

Wallace, David Foster (1986). *The Broom of the System*. Boston: Little, Brown.

Zwagerman, Joost (1991). *Vals licht*. Amsterdam: De Arbeiderspers.

Language Index

Name Index

Subject Index